THE MASONIC INITIATION: CENTENNIAL EDITION

HONOURING A CENTURY OF MASONIC INSIGHT, TRANSFORMATION, AND INNER ENLIGHTENMENT

W.L. WILMSHURST

MICHAEL DUNLAP

WALTER LESLIE WILMSHURST

Originally published as *The Masonic Initiation* by Walter Leslie Wilmshurst, 1924. This work is in the public domain.

Kindle Edition: 978-1-7637977-1-0

Paperback Edition: 978-1-7637977-0-3

Hardcover Edition: 978-1-7637977-2-7

Publisher: Lodge of the Ancients Publishing

Email: *publishing [at] lodgeoftheancients [dot] com*

Printed in United States and Internationally

ACKNOWLEDGMENTS

To my Father and Forefathers: Every achievement of mine is woven from the legacy you entrusted to me. I am, and forever will be, the sum of your parts.

To my family: Your unwavering love and steadfast support have been my constant foundation. Thank you for your patience, encouragement, and the light you bring to my life's journey.

To Brother Walter Leslie Wilmshurst: Across a century, your words and insights have served as a mentor and guiding light, deepening my understanding of the Craft. Your dedication to the esoteric dimensions of Freemasonry continues to inspire my path.

To our Most Worshipful Grand Master, Brother Bernie Khris Albano: Your commitment to advancing Masonic education stands as a testament to your leadership. Through your words and deeds, you are championing the pursuit of knowledge and the value of learning within our Craft.

To my Brethren of Lodge Kiama No. 35: Our shared fellowship and dedication to the tenets of Freemasonry enrich my journey daily. Your camaraderie and commitment exemplify the spirit of our lodge.

And to the many silent mentors and guardians of our ancient tradition, whose names may never be known but whose wisdom and examples resonate through the ages: You have shown the way, and your legacy is held in reverence by those who seek Truth and Light.

CONTENTS

INTRODUCTION

MASONRY AND RELIGION

This book is meant to be a sequel to, and an amplification of, my previous volume, *The Meaning of Masonry*, first published in 1922—a collection of papers issued diffidently and tentatively on the chance that they might interest some few members of the Craft in the deeper and philosophic aspect of Freemasonry. It at once met, however, with a surprisingly warm welcome from all parts of the world, and already has had to be thrice reprinted. Any personal pleasure at its reception is eclipsed by a greater gratification and thankfulness at the now demonstrated fact that the present large and rapid increase in the number of the Fraternity is being accompanied by a correspondingly wide desire to realise the significance and purpose of the Masonic system to a much fuller degree than till now has been the case. The Masonic Craft seems to be gradually regenerating itself, and, as I previously indicated, such a regeneration must needs make not only for the moral benefit and enlightenment of individuals and Lodges, but ultimately must react favourably upon the framework in which they exist—the whole body of society.

In these circumstances it becomes possible to speak more fully, perhaps also more feelingly, upon a subject which, as a large volume of public and private testimony has revealed to me, is engaging the earnest interest of large numbers of Brethren of the Craft. So I offer them these further papers, presenting the same subject-matter as before, but in a different form and expounding more fully matters previously treated but superficially and cursorily.

By "the Masonic Initiation" I mean, of course, not merely the act and rite of reception into the Order, but Speculative Freemasonry—within the limits of the Craft and Arch Degrees—regarded as a system, a specialised method of intellectual guidance and spiritual instruction; a method which to its willing and attentive devotees offers at once an interpretation of life, a rule of living, and a means of grace, introduction, and even intromission, to life and light of a supra-natural order.

Masonry being essentially and expressedly a quest after supranatural light, the present papers are schematically arranged in correspondence with the stages of that quest; they deal first with the transition from darkness to light; next with the pathway itself and the light to be found thereon; and, lastly, with light in its fullness of attainment as the result of faithfully pursuing that path to the end. In a final paper I have re-surveyed the Order's past and indicated its present tendencies and future possibilities.

In their zeal to appreciate and make the best of their connection with the Order, some members, one finds, experience difficulty in defining and "placing" Freemasonry. Is it Religion, Philosophy, a system of morals, or what? In view of the deepening interest in the subject, it may be well at the outset to clear up this point. Masonry is not a Religion, though it contains marked religious elements and many religious references. A Brother may legitimately say, if he wishes—and many do say—"Masonry is my religion," but he is not justified in classifying and holding it out to other people as a Religion. Reference to the Constitutions makes it quite clear that the system is one meant to exist outside and independently of Religion; that all the Order requires of its members is a belief in Deity and personal conformation to the Moral Law, every Brother being free to follow whatsoever form of religion and mode of worship he pleases.

Neither is Masonry a Philosophy; albeit behind it lies a large philosophical background not appearing in its surface-rituals and doctrine, but left for discovery to the research and effort of the Brethren. That philosophical background is a Gnosis or Wisdom-teaching as old as the world, one which has been shared alike by the Vedists of the East, the Egyptian, Chaldean and Orphic Initiation systems, the Pythagorean and Platonist schools, and all the Mystery Temples of both the past and the present, Christian or otherwise. The present renaissance in the Masonic Order is calculated to cause a marked, if gradual, revival of interest in that philosophy, with the probable eventual result that there will come about a general restoration of the Mysteries, inhibited during the last sixteen centuries. But of this more will be said in the final section of this book.

The official description of Masonry is that it is a "System of Morality." This is true, but in two senses, one only of which is usually thought of. The term is usually interpreted as meaning a "system of morals." But men need not enter a secret order to learn morals and study ethics; nor is an elaborate ceremonial organisation needed to teach them. Elementary morals can be, and are, learned in the outside world; and must be learned there if one is to be merely a decent member of society. The possession of "strict morals," as every Mason knows, is a preliminary qualification for entering the Order; a man does not enter it to acquire them after he has entered. It is true he finds the Order insistent on obedience to the Moral Law and emphasising closer cultivation of certain ethical virtues, as is essential to those who propose to enter upon a course of spiritual science; and this is the primary, more obvious sense in which the term "system of morality" is used.

But the word "morality," in its original, and also in its Masonic, connotation, has a further meaning; one carrying the same sense as it does when we speak of a "morality-play." A "morality" is a literary or dramatic way of expressing spiritual truth, putting it forward allegorically and in accordance with certain well-settled principles and methods (mores); it is the equivalent of a usage or "use," as ecclesiastics speak of "the Sarum use" or liturgy. In the same sense Plutarch's *Moralia* is largely a series of disquisitions upon the mores of the ancient religious Mystery-schools.

A "system of morality," therefore, means secondarily "a systematised and dramatised method of moral discipline and philosophic instruction, based on ancient usage and long-established practice." The method in question is that of Initiation; the usage and practice is that of allegory and symbol, which it is the Freemason's duty, if he wishes to understand his system, to labour to interpret and put to personal application. If he fails to do so, he still remains—and the system deliberately intends that he should—in the dark about the Order's real meaning and secrets, although formally a member of it. The Order, the morality-system, merely guarantees its own possession of Truth; it does not undertake to impart it save to those who labour for it. For Truth and its real arcana can never be communicated directly, or save through allegory and symbol, myth and sacrament. The onus of translating these must ever rest with the recipient as part of his lifework; until he makes the truth his own he can never know it to be truth; he must do the will before he can know the doctrine.

"I know not how it is" (said St. Bernard of Clairvaux of allegory and symbol) "but the more that spiritual realities are clothed with obscuring veils, the more they delight and attract; and nothing so much heightens longing for them as such tender refusal."

Masonry, then—as a "system of morality" as thus defined—is neither a Religion nor a Philosophy, but at once a Science and an Art, a Theory and a Practice; and this was ever the way in which the Schools of the Ancient Wisdom and Mysteries proceeded. They first exhibited to the intending disciple a picture of the Life-process; they taught him the story of the soul's genesis and descent into this world; they showed him its present imperfect, restricted state and its unfortunate position; they indicated that there was a scientific method by which it might be perfected and regain its original condition. This was the Science-half of their systems, the programme or theory placed in advance before disciples, that they might have a thorough intellectual grasp of the purpose of the Mysteries and what admission to them involved.

Then followed the other half; the practical work to be done by the disciple upon himself, in purifying himself; controlling his sense-nature; correcting natural undisciplined tendencies; mastering his thought, his mental processes and will, by a rigorous rule of life and art of living. When he showed proficiency in both the theory and the practice, and could withstand certain tests, then but not before he was allowed the privilege of Initiation—a secret process, conferred by already initiated Masters or experts, the details of which were never disclosed outside the process itself.

Such, in a few words, was the age-old science of the Mysteries, whether in Egypt, Greece or elsewhere, and it is that science which, in very compressed, diluted form, is perpetuated and reproduced in modern Masonry. To emphasising and demonstrating this fact, both the present and my former volume are devoted; their purpose being coupled with a hope that, when the true intention of the Order is perceived, the Craft may begin to fulfil its original design and become an instrument of real initiating efficiency instead of, as hitherto, a merely social and charitable institution. Indeed, the place and office of Masonry cannot be adequately appreciated without acquaintance with the Mysteries Masonry of antiquity, for, as a poet (Patmore) wrote who knew the latter perfectly,

Save by the Old Road none attain the new,
And from the Ancient Hills alone we catch the view!

Masonry having the above purpose, whilst not a religion, is consistent with and adaptable to any and every religion. But it is capable of going further. For an Order of Initiation (like the monastic Orders within the older Churches) is intended to provide a higher standard of instruction, a larger communication of truth and wisdom, than the elementary ones offered by public popular religion; and at the same time it requires more rigorous personal discipline and imposes much more exacting claims upon the mind and will of its adherents. The popular religious teaching of any people, Christian or not, is as it were for the masses as yet incapable of stronger food and unadapted to rigorous discipline; it is accommodated to the simple understanding of the man in the street, jog-trotting along the road of life. Initiation is meant for the expert, the determined spiritual athlete, ready to face the deeper mysteries of being, and resolute to attain, as soon as may be, the heights to which he knows his own spirit, when awakened, can take him.

Is not the present declension of interest in popular religion and public worship due—far from entirely, yet largely—not to irreligiousness, but to the fact that conventional religious presentation does not satisfy the rational and spiritual needs of a public forced and disciplined by the exigencies of modern existence to insist upon a clear understanding and a firm intellectual foothold in respect of any form of venture it is called upon to undertake? Is not the turnover of so many essentially religiously-minded and earnestly questing people from the Churches to variants of religious expression, including Masonry, due largely to that reason and to the fact that the Churches, whilst inculcating faith, offering hope, proclaiming love, fail entirely in providing what the Mysteries of the past always did—such a clear philosophical explanation of life and the Universe as provided—not proof, which in regard to ultimate verities it is impossible to offer—but an intellectual motive for turning from things of sense to things of spirit?

Nothing is further from my wish or intention in these pages than to extol Masonry at the expense of any existing Religion or Church, or to suggest competition between institutions which are not and can never be competitors, but complementaries. I am merely asserting the simple obvious facts that popular favour has turned, and will more and more turn, to that market which best supplies its needs, and that for many nowadays the Churches fail to supply those needs, or form at best an inferior or inadequate source of supply. The growing human intelligence has outgrown—not religious truth but presentations of it that sufficed in less exacting social conditions than obtain to-day, and it is calling for more sustaining nutriment.

It may be useful to recall how the position was viewed not long ago by an advanced mind racially detached from the religion and ways of the Western world. A Hindu religious Master, an Initiate, who attended the World's Congress of Religions at Chicago as the representative of the Vedantists, made an observational tour of America and Europe with a view to sympathetically understanding and appraising their religious organisations and methods. His conclusions may be summarised thus: "The Western ideal is to be doing (to be active); the Eastern, to be suffering (to be passive). The perfect life would be a wonderful harmony of the two. Western religious organisations (Churches and sects) involve grave disadvantages; for they are always breeding new evils, which are not known to the East with its absence of organisation. The perfect condition would come from a true blending of these opposite methods. For the Western soul, it is well for a man to be born in a Church, but terrible for him to die in one; for in religion there must be growth. A young man is to be censured who fails to attend and learn from the Church of his nation; the elderly man is equally to be censured if he does attend—he ought to have outgrown what that Church offers and to have attained a higher order of religious life and understanding."

The same conclusion was expressed by an eminent and ardent religionist of our own country: "The work of the Church in the world is not to teach the mysteries of life, so much as to persuade the soul to that arduous degree of purity at which Deity Himself becomes her teacher. The work of the Church ends when the knowledge of God begins." In other words, Initiation science (in a real and not merely a ceremonial sense) is needed and commences to be applicable only when elementary spiritual tuition has been assimilated and richer nourishment is called for. The same writer, though a zealous member of the Roman Church, affirms frankly and truly that in any age of the world, the real Initiate of the Mysteries, whatever his race or national religion, must needs always stand higher in spiritual wisdom and stature than the non-initiate of the Christian or any other faith.

Such testimonies as these point to—what many others will feel to be a necessity—the need of some complementary, supplementary aid to popular Religion; some Higher Grade School, in the greater seclusion and privacy of which can be both studied and practised lessons in the secrets and mysteries of our being which cannot be exhibited *coram populo*. Such an aid is provided by a Secret Order, an Initiation system, and is at hand in Freemasonry. It remains to be seen whether the Masonic Craft, in both its own and the larger ulterior interest of society, will avail itself of the opportunity in its hands. There being a tendency in that direction in the Craft to-day, the pages of this and of my former book are offered to encouraging that tendency to a fruition that could not make otherwise than for the general good.

But let those of us who are desirous to further that tendency, and to see provided an advanced system of spiritual instruction, never entertain a notion of competing with any other community, or permit ourselves a single thought of disparagement or contempt towards either those who learn or those who teach in other places. Life involves growth. The hyacinth-bulb in the pot before me will not remain a bulb, whose life and stature are to be restricted to the level of the pot it has been placed in. It will shoot up a foot higher and there burst in flower and fragrance, albeit that its roots remain in the soil. Similarly each human life is as a bulb providentially planted in some pot, in some Religion, some Church. If it truly fulfils the law and central instincts of its nature it will outgrow that pot, rise high above the pot's surface-level, and ultimately blossom in a consciousness transcending anything it knew whilst in the bulb stage. That consciousness will be one not of the beginner, the student, the neophyte in the Mysteries; it will be that of the full Initiate.

But that perfected life will still be rooted in the soil, and, far from despising it, will be forever grateful for the pot in which its growth became possible. Masonry will, therefore, never disparage simpler or less advanced forms of intellectual or spiritual instruction. The Mason, above all men and in a much fuller, deeper sense, will respond to the old ordinance "Honour thy father and mother." In whatever form, under whichsoever of the many names the God-idea presents itself to himself or his fellow-men, he will honour the Universal Father; and in whatsoever soil of Mother-Earth, or whichsoever section of Mother-Church, he or they have received their infant nurture, he will honour that Mother, even as he is bound also to honour his own Mother Lodge, seeing in each of these the temporal reflection of still another Mother, the supernal parent described as "the Mother of us all."

Upon one other point I must add a word. A writer wishing to help on the understanding of Masonry, as fully as may be, in the interests of Brethren who, as events have shown, are waiting in numbers to receive and ready to turn to account such help as may be given, is put to real anxiety to find a way of so writing that he simultaneously discharges the combined duty of extending that help and of observing his own obligations as to silence.

In my former volume I explained that, in respect of necessary safeguards, all due secrecy should be observed; and the assurance is now repeated in respect of the present one. No non-Mason need look to find in these pages any of the distinctive secrets of the Craft; no Mason, I believe, will trace in them any disloyal word or motive, or recognise in them anything but earnest anxiousness to promote the

Craft's interests to the uttermost. Moreover, the things I permit myself to say are, I conceive, exempt from silence as regards the Craft, for they are things which justly and lawfully belong to it and properly concern it; and since its members, near and far, in full measure and in many ways have proved themselves worthy of such confidence as I can show them, I feel myself justified in addressing them more intimately than before. As regards those outside the Craft, into whose hands a published book cannot be prevented from falling, what I have written consists of things already spoken about at large in other forms of expression in these days of keen search for guidance upon the dark path of human life; and let me here say that as warm, and almost as many, appreciations of my former volume have reached me from non-Masons as from within the Craft, and that it has attracted to the Order much sympathy and good-will that did not previously exist.

Doubtless there are eyes of such strictness that they regard any public mention of the Masonic subject as an impropriety. Even these I would not willingly offend; yet to allow a possible technicality to prevent the giving, to those seeking it, the only gift I can make to the Craft in return for what it has given to myself, seems to me less meritorious Masonic conduct than would be the negative virtue of keeping rigid silence when so much can usefully be said.

So I take comfort from that ancient word of wisdom which proclaims that "He that observes the wind shall not sow, and he that observes the clouds will not reap!" And though, whilst writing these pages, a morning desire to sow my seed has often been followed by an evening prompting to withhold my hand, yet the former has prevailed with me. And if of that seed, some falls upon Masonic and some chances upon other ground, who shall know whether shall prosper this or that? but I pray that both shall be alike good. For, continues the same old Sage, "truly light is sweet, and a precious thing it is for the eyes to behold the Sun"; and to-day there are drawn blinds everywhere waiting to be lifted, to let in a Sunlight that belongs to no close community, but to all men alike.

So having, I hope, brought myself to order in this respect, and marking with thankful eyes the sunrise of a new order of intelligence breaking over the Brotherhood, let me now proceed, in the one Name that is thought of under many names, to declare the Lodge open, for the purpose of considering Craft-Masonry in all its degrees.

CENTENIAL INTRODUCTION

In the hundred years since Walter Leslie Wilmshurst penned *The Masonic Initiation*, his work has continued to illuminate the path for countless Masons and spiritual seekers. Wilmshurst's profound reflections on the esoteric dimensions of Freemasonry remain as relevant today as they were when first written, offering a timeless guide to the inner journey of self-discovery and spiritual enlightenment. This centennial edition celebrates his enduring legacy while introducing new commentary to explore and expand upon his insights.

As we present this edition, it is vital to clarify that the thoughts and interpretations provided in the added commentary are solely those of the author. They should not be interpreted as representing the views of any specific Lodge, district, jurisdiction, Grand Lodge, or constitution within Freemasonry, nor of any other fraternal order. These reflections are the personal meditations of one Mason, inspired by Wilmshurst's masterpiece, shared as an invitation for readers to contemplate these subjects further.

Freemasonry today finds itself at a crossroads, navigating an increasingly secular, fast-paced, and technology-driven world. In this context, Wilmshurst's call to engage deeply with the Craft's esoteric and mystical teachings resonates more strongly than ever. His work challenges us to look beyond the surface of ritual and symbol, to embrace the transformative power of Freemasonry as a living philosophy.

This centennial edition honours Wilmshurst's original intentions while providing a contemporary lens through which his teachings can be understood and applied. The added commentary aims not only to clarify his profound ideas but also to draw connections between Freemasonry's ancient wisdom and modern thought. By weaving together historical insight, philosophical reflection, and practical application, this edition seeks to inspire today's Masons to approach their journey with renewed purpose and understanding.

Wilmshurst himself spoke of Freemasonry as a "progressive science," one that evolves with each generation while remaining anchored in eternal truths. Through these reflections, we hope to carry forward his legacy, encouraging each reader to embrace the Craft not simply as a collection of rituals and traditions but as a lifelong path of self-transmutation and service.

This centennial edition is offered with humility and reverence for Wilmshurst's original work, alongside a profound hope that it will serve as a beacon for all who seek the light of wisdom. Let these meandering thoughts, born of deep pondering upon Wilmshurst's text, inspire you to delve further into the mysteries of the Craft and discover their relevance to your own journey.

As you turn these pages, may you be reminded that Freemasonry's greatest teachings lie not in what is spoken aloud but in what is reflected upon in silence. May this edition spark within you the desire to build, to refine, and to ascend—to shape your life into a Temple worthy of the Divine.

CHAPTER ONE - THE MASONIC INITIATION

FROM DARKNESS TO LIGHT

No more needed and useful work is to be done in the Masonic Order to-day than the education of its members in the true purpose of rites of initiation, that they may the better appreciate the reason, the importance, and the seriousness, of the work the Order was designed to achieve.

Hitherto, that educative work has been grievously neglected, with prejudicial results to the Craft through the admission of candidates little adapted to appreciate its purpose. Some members have no wish to be masonically educated. They are content to be Masons in name only and are satisfied that the monotonous, mechanical repetition of unexplained ceremonies and side-lectures fulfils every requisite and conveys all that is to be known. Yet in every Lodge are to be found brethren who are asking for something more than this, who know that the Craft was designed for wider and better ends; who, as earnest seekers after Wisdom and light, entered the Order in the hope of finding them, but who too often are repelled by what they do find there or lose interest on their needs being left unprovided for. It is in the special interest of this worthier type of Mason that this address is given.

We greatly need competent, trained exponents of the meaning and symbolism of the Craft, not merely teachers of the letter of its rituals and lectures. The duty and responsibility of providing this wider instruction surely lies upon those holding the rank of Installed Master. Is not their place in that East from which real light should continually be coming, and whence they are supposed to employ and instruct in Masonic science those who sit in less or greater degrees of darkness in other symbolic quarters of the Lodge? Are they not the figurative representatives of royal Solomon, and symbolic mouthpieces of a more than human Wisdom?

Over each of them has there not been raised a most solemn petition that they may be endued with wisdom to comprehend, judgment to define, and ability to enforce obedience to the holy law declaring the conditions upon which real Initiation depends, so that they may effectively enlighten the minds of their Brethren? How many Installed Masters are conscious in their hearts of possessing, or of even striving to acquire, that wisdom, that understanding of our science, that power of raising others from darkness to light in any real and vital sense?

Now you have called me to the presidency of this large Association of Installed Masters, whose function is to further the best interests of the Craft in this district. In accepting that position of honour, can I better use it than by inviting you, my Worshipful Colleagues, to consider with me some lines upon which true Masonic instruction should be directed, so that we may combine in raising the general level of Masonic science in our respective Lodges, and at least try to justify more fully our pretension to be Masters of it?

My purpose now, therefore, is, firstly, to give some idea of what real Initiation involves, and to show how great a difference exists between it and mere formal passage through the ceremonies of the Craft. Secondly, it is to explain what Initiation meant and still means in the more secret and advanced systems out of which modern Masonry has sprung as a comparatively new branch from a very ancient tree. And lastly, it is to indicate how, and with what greater efficacy, our Lodge-work might be conducted if we better realised the true nature and purpose of the Order.

INITIATION, REAL AND CEREMONIAL

It may be a surprise to some members of our Craft to be told that our ceremonial rites, as at present performed, do not constitute or confer real Initiation at all, in the original sense of admitting a man to the solemn mysteries of the human soul, and to practical experience in divine science. The words "Initiation" and "Mysteries" have become so popularised and debased that they are nowadays used in relation to familiarising anyone with the methods of, say, the Stock Exchange, or any other pursuit with which he is unacquainted.

We profess to confer Initiation, but few Masons know what real Initiation involves; very few, one fears, would have the wish, the courage, or the willingness to make the necessary sacrifices to attain it if they did. Nevertheless, our Craft Degrees give us a rough outline and fragmentary sketch of what the real process entails, and they leave it with ourselves either to amplify that sketch by our own efforts and to make its implications such a reality that our whole life becomes transformed in consequence, or to treat it as so much ceremonial through which we are only to pass formally, leaving our old imperfect nature not a whit changed by the process.

Now, if Masonry, with its solemn prayers, assurances, and pledges, means anything, its true purpose is to promote the spiritual life and development of its members to a degree far in advance of what it accomplishes at present. Otherwise, it remains but a social formality, while its obligations and religious references are apt to lapse into profanity or even blasphemy. To prevent this, there is needed a clear grasp of the fundamental purpose of an initiatory system and the reason for its existence, after which one can proceed more advantageously to understanding its degrees and symbols in detail. For without such knowledge and understanding there can be no real power, no spiritual driving-force, behind our rites; and without that power, ceremonies are but perfunctory, inefficacious formalities.

Ceremonies were instituted originally to give an external form to an internal act; but where the internal power to perform such acts does not exist, a ceremony will avail nothing and achieve nothing. You can go on making nominal Masons by the thousand, but you will only be creating a large organisation of men who remain as unenlightened in the Mysteries as they always were. You cannot make a single real Initiate, save, as our teaching indicates, by the help of God and the earnest intelligent co-operation of those qualified to assist to the light a fellow-being who, from his heart and not merely from his lips, desires that light, humbly confessing himself spiritually poor, worthless, immersed in darkness, and unable to find that light elsewhere or by his own efforts. For real Initiation means an expansion of consciousness from the human to the divine level.

Every system of real Initiation, whether of the past or present, is divided into three clear-cut stages; since before anyone can pass from his natural darkness to the light supernal and discover the Blazing Star or Glory at his own centre, there are three distinct tasks to be achieved. They are as follows:

First, the turning away from the attractions of the outer world, involving detachment from the allurements of all that is meant by "money and metals," and the purification and subdual of the bodily and sensual tendencies. Not everyone is able or ripe for doing this; the natural life maintains a powerful hold over us, and our ingrained habits are not readily changed. Yet as long as any of these sensible attractions magnetise and chain us to physical enjoyment, so long are we "in worldly possessions" and precluded from attaining real Initiation into what is super-physical. This work of detachment and self-purification is our Entered Apprentice work, and to it, as you know, is theoretically allotted the long period of seven years.

The reason for the seven years' apprenticeship is based on the septenary principle operating in Nature. In the course of each seven years, the material particles of the human body become entirely changed and reconstituted. By a course of pure living, diet, and thought for that period, therefore, the physical organism is clarified, sublimated, and made a more efficient vehicle for the transmission of the central inner light. This is the true reason for asceticism; the gradual substitution of refined physical tissues for grosser, impure ones.

Second, the analysis, discipline, and obtaining control of one's inner world—of the mind, of one's thoughts, one's intellectual and psychic faculties. This extremely difficult task is that of the Fellow Craft stage, to which is allotted a further five years, which with the previous seven make twelve. Because of this, the candidate who had duly completed this period was said, in the ancient systems, to be mystically "twelve years old,"—a point to which we will refer again presently.

Third, the "last and greatest trial," lay in the breaking and surrender of the personal will, the dying down of all sense of personality and self-hood, so that the petty personal will may become merged in the divine Universal Will and the illusion of separate independent existence give way to conscious realisation of unity with the one Life that permeates the Universe. For so only can one be raised from conditions of unreality, strife, and figurative death to a knowledge of ultimate Reality, Peace, and Life Immortal. To attain this is to attain Mastership, involving complete domination of the lower nature and the development in oneself of a higher order of life and faculty. And he who thus attained was said to be of the mystical age of thirty years, of which also I will say more presently.

Now it is these three stages, these three labours or processes, that are epitomised dramatically in our three Degrees. Every Mason in taking those Degrees identifies himself ceremonially with what they signify; he also solemnly obligates himself to put their significance into actual practice in his subsequent life. But it is obvious that those labours are highly arduous tasks demanding the whole time, the persistent thought, and the concentrated energies of anyone who submits himself to them. They are not achieved by merely passing through a sequence of ceremonies in three successive months, at the end of which the candidate, far from being an Initiate, usually remains the same bewildered, benighted man he was before, knowing only that he has been hurried through three formal rites entitling him at last to the august title of Master Mason.

Hence we are justified in asserting that Masonry, as now unintelligently practised, does not and cannot confer real Initiation; it merely discharges certain ceremonial formalities. Nevertheless, in those formalities the earnest Mason, the diligent pursuer of the path of light, is given a clear chart of the process of spiritual self-development which he can follow up by his own subsequent exertions; and further, he is directed to a most valuable key for unlocking central truth and discovering the hidden secrets and mysteries of his own being—the key of intense aspiration to find the light of the centre.

"Does that key hang or lie?" asks one of our lectures. For most Masons, it lies. It lies rusting and unused, because they either do not desire or do not know how to use it, or have no one competent to show them how to do so. For some few, it hangs—you are taught where—and, though it is of no manner of metal, those who have found and use it, pursuing their quest with fervency and zeal, if perhaps at first with shambling feet and uncertain steps, may assuredly hope to gain admission into the Lodge of their own soul, and, when the last hoodwink falls that now blinds their vision, to find themselves there face to face with the Master of that Lodge, and in possession of every point of fellowship with Him.

A poet well schooled in the process of real Initiation has thus written of it:

Pierce thy heart to find the key
With thee take
Only what none else would take

Lose, that the lost thou mayst receive;
Die, for none other way canst live.
When earth and heaven lay down their veil
And that apocalypse turns thee pale,
When thy seeing blindeth thee
To what thy fellow-mortals see,
When their sight to thee is sightless,
Their living, death; their light, most lightless;
Seek no more ....
— Francis Thompson's "Mistress of Vision"

For it is then, and only then, that true Initiation is achieved, that the lost Word is found at the deep centre of one's own heart, and the genuine but withheld secrets of our immortal being are restored to us in exchange for the natural knowledge and faculties which, in this world of time and change, have been given us by Providence as their temporary and mortal substitutions.

THE PURPOSE OF THE MYSTERIES

We shall understand little of the purpose of Masonry unless we know that of the older systems out of which it issued. That purpose was to promote and expedite the spiritual evolution of those who desired the regeneration of their nature and were prepared to submit to the necessary discipline.

Thus, the work of the Ancient Mysteries was something vastly more serious and momentous than merely passing candidates through a series of formal rites as we do today. Their great buildings, which still survive, were assuredly not erected at such immense labor and skill merely to provide convenient meeting places, like our modern Lodge premises, at which to administer a formal rite at the end of a day devoted to business and secular pursuits. The mass of Initiation literature and hieroglyphs available to us reveals how drastic and searching was the work to which candidates were subjected under the expert guidance of Masters who had previously undergone the same discipline and become competent to advance their juniors.

With them, the work was a difficult but exact science, claiming one's whole time and energies; it was the highest, greatest, and holiest of all forms of science—the science of the human soul and the art of its conversion from a natural to a regenerate supernatural state. Reminiscences of the dignity of this work still survive in our references to Masonry as the "noble science" and "royal art," terms meaningless today, although each newly made Mason is charged to make daily progress in Masonic science and everyone installed into the chair of a Lodge is termed a Master of Arts and Sciences.

But this secret immemorial science could be imparted only to those morally fit and spiritually ripe for it, as not all men yet are. It was meant only for those bent on passing from the moral and intellectual darkness in which normal humanity is plunged, to that light which dwells in their darkness, though that darkness comprehendeth it not until it is opened up at their centre. It was solely for those who sought the way, the truth, and the supernatural life, and were ready to divest themselves of the "money and metals" of temporal interests and concentrate their energies upon the evolution of the higher principles of their nature, which is possible only by the abnegation and surrender of their lower tendencies.

Evolution, nowadays recognised as a universal process in Nature, is sometimes supposed to be a modern discovery. But the ancient Wisdom-teaching knew and acted upon it ages before modern scientists discovered it in our own day. It recognised that in all the Universe there is but one Life broken up and differentiated into innumerable forms, and evolving through those forms from lesser to greater degrees of perfection. In Masonic metaphor, it saw Nature to be the vast general quarry and forest out of which individual lives have been hewn like so much stone and timber, which, when duly perfected, are destined to be fitted together and built into a new and higher synthesis, a majestic Temple worthy of the Divine indwelling, and of which Solomon's temple was a type.

All life has issued out of the "East," i.e., from the Great World of Infinite Spirit, and has journeyed to the "West" or the Little World of finite form and embodiment, whence, when duly perfected by experience in those restricted conditions, it is ordained to return to the "East." Hence, when our Entered Apprentice is asked in the lecture, whence he comes and whither he goes, he replies that he is on his way back from the temporal West to the eternal East. The answer corresponds with a fuller one to be found in the surviving records of the early British Initiates, the Welsh bards, where to the same question the following reply is made:

> *"I came from the Great World, having my beginning in Spirit. I am now in the Little World (of form and body) where I have traversed the circle of strife and evolution, and now, at its termination, I am man. In my beginning, I had but a bare capacity for life; but I came through every form capable of a body and life to the state of man, where my condition was severe and grievous during the age of ages. I came through every form capable of life, in water, in earth, in air. And there happened to me every severity, every hardship, every evil, every suffering. But purity and perfection cannot be obtained without seeing and knowing everything, and this is not possible without suffering everything. And there can be no full and perfect Love that does not provide for its creatures the conditions needful to lead to the experience that results in perfection. Every one shall attain to the circle of perfection at last."*
>
> *—From Barddas; the ancient initiate tradition of Welsh Druidic*

LIFE, then, was seen as broken up and distributed into innumerable individualised lives or souls and as passing from one bodily form to another in a perpetual progression. (In Masonic metaphor, those individualised souls are called "stones," for stone or rock is an emblem of what is most enduring, and the stones are rough ashlars or perfect cubes accordingly as they exist in the rough or have been squared, worked upon, and polished.) The bodily form with which the soul becomes invested upon entering this world (symbolised by the Mason being invested with the apron) was seen to be transient, variable, perishable, of small moment compared with the life or soul animating it. Yet it was of the greatest importance in another way, since it provided a fulcrum point or point of resistance for the soul's education and development. It was, as we still term it, the "tomb of transformation"; the grave into which the soul descended for the purpose of working out its own salvation, for transforming and improving itself, and ascending out of it the stronger and wiser for the experience. Thus, life was seen as one continuous stream, temporarily checked by the particular form that clothed it, but flowing on from form to form to ever new and higher conditions; slumbering in the mineral, dreaming in the plant, waking in the animal, and reaching moral self-consciousness in man.

But does the ascending process end there? Is man as he is now, the goal, the last word, of evolution? Surely, no. As a Persian Initiate once wrote:

I died as a mineral and became a plant.
I died as a plant and rose to animal.
I died as an animal and became man.
Why should I fear? When did I ever grow less by dying?
Yet once more I shall die as man, to soar
With angels blest. But even from angelhood I must pass on.
I shall become what no mind e'er conceived!

Now, in order that evolution from lower to higher degrees of life may take place, some force must previously have been involved in living organisms that makes their evolution possible. You cannot have evolution without involution. A seed would never grow unless it held within it the force which expands it into a plant with a glory of leaf, flower, and fruit. An acorn contains in itself the possibility of the oak. A bird's egg conceals within its fluids the miracle of the feathered bird and the skylark's song. Place any of these in appropriate conditions, and the latent life-force will evolve naturally to its preordained limit. The growth may even be artificially accelerated by methods of intensive culture.

What now of man? Man also contains within him a life-force, a "vital and immortal principle" as Masonry calls it, which has not yet expanded to full development in him, and indeed in many men is scarcely active at all. Man, too, has that in him enabling him to evolve from the stage of the mortal animal to a being immortal, superhuman, godlike. Man is evolving towards a far-off divine event in common with all Nature. But how slowly! And how greatly he thwarts and retards his own development by indulging his gross mortal body and its sensual tendencies, instead of repressing them and cultivating his latent higher principles! Human nature, it is commonly said, continues always the same; its weaknesses and vices are those of thousands of years ago, and looking back over the centuries there is little perceptible improvement in the mass despite our boasted progress and civilisation.

Can this long, slow process of human evolution be expedited? Is there a method of intensive culture that can be applied to man; one that will more quickly lift him clean above his present level and transform the sensual, benighted, human animal into an illuminated godlike being?

To this the answer of the Ancient Mysteries was "Yes, there is. Human evolution can be accelerated; if not at present in the mass of humanity, yet in suitable individuals. Human nature is perfectible by an intensive process of purification and initiation. There is a royal science of spiritual advancement, and an art of living, by which the latent, undeveloped divine Life-principle in man can be liberated from the veils of darkness in him now obscuring it and brought forward into full play. If suitable candidates will but make the requisite sacrifices and submit to the necessary discipline, they can be brought in their present lifetime from darkness to light; they can be raised to a higher degree of humanity than is otherwise possible to them, and from that position they in turn will be able to raise others to the same degree and so gradually increase the spiritual stature and powers of the whole race."

The work of the Ancient Mysteries was, therefore, a "perfecting" work, or a work of initiation introducing men to a new order of life, since it was designed to make imperfect beings whole and perfect by completing their evolutionary possibilities. The Greek word for this (teleios) has the twofold meaning, "to make perfect" and "to initiate." It occurs constantly in the Scriptures, the greatest text-book of Initiation-science that exists. They speak of "the just made perfect"; "be ye perfect as your Father in heaven is perfect"; "we speak wisdom (initiation science) to such as are perfect (or initiated)."

This perfecting work was for all men alike, of whatever race, language or religion, as Masonry is to-day. For all are brethren, and upon an equal footing in respect of this work, though not all men are necessarily ready to undertake it at the same moment; all their religions are but so many radii of one circle, designed to lead them from the circumference and surface of life to the one light at its centre. The qualifications of a candidate for the Mysteries were precisely those provided for Masonic candidates to-day. The one dominant wish of his heart in asking for admission had to be a yearning desire to pass from his natural blindness to the innermost light, and to have his old imperfect nature revolutionized and transformed.

Let me quote one of the oldest prayers in the world, still used in the East by those seeking real Initiation. In its original Sanskrit it consists of but six words, which may be Englished thus:

From the unreal, lead me to the Real!
From darkness, lead me to light!
From the mortal, bring me to Immortality

It expresses the desire that should be not only upon the lips but burning in the heart of every candidate the world over, under whatever system of Initiation he may come. Without that desire as the deepest urge of his heart no real Initiation is possible, nor is any candidate properly prepared to ask for it. No one can expect to come to the revelation of the supernatural light or to be raised to the sublime degree of a Master-soul, who is content with his present life as it is, who regards himself as not in darkness but as already enlightened, or supposes his present mortal existence to constitute real life.

Only by perceiving the unreality and impermanency of the present world and its interests can one really begin to detach himself from it and divest himself, in thought and desire, of its "money and metals." So long as one carries these with him or remains in any sense "in worldly possessions," so long he darkens his own light and automatically defers his own initiation into it.

They mean not merely one's cash and temporal belongings. They include all that clogs and clings to us from our immersion in the outer world; our intellectual possessions, our stores of notions, beliefs and preconceptions about truth, and the mental habits and self-will we have acquired, even with the best motives, in our state of darkness.

All these constitute our "worldly possessions," and they are not our real wealth but our limitations. It is a paradox, but a true one, that we can only gain by giving them up. Their attraction must cease if that high light we profess to seek is ever to be found, and the aspirant for it must stand at the door of the Mysteries in the deepest sense a poor candidate in a state of darkness, content to be as a child and surrender himself to an entirely new order and rule of life.

Few are prepared for this task of self-divestment of all that, as experienced men of the world, they have clung to and built into their mental fabric. How many of those who ceremonially profess to do so would be ready or content to do it really? On being told of this prerequisite to Initiation they would go away sorrowful, for they have great possessions, and are not yet prepared to give them up for something intangible.

In a like sense the candidate had to be a free man; free in a moral rather than in a civil sense; voluntarily offering himself for the work and free from all attachments hindering its achievement; and so becoming also free to the goodly fellowship of all other initiates the world over and free from any less worthy intercourse. He had to be of full age; that is, in full bodily and mental maturity so as to be fit for the disciplines awaiting him, and spiritually mature (as not everyone is) for undertaking the final stages of his evolution. Sound judgment, a sound mind in a sound body, was also essential in view of the demands made on the mental and psychic faculties, involving the risk of insanity to the mentally unstable. Strict morals (or chastity) were imperative, since the task of self-transformation involves physiological changes in the bodily organism necessitating the utmost personal purity and continence.

And he had to be of good report. This does not mean of good reputation. It means that on being tested by the initiating authorities he must be found spiritually responsive to the ideals aimed at and "ring true," giving back a good sound or report like a coin that is tapped to determine its genuineness. In the wonderful Egyptian rituals in the Book of the Dead, one of the titles always found accorded to the Initiate was "true of voice." This is the same thing as our reference to possessing the "tongue of good report." It does not mean that he was incapable of falsity and hypocrisy, which goes without saying, but that his very voice revealed his inherent spirituality and his own speech reflected and was coloured by the divine Word behind it. The vocal and heart nervous centres—"the guttural" and "the pectoral," as we say—are intimately related physiologically.

Purity or impurity of heart modifies the tonal quality and moral power of one's speech. The voice of the real Initiate or saint is always marked by a charm, a music, an impressiveness, and a sincerity absent in other men; for he is "true of voice"; he possesses the "tongue of good report."

The rule of the Ancient Mysteries was, and still is in other systems, that twelve years of preparation should elapse before the last great spiritual experience was permitted that brought the candidate to the light at his centre and qualified him for Mastership, though less sufficed in appropriate cases. As the result of his purification and labours he had become an illuminate and he was mystically said to be twelve years old. From a rough ashlar he had become a polished perfect cube, a stone meet for building into the "holy city" which we are told lieth foursquare and has twelve gates that are always open. For all the parts of his organism were now equalised and balanced, and all his gates (or channels of intercourse with the divine world), no longer shut and clogged by the darkness of his former impurities, lay open for the passage through them of the true light. In Masonry, this condition is called the "hour of high twelve"; and he who has attained it will be, like Hiram, in constant communion with, and adoration of, the Most High.

Similarly, when the candidate had advanced still further to the sublime degree and powers of Mastership he was said to be thirty years old. You will find these mystical ages referred to in the third Gospel, where we are told (Luke ii, 42) of the Great Exemplar being twelve years old and so illuminated that His wisdom confounded the academic but unenlightened teachers of the Temple; and again (Luke iii, 23) that He "began to be about thirty years old," at which period began his work as a Master, which continued for another three years and manifested such works and teaching as are possible only to a Master. Thirty-three years was, in the Mysteries, the mystical duration of life of every initiate who attained Mastership.

That period has no relation to bodily age; it is based on considerations we need not now enter into but referring to the completion of human evolution, when it can be said of the soul's travail "It is finished," "He hath wrought the purpose through of That which made him man." It is for this reason that the Ancient and Accepted Scottish Rite of Masonry extends to 33 Degrees, in perpetuation of the original secret tradition.

Of the detailed methods employed in assisting properly qualified candidates to the light of the centre, whether in the ancient systems or at the present day, and of the wonderful change wrought by them in the candidate himself, nothing can be said publicly; these are matters belonging to silence. The secrets and mysteries of real Initiation can never be fully communicated except in the course of the process itself. They are not disclosed in Masonry at all. Our teaching refers to them as being "serious, solemn and awful," but leaves them at that and provides various substituted ones which have no value save for ceremonial use, and as indications that more genuine ones exist which qualified Brethren will come to know when time and circumstances warrant. To all others they will remain sealed. That time and those circumstances depend upon our own desire and efforts. It is an ancient maxim of the science that "when the disciple is ready, the Master will be found waiting" to help on his advancement, and in accordance with this our teaching expressly declares that the purpose of the Mason is to seek a Master and from him to gain instruction. The earnest Masonic disciple whose heart and thought are steadfastly set towards the light may assuredly count upon finding himself led sooner or later to a real Initiate capable of helping him to it and of revealing so much of the real secrets as he is qualified to know.

Real Initiates exist at all times, in this country and elsewhere, for the science is not restricted to any nation or creed but is universally diffused over the earth's surface. They are, of course, not numerous and they are to be met with only by those competent to recognise them. They live a hidden life; in the world but not of it. They never seek publicity or honours; they never even disclose the fact that they are Initiates. This is the true Masonic secrecy and humility; the greatest among men are content to be as those that are least. The world little suspects what it owes to its hidden Initiates.

It would be interesting to say something of them, but time permits of my speaking only of a single case, and I will illustrate the universality of the science by referring (though reticently) to one who is not of our country, colour, or creed.

There lives in a distant part of our Empire a man who is in the fullest sense a Master Mason. Years ago he embarked upon the great quest of light, and after the necessary self-preparation under another Master he attained that great spiritual experience which changed his whole nature and raised him finally and permanently from darkness to light. You may like to know how the daily life of such a man is spent, for it conforms literally with the rule of our symbolic working tool, the 24-inch gauge, in its application to the 24 hours of the day. For at least two hours each day he withdraws entirely from all external affairs, tyling his door as it were against their intrusion, and opens the Lodge of his soul to its central depths, passing into blissful, ecstatic communion with the Most High. It is his "hour of high twelve." For another two hours a day he sleeps; that brief period, with a minimum of simple food, sufficing to rest and recuperate his bodily energies, since his real rest and sustenance are drawn from the supernatural peace and bread of life that come to him from his Centre. The remaining twenty hours of the day are devoted to unflagging labour in the interests of his countrymen and in the spiritual advancement of those brought under his guidance. You may suppose that he is a recluse living an unpractical life in a cell or a forest. On the contrary, he is a prominent man who has been knighted for his public service, a King's Counsel, Attorney-General for a large province, a cultured scholar in English and other languages, and the writer of some important books. I have asked British Government officials who have worked with him for years whether they have found anything distinctive in him; but they had detected nothing and were utterly blind to the extraordinary spiritual power and saintliness behind his formal exterior. He is one of those who has found, and lives from, the divine centre of his being —that point from Darkness which a Master Mason cannot err—and accordingly possesses wisdom and powers beyond the imagination of the uninitiated world.

THE IDEAL LODGE

And now, Brethren, from what has been said of the ancient and royal science you may see how faithfully our Craft perpetuates the world-old system of elevating men to a higher order of life than they normally experience, and at the same time you may judge how far it falls short in understanding that science and carrying its intentions into practice.

Are we always going to be content with making merely formal Masons and maintaining a merely social and philanthropic society? If so, we shall remain no different men from the popular world who are not Masons. Or are we wishful that the Craft should fulfil its purpose of being a system of real initiating efficiency by awaking the undeveloped spiritual potentialities of its members and raising them to a sublimer level of life? If so, we must educate ourselves more deeply in its meaning. Let me indicate how things would go if our work were conducted upon more intelligent lines. It is too much to expect any marked or sudden change to take place in old methods or habits, and resistance to any improvement may always be expected from some who are satisfied with things as they are. Nor can improvement be forced upon anyone; to be advantageous it must come spontaneously. But many Brethren and many Lodges sincerely desire it, and so let me offer you a picture of what an ideal Lodge would be; you may then consider how far it may be practicable to attempt to conform to that ideal.

In the first place, Lodge meetings would be primarily devoted to what we are taught is their chief purpose, namely, to expatiating on the Mysteries of the Craft and educating Brethren in the understanding of them. This is now never done; largely because we are without competent instructors. We suppose that our side-lectures are sufficient instruction. This is not the case. There are additional large fields of knowledge that Masons must explore if they wish to learn this science, while our official lectures are themselves packed with purposely obscured truths that are left to our own efforts and perspicuity to discover, but the purport of which at present remains entirely concealed.

The duly opened Lodge would be a sanctuary of silence and contemplation, broken only by ceremonial utterances or such words of competent and luminous instruction as the Master or Past Masters are moved to extend. And the higher the degree in which it is opened, the deeper and more solemn would be the sense of excluding all temporal thoughts and interests and of approaching more nearly that veiled central light whose opening into activity in our hearts we profess to be our predominant wish.

In such circumstances each Lodge meeting would become an occasion of profound spiritual experience. No member would wish to disturb the harmony of such a Lodge by talk or alien thought. No member would willingly be absent. If he were, save from necessity, it would indicate that, though entitled to wear the apron in a literal sense, he was temporarily not properly clothed in his mind and intention to be qualified to enter the Lodge. Every one would regret when such a meeting closed and it became necessary to be recalled from such peace and refreshment to the jars and labours of the outer world.

The admission of a new candidate would be a comparatively infrequent event. For no one would be received to membership save after the fullest tests of his genuine desire for Masonic knowledge and of his adaptability to it.

The conferment of the different degrees would be at much longer intervals than is now authorised, so as to ensure their being assimilated and understood, as is impossible at present. And upon the notable occasion of a degree being conferred, those present would be not merely passive spectators of the rite. They would have been educated to become active though silent helpers in it by adding the force of their united thought and desire to the spoken word, and so creating such a tense and highly charged atmosphere that an abiding permanent uplift in the candidate's consciousness might be hoped for. For the efficacy of rites like ours does not depend solely on the Master who performs them. He is the mouthpiece for the time being of all those present, but it is the whole assembly that should really be acting; forming, as it were, a battery of spiritual energy, and drawing the new Brother into vital fraternity with itself. Great power resides in strong collective thought and intention, and when these are focused and concentrated upon a candidate properly prepared in heart and mind for our ministrations, we might hope to induce in him something like real initiation; but otherwise he will be listening to but a formal recital of words.

It follows that we should never hear such things as the usual talk about "making one's Lodge a success," or as personal praise to anyone for having performed his work creditably. Whether our work is really done well, in the sense of being spiritually effective, God alone knoweth, to whom all gratitude should be rendered for any good achieved; while the only worthy success for a Lodge is its capacity for vitally affecting the lives of those who enter it and transforming their mental and moral outlook.

The Lodge-room should be holy ground; a Temple consecrated to Masonic work and used for it exclusively. For it is a symbol of the temple of the human individual, and we who are taught the necessity of every intending initiate's excluding money and metals from his thought, and who have before us the significant example of a Master who vigorously scourged all money-changers out of the Temple, should surely conform to those lessons by keeping our symbolic temple sanctified and entirely free from secular use. There is a practical advantage in so doing, for premises continually devoted to a single purpose become, as it were, charged and saturated with the thought and ideals thrown off by those who habitually so use it. A permanent spiritual atmosphere is created, the influence of which appreciably affects those who enter it, and the possibility of the efficacious initiation of candidates is thereby greatly increased; whereas that atmosphere becomes defiled, and any spiritual influence stored in it neutralised, by promiscuous use.

Visiting other Lodges would no longer be for social reasons, but, as in ancient times, solely with a desire to enlarge one's Masonic knowledge and experience, to share their spiritual privileges, or even to bring spiritual reinforcement to Lodges needing such help. No practice is more beneficial than intercourse between those of different Lodges engaged in a common work, and no right is more firmly established than that of any seeker of the light to claim and be given hospitality and assistance conducing to that end. But our modern practice of mass-visiting is calculated to disturb the true work we ought to be doing, and is somewhat of an abuse and travesty of a privilege dating from antiquity, when occasional representatives of one school of the Mysteries journeyed, often long distances, to another in a different land to enlarge their own knowledge or impart it to those they visited.

Promotion to office in the Craft would not be by rotation or from seniority of membership or social standing in the outside world. It would depend entirely upon spiritual proficiency; upon ability to impart real illumination to candidates and advance the true work of the Craft. The little jealousies and heartburning that now occur at the annual promotions would be impossible; such things belong to the base metals in our nature, which ought long ago to have been got rid of in anyone really qualified for office. Did we better realise the serious nature of Initiation work, we should often shrink in humility too from accepting positions we are now eager to seize. Remember that in leaving the outer world and passing the portal of the Lodge into the world within, all values change; all questions, and even all sense, of personality should cease. You become engaged not in a personal task but in a common fraternal work before God, in whose sight all are equal and who will act through such instruments as seem good to Him. Therefore "let him that is greatest among you be as he that is least"; it may well be that the apparently least among us is often likely to be the more efficient workman.

These, I know, are lofty ideals, largely impracticable at the moment, and I have no wish to alienate any Brother's interest in the Craft by imposing a standard beyond his present capacity and desire. Yet Brethren to whom the ideal appeals, and to whom it is both desirable and practicable, might unite in meeting with the intention of conforming to it, and here and there even a small new Lodge might be formed for that special purpose, leaving other Lodges to work on their accustomed lines.

Is Masonry, throughout, anything but a lofty ideal, which so far we have made little serious attempt to realise? The main difficulty before us is that the true work of the Craft contemplates a much greater detachment from the things and the ways of the outer world than we are at present willing, or perhaps able, to allow. So we compromise with ourselves, and seek to combine the outer secular life with the inner ideals of the Craft. The two conflict, and no man can efficiently serve two masters. We must choose whom we will serve.

Still the ideal is before us, a glimmering light in a dark, distracted and dying world, and it rests with ourselves whether it remains a glimmer or whether we strive to fan it into a blaze of fact. For those who desire merely a social and sociable organisation, garnished with a little picturesque ceremonial and providing opportunity for a little amusement and personal distinction, Masonry will never be more than the formality it long has been and still is for many, and they themselves will remain in darkness as to its meaning, its purpose, and its great possibilities.

But for those who are not content with vanities and unrealities, who desire not a formal husk but the living spirit, and are bent on plumbing its well-guarded secrets and mysteries to their depth and living out its implications to the full, Masonry may well come—as for some it has come to be the chief blessing and experience of their lives; it may yield them even the last secret of life itself. It may fulfil for them the ancient prayer of the Eastern Initiates we just now spoke of, by leading them from the unreal to the supreme Reality, from darkness to light ineffable, from the things of time and mortality to things immortal. They may find it a ladder of truth and world-escape set up for them in the wilderness around them, and their Lodge a place of unfolding vision where, with the Hebrew patriarch, they will exclaim: "This is none other than a house of God and a gate of heaven!"

REFLECTION: AWAKENING TO THE VEIL

EDUCATION AND EVOLUTION IN FREEMASONRY

The pressing need for education within Masonry remains a fundamental challenge today, deeply tied to the question of purpose. Freemasonry's full potential is not realised through ritual proficiency alone but through genuine engagement with the philosophy and meaning embedded within its traditions. Historically, ancient centres like Alexandria, Athens, and Timbuktu became sanctuaries for the pursuit of wisdom and enlightenment, where learning and contemplation were paramount. Similarly, Freemasonry was conceived as a refuge for intellectual and spiritual transformation. However, this sacred focus on wisdom has diminished in the modern age, where societies often prioritise commerce and technology. Without intentional instruction, Freemasonry risks becoming a mere echo of its original design, prioritising form over substance.

Masonic education transcends mere knowledge transfer, guiding each member on a deeply personal journey of self-discovery. Ritual achieves its highest purpose when it transforms into a "living myth," immersing the individual in a narrative that shapes their identity and sense of purpose. As Joseph Campbell profoundly observed in *The Power of Myth,* "A ritual is the enactment of a myth. By participating in the ritual, you are participating in the myth." This transformation depends on the educational dimension of Masonry, which breathes life into its symbols and practices. Lodges that neglect this vital aspect risk diminishing the Craft's transformative power, leaving Masons to encounter only the outward form of ritual, rather than the wisdom and light they seek.

Many Masons enter with the hope of uncovering wisdom and light, yet may find themselves disillusioned if rituals are performed merely as outward forms, devoid of introspection and philosophical depth. Such a journey feels incomplete, lacking the profound engagement necessary for personal growth.

The future of Freemasonry depends on revitalising its dedication to education. Modern technology offers unprecedented opportunities to connect Masons globally through online courses, virtual lectures, and study groups. By incorporating these tools, Freemasonry can reinvigorate its members' journeys, inspiring them to explore the Craft as a transformative and lifelong pursuit rooted in the wisdom of both tradition and innovation.

Ultimately, education within Freemasonry transcends the understanding of ritual. It represents a return to the Craft's original purpose: a sanctuary where members uncover profound mysteries about themselves and the universe. Like the ancient sages who dedicated temples to wisdom, Masonic education is a personal journey and a collective duty—to one's Brothers and the Craft.

GUARDIANS OF THE LIGHT: THE SACRED ROLE OF INSTALLED MASTERS

In the pursuit of Masonic education, the Installed Master plays a pivotal role within the Lodge—a position defined not merely by authority but by deep responsibility. More than an honorific title, the role embodies wisdom and carries the charge to lead brethren in ritual precision and understanding. This role is far more than a leader's; it symbolises a custodian of wisdom who guides others on their Masonic journeys.

The Master is entrusted with upholding the Lodge's spiritual and educational essence, yet this responsibility is collective rather than solitary. Like a master builder who relies on skilled craftsmen to complete a structure, the Installed Master draws upon the Lodge's combined wisdom. True leadership in Masonry thrives on collaboration, as the Master encourages each member to contribute to the Lodge's intellectual and spiritual growth.

Contemporary challenges, however, test this ideal. In some jurisdictions, the tradition of gradual progression through Masonic degrees is occasionally shortened, allowing candidates to complete all degrees in a single day. While intended to address declining membership, this practice risks undermining the profound, transformative journey that slower, reflective progression provides. The absence of such a journey can lead to a superficial understanding of Masonry's depths.

Moreover, expedited advancement often impacts Lodge leadership quality. At times, newly raised Master Masons are quickly moved through offices and into the role of Worshipful Master without the depth of preparation such a position demands. This rapid progression can detract from the educational strength of the Lodge, as an unprepared Master may lack the understanding needed to guide others effectively. If left unchecked, this cycle perpetuates a lineage of leaders without full initiation into their roles.

A Master who has thoughtfully observed and learned through each degree arrives in the East with a keen understanding of his Lodge's collective knowledge. By the time he assumes this leadership role, he ideally holds a "mental map" of each Brother's talents, knowing whom to consult for insights into ritual, history, or philosophy. This dynamic portrays the Master as a beacon of shared knowledge—a facilitator rather than a dictator of the Lodge's intellectual life. Here, the Master leads not by overshadowing others but by creating a collaborative environment where each Brother's strengths are recognised and utilised.

This collaborative model also fosters mentorship within the Lodge. New members, observing the diverse expertise within the Lodge, are encouraged to seek guidance and refine their unique strengths. While the Master is endowed with wisdom, his role extends to coordinating and nurturing the collective wisdom of his Brethren, exemplifying the Lodge as a unified body of growth and support. In this sense, leadership transcends individual authority, representing a shared journey toward upliftment and enlightenment.

Thus, the Master's role becomes dual: to inspire by example and to empower by recognising and elevating each Brother's strengths. In this way, the Lodge reflects the wider Masonic ethos, where personal growth contributes to the collective whole. Balancing leadership with cooperation, this structure embodies Freemasonry's essence—a tradition where each Brother's development enhances the unity and enlightenment of the entire Lodge. Through this collaborative spirit, the Master transforms the Lodge into a sanctuary of learning, support, and shared illumination.

Ultimately, the Master is not the sole bearer of wisdom but the conductor of a harmonious symphony of understanding, guiding the Lodge toward unity and insight. This vision of collective enlightenment lies at the heart of Masonry—a tradition that sustains its relevance across generations by fostering shared growth and wisdom. Through this role, the Master is a custodian of ritual and Masonic education, ensuring the Lodge's vitality and purpose remain meaningful for future generations.

Wilmshurst's opening in The Masonic Initiation speaks directly to the essence of Freemasonry, urging us to perceive its rites as more than ceremonial formalities. Rather, the Craft is portrayed as a living tradition that fosters self-knowledge, discipline, and a relentless quest for inner illumination. Masonic work is not merely a procession of symbols and rituals but a lifelong journey that invites each initiate to delve into a deeper understanding of their own nature and the universe. This journey emphasises self-reflection and internal growth, presenting Freemasonry as a path of continual self-improvement.

The Lodge itself acts as a reflective space for this inner work. Each degree is seen not as a standalone achievement but as a segment of a cohesive journey that guides the initiate toward spiritual advancement. Through this progression, each member is encouraged to commit to a path that requires courage, humility, and a willingness to engage with profound truths. The Craft's symbols offer a structured pathway for those ready to labour in pursuit of wisdom, transforming the Masonic experience into a path of personal and spiritual transformation.

Freemasonry's symbols and teachings are far from relics of the past; they are preserved tools meant to awaken a deep sense of purpose within each Mason. Wilmshurst suggests that when these symbols are approached with genuine intent, they promote inner growth, foster an expansive understanding of our place in the cosmos, and broaden one's vision of life itself. For those seeking more than a superficial understanding, these symbols become gateways to experiences that enrich the soul, guiding the individual toward higher truths and personal transformation.

In this view, Freemasonry's legacy lies in its dedication to self-discovery, and the spirit's transformative journey reminds Masons to engage with their work not as passive participants but as genuine seekers, willing to explore the mysteries within. Freemasonry's purpose, embedded within its symbols and teachings, is both personal and universal: to inspire, uplift, and guide those who seek enlightenment, making the journey an ongoing unfolding of wisdom rather than a finite goal.

UNVEILING THE THRESHOLD: REAL VS. CEREMONIAL INITIATION

In examining true initiation, we encounter an archetypal journey central to human experience across cultures and ages. Authentic initiation rites transcend mere societal rituals; they represent profound transformations of the self, awakening individuals to a reality beyond the mundane. Such rites compel the aspirant to confront and transcend personal limitations, connecting them to a shared tradition that unites humanity with the divine. This concept aligns with the heart of Masonic initiation, where each degree is not a mere formality but a symbolic enactment of inner truths—a journey from darkness to light, mirroring the transformative rites practised by ancient societies.

True initiation has traditionally marked pivotal moments in an aspirant's life, symbolising a 'new birth'—a shift in consciousness that unveils both personal potential and responsibility. Historically, these rites took place "when the sun was at its meridian," embodying the pinnacle of spiritual illumination. They required more than mere attendance; they demanded a willingness to undergo a transformation, setting authentic initiation apart from formalised ritual. As the sun's zenith illuminates with its fullest light, these ancient rites also offer enlightenment to those prepared for the journey. Drawing from these time-honoured traditions, Freemasonry invites members to enter a lineage of light shaped by the wisdom of ancient cultures.

Our Craft, therefore, is a mosaic of these luminous insights, a tapestry woven from the wisdom of countless civilisations. Masonic rituals echo these ancient heights, reminding us of an inheritance transcending time and place. Each degree extends an invitation to join a universal story that distils centuries of wisdom into symbols and allegories. These symbols resonate with the peaks of ancient understanding, inviting us to experience a "gradual unfolding of Truth" within ourselves—a journey that transcends the Lodge's walls and continues as a lifelong quest for light.

True initiation is a convergence of outer form and inner substance, aligning the visible with the invisible, the temporal with the eternal. Though expressed through physical Degrees, the Masonic journey beckons each member to undertake an inner path toward wisdom and personal evolution. This transformation does not occur through the mere repetition of gestures or words but requires introspection, sacrifice, and a dedication to embodying the ideals of the Craft. Masonic initiation challenges us to move beyond ceremony into a genuinely transformative experience that enlivens the deeper teachings, making them real and meaningful in our lives.

This distinction between ceremonial and real initiation is foundational to understanding Masonry's journey. Rituals serve as blueprints, guiding us along a path trodden by countless initiates across ages and cultures. Yet without the personal commitment to internalise these teachings, the rites remain hollow performances. True initiation is not just an intellectual exercise; it is a transformative experience that connects us to greater mysteries and elevates our perception of existence.

In drawing this distinction, Masonic initiation invokes the wisdom of ancient schools that shaped its symbolic language and ethical foundation. Just as we honour our forebears, so are we called to honour the traditions—Egyptian, Greek, Chaldean, and Eastern—that infused Freemasonry with its symbols and insights. This reverence is active, not passive; it calls us to engage deeply with these teachings, allowing them to inspire and elevate our practice today. By connecting with this ancient light, we find ourselves part of a lineage that has carried forward insights into the mysteries of existence across centuries.

Masonic initiation synthesises individual and collective evolution within this framework, inviting us to join an enduring journey that has enriched humanity. Initiation rites across cultures share a common purpose: to draw the aspirant beyond personal limitations and into a greater awareness of universal unity. Similarly, real initiation in Freemasonry leads each Mason to recognise their place within a continuum of seekers, each drawn toward the light of wisdom and truth. Our ceremonies, therefore, are not simply scripts to follow but transformative processes that connect us to universal truths woven across time.

True initiation transcends linear knowledge, offering the initiate a wisdom that surpasses language and a light that illuminates the soul. As candidates progress through the degrees, they are not merely advancing in rank but crossing symbolic thresholds of consciousness, drawing closer to the Blazing Star representing the ultimate truth. This journey resembles an inner alchemy, as much a call to transmute the self as a formal rite. It requires intellect and a heartfelt commitment to one's highest evolution.

In this light, Freemasonry offers a profound path, a vessel carrying forward the legacy of ancient Mysteries. The Craft invites each Mason to seek true initiation beyond external symbols and spoken words, leading toward a personal enlightenment that embodies humanity's finest potential. Honouring the father and mother traditions that shaped our Craft, we are also called to walk this path with renewed purpose, breathing life into a timeless journey. True initiation is not merely a historical remnant; it is a living tradition that calls us to cultivate wisdom, compassion, and understanding in a world that needs these qualities as much as ever.

Wilmshurst presents initiation as far more than a ceremonial rite—it is an intricate process of spiritual awakening. At its core lies a transformative journey, an invitation to discover the light within and align oneself with the truth. This path begins not with superficial mastery of symbols but with a profound, inward commitment to seeking meaning self-knowledge, and a connection with a reality that transcends the ordinary.

Initiation involves revelation and concealment, with the soul gradually "unveiled" through ritual, discipline, and reflection. Each degree represents a stage of this transformative journey, guiding the initiate from darkness toward light. The symbols and allegories of Freemasonry serve as tools for exploring deeper truths, offering a structured framework for personal and spiritual growth. These teachings, rooted in timeless wisdom, encourage initiates to look beyond the surface and engage with the Craft as a means of self-discovery and enlightenment.

For Masons, initiation opens a doorway to the hidden mysteries within themselves and the universe. It challenges each member to go beyond a surface understanding, urging them to seek deeper truths through contemplation, study, and practice. The Fellow Craft Degree, for example, highlights the importance of the liberal arts and sciences—not merely as intellectual pursuits but as tools for perceiving the divine order in all things. This aligns with the practices of ancient wisdom traditions, where learning served as a vehicle for both intellectual and spiritual awakening.

In Freemasonry, initiation is unique in its emphasis on personal accountability and continuous growth. It is not simply bestowed by the Lodge; it must be earned through the initiate's dedication and effort. The journey begins in the Lodge but extends far beyond its walls, unfolding in the quiet sanctum of the heart and mind. This process of self-transformation requires active engagement with the symbols and lessons of the Craft, evolving from ritual performance into a profound inner alchemy.

Freemasonry must inspire its members to actively engage with its teachings, ensuring the rituals remain alive with meaning and purpose. The challenge of modern Masonry lies in balancing tradition with innovation, particularly in an era of virtual learning and online communities. While these tools offer new opportunities for engagement, they must not overshadow the personal, experiential elements that make initiation meaningful.

The purpose of Masonic initiation is not a finite goal but a lifelong process of self-refinement. Each degree is a step on an endless journey, guiding the Mason to new insights and unveiling deeper mysteries within the Craft and themselves. This progression mirrors the process of individuation, where one seeks to harmonise all aspects of the self to achieve wholeness. Through this journey, the initiate embraces both the light and shadow within, striving toward a balanced and enlightened state of being.

As initiates move forward, they are called to embody the teachings of Freemasonry in their lives, contributing to the spiritual evolution of their Lodge and the Craft as a whole. By committing to this path of growth, each Mason affirms the timeless relevance of Freemasonry, bringing its principles of wisdom, compassion, and understanding to a world in need. Initiation, in this sense, is not a rite to complete but a discipline to live by—a call to continually seek the light and, in doing so, to become an example of that light for others.

THE THREE VEILS: A PASSAGE INTO TRUE ILLUMINATION

In Freemasonry, initiation transcends ceremonial progression; it represents a journey through three Veils, each symbolising a stage of inner mastery. These Veils guide the Mason from worldly consciousness to a profound understanding of self and universe. Beginning with self-discipline and culminating in unity with the divine, this journey mirrors the progression from Entered Apprentice to Master Mason. Resonant with initiatory traditions across cultures, the Veils offer insight and transformation, encouraging continuous growth in wisdom and virtue.

THE FIRST VEIL: LAYING THE FOUNDATION (ENTERED APPRENTICE)

The first veil, embodied by the Entered Apprentice degree, introduces the principle of self-circumscription—disciplining one's passions and actions. Self-control establishes a foundation for spiritual growth in the same way a cornerstone stabilises a structure. This stage calls for a life shaped with intention and purpose, laying the groundwork for the Masonic journey. This foundational work is not merely about restraint but about aligning one's life with virtues like temperance and mindfulness, ensuring that every action furthers spiritual progress.

In today's fast-paced, ego-driven world, the first veil offers a powerful reminder to slow down, cultivate discipline, and seek meaning beyond material pursuits. It serves as a cornerstone for personal growth, emphasising the importance of self-awareness and intentional living as essential to the path of enlightenment.

THE SECOND VEIL: THE PURSUIT OF KNOWLEDGE AND WISDOM (FELLOW CRAFT)

The second veil, represented by the Fellow Craft degree, invites the Mason to seek knowledge and apply it with discernment, transforming information into wisdom. This stage introduces the liberal arts and sciences as tools to perceive the divine order within creation. These disciplines, encompassing grammar, rhetoric, logic, arithmetic, geometry, music, and astronomy, guide the Mason toward truths extending beyond physical perception, offering insights into the natural and metaphysical worlds.

This pursuit of wisdom is not solely intellectual; it bridges the physical and spiritual, inviting the initiate to sense the interconnectedness of existence. Geometry, for example, symbolises cosmic harmony, revealing the unity within creation. This veil emphasises the transformative power of learning, challenging the Mason to use knowledge as a means to illuminate higher truths.

In the modern era, Masonic education faces unique opportunities and challenges. While digital platforms have increased accessibility to Masonic teachings, balancing these resources with personal mentorship ensures that the wisdom of the Craft is shared authentically. The second veil reminds us that knowledge must be pursued with depth and intention, fostering a path of continuous enlightenment.

THE THIRD VEIL: TRANSCENDENCE OF THE PHYSICAL REALM (MASTER MASON)

The final veil, embodied by the Master Mason degree, represents the transcendence of material attachments in pursuit of spiritual liberation. This stage confronts the inevitability of mortality, guiding the initiate to recognise that true freedom lies beyond the physical world. Only by surrendering worldly attachments can one fully unite with the divine. This veil signifies the culmination of the Masonic journey, where the spirit seeks unity with the eternal—a passage from the transient to the timeless.

The third veil offers a transformative perspective in a society often consumed by material success and external validation. It challenges each Mason to look inward, shifting their focus from external achievements to spiritual growth. This stage calls to embrace mortality as a step toward immortality, aligning one's path with eternal truths.

A profound invocation aligns with this veil's teaching:

ॐ असतो मा सद्गमय ।
तमसो मा ज्योतिर्गमय ।
मृत्योर्मा अमृतं गमय ।
ॐ शान्तिः शान्तिः शान्तिः ॥

Oṁ asato mā sadgamaya
tamasomā jyotir gamaya
mrityormāamritam gamaya
Oṁ śhānti śhānti śhāntiḥ

Om,
Lead me from the unreal to the real,

Lead me from darkness to light,
Lead me from death to immortality.
May peace be, may peace be, may peace be.

This timeless mantra embodies the heart of Freemasonry's philosophy, reminding each Mason that the pursuit of truth and enlightenment is universal. It calls the Mason to transcend physicality and embrace spiritual refinement, aligning their journey with an eternal quest for light and wisdom.

ALCHEMY OF THE SOUL: A JOURNEY OF SPIRITUAL REFINEMENT

The three Veils are not merely ritualistic stages but living symbols of the spiritual refinement underpinning Masonic initiation. From foundational self-discipline to the pursuit of wisdom and ultimate transcendence, these stages guide the Mason toward self-transformation and a deeper connection with the divine. Each veil challenges the Mason to cultivate humility, dedication, and an openness to the Craft's teachings, ensuring that the journey is as significant as the destination.

Through study, prayer, and meditation, Masons progress toward inner light, discovering insights that transform both the self and their understanding of the universe. These Veils remind us that Freemasonry's ultimate purpose is not only to impart knowledge but also to inspire a lifelong quest for truth and enlightenment—one that brings harmony to the individual and to the broader tapestry of human existence.

The progression through the three degrees of Masonic initiation is no arbitrary sequence; it embodies ancient wisdom that true enlightenment is achieved only through deliberate, incremental growth. These degrees represent transformative passages, inviting each Mason to live with increasing awareness and gradually unveil the mysteries within themselves. This journey emphasises that illumination is not instantaneous but is revealed over time through layers of experience, reflection, and introspection.

This symbolic journey through the degrees highlights the importance of patience and preparation. Each degree presents an opportunity to align outer actions with an evolving inner self, preparing the initiate for the next stage. True growth is not rushed; understanding must take root and mature before the next layer of wisdom can be revealed. Such gradual progression reflects a universal spiritual principle: profound transformation occurs cyclically and progressively, not through sudden revelation. In this way, Freemasonry mirrors other traditions where wisdom arises from steady, considered work that shapes intellect and spirit.

The degrees serve as transformative stages, cultivating a Mason's understanding of self and the universe. Each step builds upon the last, supporting the initiate's ascent and encouraging re-engagement with the teachings of the Craft. The journey requires setting aside ego and self-interest, embracing humility, and being open to truths that lie beyond material concerns. Each degree is a threshold that challenges the initiate to refine their character and deepen their commitment to the path.

This emphasis on gradual growth is not unique to Freemasonry. Many mystical traditions reflect similar pacing. In Kabbalistic teachings, for example, the ascent of the Tree of Life symbolises the soul's progressive refinement, with each level representing greater awareness and divine connection. Such teachings emphasise that spiritual insight is not achieved through shortcuts but through deliberate, meditative progression. Similarly, Freemasonry insists on the importance of patient, methodical work, rejecting the notion of instant gratification in favour of enduring personal transformation.

The Masonic philosophy of gradual learning offers a valuable counterpoint. Modern society often prioritises speed and convenience, yet the Craft reminds us that depth and contemplation are essential to enlightenment. Research consistently shows that knowledge and insight are better retained when acquired through deliberate and intentional efforts rather than rushed, surface-level engagement. This aligns with Freemasonry's focus on patience and dedication as the true paths to self-discovery.

The work of Freemasonry, symbolised by returning to the quarries, is not merely about labour in the physical sense; it is the inner task of refining one's character and spirit. This ongoing process of cyclic return—of labour and refreshment—enables each Mason to grow personally while contributing to the collective work of uplifting humanity. Through this journey, the Mason learns to approach each degree with renewed focus, shedding assumptions and discovering illumination in the process. By the final veil, the journey becomes the revelation, teaching the Mason to find wisdom not in final answers but in the unfolding mystery.

The degrees of Freemasonry are far more than symbolic markers; they are manifestations of a universal truth: enlightenment requires patience, dedication, and courage. Each stage is essential, every pause purposeful, and each veil a sacred passage inviting trust in the gradual ascent. This steady and deliberate approach reminds Masons that the light they seek is not found in haste but through intentional steps taken when the soul is ready to receive it. Through this timeless process, Freemasonry imparts not just knowledge but the enduring wisdom to embrace the journey as its own reward.

THE MYSTERIES AND THE MAP OF THE SOUL

In his exploration of Freemasonry, Wilmshurst aligns it with the ancient Mystery Schools, whose initiatory practices have guided seekers toward spiritual awakening for millennia. These Mysteries were not mere rites but profound inner journeys aimed at unveiling hidden knowledge, aligning the inner and outer self, and fostering spiritual evolution. From the sacred sanctuaries of Egypt to the groves of Eleusis, these traditions invited initiates to glimpse and ultimately embody the Divine. Wilmshurst frames Freemasonry as a continuation of this transformative legacy, not merely a fraternal order but a modern embodiment of these age-old practices.

The ancient Mysteries served as sanctuaries for the soul, preserving the sacred science of transformation. They demanded humility, discipline, and devotion. In Egypt, initiations symbolised life's progression through rebirth, death, and renewal, urging the aspirant to shed the layers of self and glimpse truths beyond the material plane. These rites offered insights into cosmic order, revealing the initiate's higher purpose. Similarly, Freemasonry's rituals encourage a deeper understanding of life's spiritual dimensions, using symbolic "deaths" and "rebirths" to guide the Mason toward personal and universal truths.

In Greece, the Eleusinian Mysteries centred on the myth of Demeter and Persephone, symbolising a descent into the Underworld and a return to light. This narrative reflected the universal cycle of death and renewal, a journey echoed in Freemasonry's teachings on transformation and rebirth. Such traditions highlight that enlightenment requires a descent into the self before ascending to greater understanding—a journey of both confrontation and renewal.

Freemasonry continues this purpose, guiding initiates toward awakening and inner understanding. Its symbols and rituals are not mere allegories but tools for profound transformation. Objects like the rough and perfect ashlars, the Square and Compasses, and the Blazing Star serve as signposts for personal refinement, encouraging the Mason to uncover their divine potential. These tools are catalysts for an inner alchemy that transforms the unrefined self into an illumined being.

The Mysteries' purpose extends beyond personal enlightenment, uniting diverse seekers under a shared quest for wisdom. Freemasonry encourages its initiates to recognise the common roots of sacred traditions, each offering unique perspectives on the Divine. Mystical teachings from Sufism, Buddhism, Kabbalah, and other traditions reflect Masonic philosophy's universal truths, emphasising transcendence, unity, and the dissolution of illusion. This alignment positions Freemasonry as a bridge, fostering harmony and understanding among diverse paths to enlightenment.

The Mysteries also serve as a mirror, reflecting the initiate's divine nature and providing a map for realising it. Freemasonry's symbols guide the initiate to strip away layers of distraction and limitation, moving from ignorance to wisdom and isolation to unity. The journey is one of unveiling the light within, leading to the integration of the unconscious and conscious self in pursuit of wholeness.

By situating Freemasonry within the tradition of the Mysteries, Wilmshurst challenges Masons to reclaim their Craft's transformative purpose. In its ideal form, Freemasonry is not simply a social order but a sanctuary for personal evolution. It offers tools for awakening, urging initiates to ascend beyond the ordinary and realise their divine potential. The ancient Mysteries were not meant to comfort or entertain but to challenge and elevate the soul—a mission that Freemasonry continues.

Freemasonry's alignment with the Mysteries reveals it as a living tradition, a means of continuity that connects modern initiates to a lineage of seekers throughout history. Each Lodge becomes a place of discovery, where the mysteries of existence are explored, and members are inspired to transcend the mundane. By deeply engaging with its symbols and rituals, Freemasonry fulfils the ancient promise of the Mysteries: to guide individuals toward their highest potential, cultivate wisdom, and inspire compassion.

By embracing its transformative purpose, the Craft calls each Mason to embark on a timeless journey of self-discovery and spiritual awakening, drawing ever closer to the Divine. In this way, Freemasonry becomes a sanctuary of transformation, offering enlightenment and unity to a world searching for meaning.

BLUEPRINTS OF BEING: EVOLUTION AND PERFECTION

Wilmshurst reaffirms that Freemasonry can fulfil the ancient promise of the Mysteries by guiding individuals toward their highest potential, cultivating wisdom, and inspiring compassion. By embracing this purpose, Freemasonry moves beyond merely preserving its past; it becomes a source of light for the present and future, a sanctuary of transformation that calls each Mason to become a seeker, drawn ever closer to the Divine.

Through its teachings and degrees, Freemasonry bestows upon its initiates a profound awareness, paired with a significant responsibility—symbolised as the Masonic Intention. This power of intention, akin to the wisdom of the ancient Mysteries, comes with a duty. For Masons, this responsibility is twofold: it includes a moral obligation to act with wisdom and integrity and the craft of responding precisely to life's circumstances, beautifully encapsulated by the symbolism of the chisel.

In this context, the chisel transforms "responsibility" into "response-ability"—the Mason's refined capacity to act intentionally and skilfully. As each Mason wields this symbolic tool, they learn that their Masonic Intention, when directed with discernment, allows them to face life's challenges with precision and purpose. This response-ability elevates the Mason's actions, enabling them to embody the teachings and to approach life's trials as opportunities for growth and service.

Wilmshurst highlights gradual spiritual evolution as a journey towards perfection in character and understanding. He invokes the Greek concept of teleios, which represents a journey towards completeness and aligns with the soul's pursuit of inner wholeness. This notion resonates with the Masonic call to reach one's highest potential. Unlike sudden enlightenment, this path requires dedication, reflection, and the careful application of wisdom, making Masonic initiation an ongoing journey of self-mastery that challenges each Mason to evolve intellectually, spiritually, and morally.

This gradual process also aligns with contemporary insights into the nature of consciousness and observation. The observer effect in quantum mechanics suggests that particles behave differently when observed, indicating that consciousness influences reality. In this light, the Masonic practice of conscious intention and disciplined response mirrors the observer effect, where an initiate's awareness actively shapes their growth and experiences. Scientific research on consciousness supports the idea that awareness plays a profound role in shaping perception and reality. Through intentional engagement with Masonic principles, each Mason shapes their own "inner universe," which aligns individual perception with higher truths.

This perspective parallels Masonic teachings on intention and inner transformation, reinforcing that focused work within the Craft influences personal reality and collective spiritual progress. Each degree provides the Mason with symbolic tools to shape their responses to life, refining their inner nature. In this way, Masonic symbols and rituals are more than ceremonial acts; they are methods for cultivating disciplined intention, where focused awareness shapes one's journey.

Albert Mackey states, "The true secret of Masonry lies not in its rites and ceremonies, but in its ethical teachings. It seeks to elevate the mind, expand the moral vision, and awaken the latent divinity within man." This alignment, achieved through the practice of response-ability, becomes a form of "spiritual alchemy," transforming personal limitations into refined qualities of wisdom, compassion, and peace.

Rosicrucian teachings similarly emphasise that spiritual growth is achieved through continuous, conscious refinement, as noted by Max Heindel, "The purpose of life is not merely to gather experience but to extract from it the essence of growth, refining consciousness until it aligns with the divine." This journey, often compared to an alchemical process, illustrates that transformation is gradual, layered, and powered by focused intention and an active commitment to self-development. These teachings provide practical insights for Masons, showing that steady self-improvement and mindful action elevate the human experience to deeper understanding.

This framework extends to the broader concept of initiation, where the discipline to respond with precision elevates the Mason's journey beyond personal achievement and into service to humanity. Masonic evolution is an individual and collective endeavour; each Mason contributes to a greater universal harmony by transforming their character. In guiding individuals to direct their intentions with wisdom and care, Freemasonry upholds the ancient ideal that inner work profoundly affects the whole, reflecting the interconnectedness of consciousness.

Freemasonry thus provides a sacred path where each tool, degree, and symbol cultivates knowledge and the Masonic Intention to meet life's demands with responsibility and precision. Each step on this journey reminds Masons that the light they seek is an inner flame and a shared beacon that grows brighter as each Mason hones their response-ability, contributing to the Craft's ancient legacy of enlightenment and virtue.

WHEN THE STUDENT IS READY

Wilmshurst contends that the ideal candidate for Masonic initiation possesses a profound yearning for light and truth, driven by an inner calling rather than mere curiosity or social motivations. This ideal goes beyond superficial qualifications such as maturity or moral soundness; it centres on spiritual readiness and the willingness to embark on a transformative inner journey. Such readiness signifies a commitment to growth and the courage to engage with a process that is not simply a series of rituals but a deeply personal encounter with the self.

In an era of easily accessible information, the esoteric knowledge and symbols once closely guarded by Freemasonry are now widely available to those who seek them. However, this accessibility brings the risk of superficial understanding, which can undermine the profound essence of the Masonic path. While a candidate might encounter the symbols or rituals of Freemasonry online, this does not equate to the lived and internalised wisdom that true initiation imparts. The notion of instant understanding, prevalent in the digital age, starkly contrasts with Freemasonry's emphasis on gradual progression, symbolised by the winding staircase—a representation of the deliberate and challenging ascent toward enlightenment.

The winding staircase serves as both a literal and symbolic reminder of the trials faced by seekers throughout history. It reflects the personal challenges and symbolic tests that Masonic candidates must encounter. Like Odysseus navigating trials or Arjuna confronting inner conflict, the Mason progresses step by step, requiring patience, discipline, and self-reflection. Like the ascent of the staircase, wisdom is cumulative, and insights cannot be prematurely gained or rushed.

This concept aligns with Carl Jung's assertion, "One does not become enlightened by imagining figures of light, but by making the darkness conscious." Jung's insights resonate with Freemasonry's emphasis on self-purification and ego transcendence, where the initiate must confront hidden aspects of themselves—what Jung terms the shadow—and integrate them into conscious awareness. This process mirrors the Masonic journey, where each degree requires the initiate to shed ego attachments and deepen their understanding, fostering a balance between light and shadow.

In Jungian psychology, this transformative process is called individuation—a unification of the conscious and unconscious mind that leads to personal wholeness. Within the Masonic framework, individuation occurs through the degrees that guide the initiate to confront and integrate their aspirations and inner conflicts. The Masonic path becomes a symbolic alchemy, where the initiate refines their base nature into an enlightened state. Each ritual builds upon the last, cultivating a journey toward wholeness and revealing the Craft's true "secrets" through personal growth.

This distinction is crucial: while Freemasonry's outward symbols and rituals may be studied by anyone, its deepest mysteries remain hidden from all but those who truly walk its path. These secrets are not encapsulated in words or diagrams but in the transformative power of initiation, which unfolds only through introspection, courage, and the willingness to confront inner darkness. While symbols can be understood intellectually, their profound significance reveals itself only to those who embody the teachings through personal reflection and deliberate action.

Freemasonry protects its mysteries not by secrecy but by demanding genuine effort and inner work. The most profound insights of the Craft are accessible only to those who are ready to undertake the long and often challenging journey of self-knowledge and spiritual evolution. The ideal candidate is not someone seeking instant solutions but one dedicated to a lifelong pursuit of wisdom, growth, and transformation. Such a candidate honours the path of those who have walked the winding way before, understanding that initiation is not a destination but an ongoing process of becoming.

In the Masonic journey, readiness to act with intention is as important as readiness to observe. Jung frames this path as the realisation of the self—the fullest expression of one's nature, where the initiate aligns consciously with their divine potential. The journey is psychological and spiritual, revealing the depths of human potential and the universal principles that have shaped Freemasonry throughout history. Through this inward journey, the Mason unlocks the potential for enlightenment and unity with the divine light that the Craft represents.

This inward focus is central to Freemasonry's ideal and challenges each candidate to engage in authentic, disciplined work. Candidates may mistakenly equate knowledge with wisdom in a world dominated by immediacy. True initiation, as Wilmshurst and Jung suggest, requires more than acquiring information; it demands that the candidate live, experience, and gradually uncover the mysteries of the Craft through rigorous self-exploration. Freemasonry reminds us that genuine knowledge is not handed down but earned through the transformative process of inner work and self-mastery.

SYMBOLIC AGES AND THE TIMELESS JOURNEY

The symbolic ages of twelve and thirty in Freemasonry provide profound insight into the timeless journey of personal evolution while highlighting the diminishing role of rites of passage in modern society. Historically, such rites were integral to many cultures, marking significant transitions in an individual's life and preparing them for the responsibilities and challenges of adulthood. Today, these rites have largely disappeared outside the contexts of mystical orders or religious traditions, leaving a void in the structures that once guided young people toward meaningful maturity.

In traditional societies, the age of twelve often marked a readiness to engage with sacred knowledge and assume greater responsibility. For instance, a bar or bat mitzvah symbolised this transition in Judaism, as young individuals took on moral and spiritual duties within their community. Similarly, the Native American vision quest was a sacred rite through which adolescents sought clarity of purpose and connection to their community by spending time in solitude with nature. These ceremonies were pivotal, often accompanied by mentorship from elders, who helped the initiate understand their role within a larger, interconnected world.

While some cultural rites of passage persist, contemporary society has shifted its focus toward education and training designed primarily to serve economic goals. Youth are often prepared for competition and commerce, leaving little room for exploring deeper questions of identity, moral responsibility, or spiritual purpose. Cities once renowned for celebrating arts, philosophy, and spiritual reflection—such as Athens or Alexandria—have largely been replaced by centres of commerce, where cultural and contemplative spaces are secondary to economic activity. This shift signals a loss of focus on inner development, with many young people left to navigate questions of purpose and identity on their own in a landscape that prioritises measurable achievement over wisdom or compassion.

Freemasonry, as Wilmshurst emphasises, offers a transformative journey that stands in contrast to these societal trends. The symbolic ages of twelve and thirty in Masonic initiation signify readiness for inner growth and cultivating virtues that transcend material success. These milestones represent not chronological age but spiritual and moral development stages, calling initiates to reflect on personal responsibility and self-knowledge. Within the Craft, the journey through these stages is not about achieving specific markers but about actively engaging in the cultivation of character and alignment with deeper truths. It is a journey that prioritises the development of moral insight and personal responsibility over external accomplishments.

Contemporary psychological and sociological discussions increasingly acknowledge the absence of meaningful rites of passage in modern society. This absence has been linked to a sense of aimlessness or delayed maturity in young adults. Rites such as graduation or obtaining a driver's license often lack the depth and experiential transformation associated with traditional rites of passage. Psychologist Michael Gurian highlights the necessity of structured rites of passage, suggesting that young people may struggle to develop a clear sense of identity and purpose without them. This recognition underscores the potential value of Masonic initiation as a living tradition that addresses these gaps by offering a framework for deliberate, progressive self-development.

In a world that has largely moved away from these meaningful transitions, Freemasonry preserves a structured path rooted in the symbolic ages. These ages serve as calls to continuous growth and reflection, offering initiates tools and symbols to explore their potential and purpose. Freemasonry mirrors the ancient tradition of building one's character with the same care as constructing a physical temple. By advocating for inner development over commercial success, the Craft champions wisdom, compassion, and responsibility as the cornerstones of a fulfilling life.

Honouring these symbolic ages elevates Freemasonry beyond a series of degrees; it manifests values that once held inner growth and self-mastery in the highest regard. The Craft encourages each Mason to pursue their fullest potential, fostering personal evolution and collective harmony. In a modern world often preoccupied with external success, Freemasonry remains a unique sanctuary, preserving the ideals of light, wisdom, and self-transformation. It reminds us that true growth is not measured by outward achievement but by the depth and commitment of one's inward journey.

INVISIBLE LUMINARIES: HIDDEN LIVES OF TRUE INITIATES

In Wilmshurst's view, the life of a true Initiate is often hidden and unrecognised by the world, yet this concealed path holds immense spiritual power. He describes a quiet strength, cultivated in humility and dedicated to service, that aligns the individual more closely with the ideals of the Craft. The path of the true initiate is a life committed to growth, not for public recognition but for the profound internal shifts it creates, echoing the paths of mystics and sages across traditions—from Rumi to Swami Vivekananda.

This notion of the hidden life is deeply symbolic, suggesting that the real work of Masonry lies not in the visible symbols or rituals but in the subtle transformation within. Like the alchemists who sought to transmute base metals into gold, true Initiates turn their focus inward, transforming their basest qualities into virtues and striving to achieve harmony between the outer and inner worlds. The path of the initiate, often unseen, teaches that spiritual advancement is not measured by external accolades but by the quiet, persistent effort to align oneself with the Divine.

Manly Palmer Hall, in The Lonely Ones, captures this theme of the solitary, often hidden journey in words that resonate deeply with the Masonic ideal: "The truly wise person finds his satisfaction in the inward realisation of his heart. It matters little to him that others do not know or recognise him, for he is sufficient unto himself". Hall suggests that genuine wisdom leads to independence from the need for external validation, emphasising that the real fruits of the spiritual path are self-knowledge and inner peace. This aligns closely with Wilmshurst's concept of the initiate whose life of service and transformation unfolds quietly, often unknown even to those around them.

The hidden life is a model for all Masons, reminding us that the most powerful transformations occur beyond the public eye. Just as Rumi sought unity with the Divine, the Masonic journey encourages a life of introspection and devotion, lived in quiet strength. Hall echoes this sentiment, writing, "Each person must find his own way into the mysteries, and it is a lonely journey that he must make alone". This reflection underscores the solitary nature of the Masonic journey and the responsibility each initiate bears to forge their own path, supported by tradition but reliant on personal commitment and courage.

For Wilmshurst, the hidden life is not merely a passive existence but a life actively engaged in self-refinement and service to a higher calling. True Initiates work tirelessly not for recognition but for cultivating inner virtues, knowing that their efforts often resonate beyond their own lives. As Hall observes, "We serve best by living the truth, quietly and steadfastly, without ever seeking to convert others to our way". This reflects the Masonic principle that one's journey toward light and truth is a personal path, and its true value lies in quiet integrity rather than overt display.

The true impact of an Initiate's life often resonates long after they are gone, leaving an invisible legacy of wisdom and virtue that, though unheralded, profoundly influencing those they encountered. In this, the path of the hidden life speaks to the enduring mystery of Masonry itself: that its real power lies not in what is seen but in the transformative journey each Brother and Sister undertakes within. In such a life, Masons find a profound alignment with the words of Hall as they strive to become "like the sun, which gives light without expectation of praise or acknowledgement". Here, the Masonic journey is framed as one of quiet resilience, a path that, while hidden from the world, is guided by the inner light of truth and wisdom, enriching the lives of others even without their knowing.

THE LODGE AS SANCTUARY: REFLECTION OF THE DIVINE PLAN

We are entrusted with an extraordinary opportunity to explore the depths of our Craft, to bring its timeless principles to life, and to discover within it a path to enlightenment and profound purpose. Wilmshurst's vision of the Ideal Lodge invites us to reflect on the potential within our own Lodges and our personal journeys. It is not a critique but a hopeful and inspiring reminder of what we can achieve when we dedicate ourselves to the higher ideals of Freemasonry.

The Lodge, as Wilmshurst envisions it, is a sanctuary. In this sacred space, silence, contemplation, and unity allow us to focus entirely on the spiritual and philosophical work of the Craft. Each meeting becomes an occasion to align ourselves more deeply with the central light we all seek, creating a haven of peace and profound reflection amid the distractions of the outer world. Imagine entering a Lodge where every action, every word, and every thought is charged with purpose, inspiring us to be the best versions of ourselves.

In this space, the initiation of new candidates would take on an elevated significance. Candidates, carefully prepared and truly ready for the journey, would find their experiences deeply transformative. Degrees would unfold at a pace that allows the lessons to resonate, providing time for introspection and genuine growth. When we confer degrees, we will not be as passive participants but as an active and unified body, focusing our collective energy to create an atmosphere of inspiration and enlightenment. In doing so, we would amplify the initiation's potential, helping the candidate connect with the deeper truths that Freemasonry seeks to reveal.

Our work as Masons would centre on education and exploration, delving into the mysteries of the Craft with curiosity and reverence. Beyond the official lectures, which often point toward deeper truths, we would encourage one another to seek out the wisdom hidden within the symbols and rituals, sharing insights and learning together. Through this commitment to understanding, we would find greater meaning and fulfilment in our Masonic journey.

The leadership within the Craft would also reflect these ideals. Advancements would be guided by spiritual readiness and the ability to inspire and support others. This approach would ensure that our Lodges are led by those most committed to Freemasonry's transformative purposes, fostering a culture of humility, mutual respect, and shared dedication to the Craft's mission.

While achieving this ideal may require time and effort, it is important to recognise that progress is made in steps, not leaps. The light of Wilmshurst's vision reminds us that even small, deliberate changes can bring us closer to realising Freemasonry's deeper purpose. For those of us who feel called to embrace this vision, it provides a hopeful path forward—one that honours the traditions of the past while inspiring us to grow and adapt in meaningful ways.

As we conclude this reflection, we are reminded that Freemasonry is not static; it is a living tradition, one that continues to evolve as we, its members, bring it to life. The Ideal Lodge is not an unreachable standard but an aspiration—a guide that challenges us to rise to our potential. Through dedication, intention, and unity, we can transform our Lodges into spaces of genuine light and wisdom, enriching our lives and the lives of those around us.

Freemasonry offers us a ladder toward truth and understanding, a path from the mundane to the divine. In striving toward the ideals presented here, we honour our Craft and ourselves, turning its principles into lived experiences that uplift and inspire. Together, we can ensure that our Lodges become places where light shines brightly, transformation is real, and the journey toward enlightenment becomes not just possible but profoundly rewarding.

CHAPTER TWO - THE MASONIC INITIATION
LIGHT ON THE WAY

"They went up with winding stairs into the middle chamber,
and out of the middle into the third." — 1 Kings vi, 8

"Does the road wind up-hill all the way?" Yes, to the very end.
"Will the day's journey take the whole long day?" From morn to night, my friend!
"But is there for the night a resting-place? A roof for when the slow dark hours begin? May not the darkness hide it from my face?"
You cannot miss that Inn. — Christina Rossetti

In the previous paper we have spoken of the transition from darkness to light made by those who seek to effect the reconstitution of their natural being and to develop it, by the science and methods of Initiation, to a higher and ultra-natural level.

It has been made clear that that transition must necessarily be gradual, and that, though ceremonially dramatised in three Degrees which can be taken in successive months, to realise the implications of those Degrees in actual life-experience may be a lifetime's work;

perhaps more than a lifetime's. The Apprentice who has entered himself to the business of rebuilding his own soul has much to learn and to do before he becomes even a competent Craftsman in it; the Craftsman, in turn, has much to do and far to journey before he can hope for complete Mastership.

The work of self-transmutation is a strenuous one, not suddenly or hurriedly to be performed, and one needing hours of refreshment and passivity as well as hours of active labour, to each of which he will find himself duly summoned at the proper time. There is much to be learned in regard to the secrets of his own nature and the principles of intellectual science, which only gradually, and as the result of patience and experience, can become revealed to his view. There is a superstructure to be raised, perfect in all its parts; a work involving much more than is at first supposed. There are tests and ordeals of a searching character to be undergone on the way.

A measure of light, a first glimpse of the distant Promised Land, may come to the eager sight of the properly prepared candidate from the first moment of his entrance upon the work, but he must not suppose that he has yet fully captured it and made it permanently his own. It is something, however, to have felt that a veil has been suddenly withdrawn from his previously darkened sight and that he has become able to distinguish between his former benightedness and the goal lying before him.

We will entitle this present section, therefore, “light on the Way," and make it treat of a variety of matters calling for the aspirant's attention as he pursues the way that intervenes between his first glimpse of the light and its ultimate realisation; and in a subsequent section we shall speak of light in its fullness of attainment. We will supplement our previous explanation of Masonic doctrine by dealing with further symbols and passages in the rituals, with which every Mason is familiar formally and by the outward ear, but the significance of which too often passes unexplained and unobserved.

The expositions in this Section are offered not only for the private reflection of members of the Craft, but with the suggestion that they may serve as material for collective meditation by Brethren in open Lodge or at Lodges of Instruction. For those upon the path to real Initiation, meditation is essential. For meditation opens a window in the mind through which light streams into the understanding from the higher, spiritual principle in ourselves; which window is symbolised by the dormer-window in the emblematic Temple of Solomon, through which came light to those ascending the stairway that wound inwardly to the middle chamber leading to the central sanctuary where alone light in its fullness was to be found.

The practice of meditation, moreover, whether personal or collective, conduces to that quietness and control of the normally restless, wandering mind which are indispensable for the apprehension of deep Truth. Ancient Lodges, we are told, were wont to meet on the highest hills and in the lowest valleys; and in an old Instruction-lecture it is explained that those expressions are meant to be figurative and relate less to actual places than to the spiritual and mental condition of those assembled. To meet in the valley implied being in a state of sheltered passiveness and tranquility, when the minds of the Brethren surrendered themselves to quiet collective thought on the subject of their work; and thus, being "led beside still waters," they became, like the limpid unruffled surface of a lake, a clear undistorting mirror for the reflection and apprehension of such rays of light and truth as might reach them from above. To meet on the high hills, on the other hand, implied the more active work of the Lodge and the performance of it upon the superphysical planes—the "hills" of the spirit; for the real work of Initiation is only there accomplished, and is no longer a ceremonial formality.

There are times for work and times for repose in the Craftsman's task—times of labour and refreshment—and to perform that task efficiently both must be utilised. Modern Lodges, in the general imperfect conception of Masonry, follow merely the rush and hustle methods of the outside world, which, of course, inside the Lodge have no place and ought no longer to be emulated. They are busy enough on the active side, but they provide no opportunity for cultivating the equally necessary passive aspect of the work. It would be found eminently advantageous, therefore, if Lodges which desire to realise true Masonry adopted the practice of collectively contemplating points of symbolism and teaching; devoting certain meetings to this special purpose, and then, without more discussion than is necessary and helpful, quietly and earnestly concentrating attention upon the significance of some symbol or point of doctrine brought before them.

For those seriously engaged in the ascent of the winding staircase, the following expositions may perhaps serve as helpful rays of light from the dormer window. They are necessarily brief and merely elementary introductions to phases of the science which, as the aspirant proceeds, he will find inexhaustible and claiming not cursory notice but his constant deep attention. May they, however, be as a lamp to his feet and a light upon the spiral path to lead him to his own middle chamber, and help to guide him to that final central sanctuary where the light itself shines in fullness and waits to be found.

"THE KNOWLEDGE OF YOURSELF"

It has already been shown that the structure and appointments of the Lodge are symbolic; that the Lodge is a representation both of the Universe and of man himself as a Microcosm or the Universe in miniature; that it is an image of his own complex constitution, his heavens and his earth (his spirituality and materiality) and all that therein is.

By contemplating that image, therefore, the Mason learns to visualise himself; he is given a first lesson in that self-knowledge in the full attainment of which is promised the understanding of all things. "Know thyself," we have said, was written over the portals of the ancient temples of Initiation, self-knowledge being the aim of their intention and the goal of their purpose. Masonry perpetuates this maxim by recommending self-knowledge as "the most interesting of all human studies." It is the tersest, wisest of instructions, yet little heeded nowadays, and it is incapable of fulfilment unless undertaken in accordance with the ancient science and with a concentration of one's whole energies upon the task.

It involves the deepest introspection into oneself and perfect discrimination between what is real and permanent, and what is unreal and evanescent in ourselves. As aspirants to the Mysteries could not learn the secrets of the Temple without entering it, learning its lessons, undergoing its disciplines, and receiving its graduated initiations, so no one can attain self-knowledge save by entering into himself, distinguishing the false from the true, the unreal from the real, the base metal from the fine gold, sublimating the former into the latter, and ignoring what is negligible or superfluous. The very word Initiation primarily derives from the Latin *in ire*, to go within; and thence, after learning the lessons of self-analysis, to make a new beginning (*initial*) by reconstructing one's knowledge of life and manner of living. The 43rd Psalm restates the same instruction: *Introibo ad altare Dei*, "I will go in to the divine altar." Similarly, the Masonic Initiation contemplates a going within oneself, until one reaches the altar or centre, the Divine Principle or ultimate hidden basis of our being. To know the anatomy and physiology of the mortal body is not self-knowledge. The physical fabric of man is a perishing self, mere dust and shadow, projected from vitalising forces within it, and without permanence or reality.

To understand the nature and mechanism of the mind, emotions and desires, is useful and necessary, but is not self-knowledge, for they, too, are transient and, therefore, unreal aspects of the deeper real self. The personality we present to the world is not our real self. It is but a mask, a distorting veil, behind which the true self abides hiddenly and often unknown to our unreal surface self, unless and until it be brought forward into consciousness, displacing and overriding the notions and tendencies of the natural, but benighted, superficial self. Until then its "light shineth in darkness and the darkness comprehendeth it not." To bring it forward out of its veils of darkness, to "comprehend" and establish it permanently in our awareness is, and has ever been, the purpose of all Initiation.

But this cannot be achieved until the outer bodily and mental vestures have been purified and a voluntary dying or effacement of everything in us alien to, or conflicting with, the real self has been suffered; all which is implied by the teaching of our three Degrees respectively.

True self-knowledge is unobstructed conscious union of the human spirit with God and the realisation of their identity. In that identic union the unreal, superficial selves have become obliterated. The sense of personality is lost, merged in the Impersonal and Universal. The little Ego is assumed into the great All, and knows as It knows. Man realises his own inherent ultimate Divinity, and thenceforth lives and acts no longer as a separate individual, with an independent will, but in integration with the Divine Life and Will, whose instrument he becomes, whose purposes he thenceforth serves. This is "the great day of atonement," when the limited personal consciousness becomes identified or made at one with one's own divine, omniscient, vital and immortal Principle, which each must realise as the high priest of his personal temple and after many washings and purifyings against the contrary tendencies of his former unregenerate nature. This was the secret supreme attainment hinted at in the cryptic maxim "Know thyself!" Each of us may judge for himself whether he has yet reached it.

To find our own Centre, our real self, involves, therefore, a turning inwards of our previously externalised faculties of sense and thought, and an introspective penetration of the outlying circumferential elements of our nature until the Centre is found. This task is figured by our ceremonial perambulations and by the path of the winding staircase leading from the ante-rooms and forecourts of our nature to the Centre, up which the aspirant must ascend, asking, seeking, knocking, all the way; being subjected from time to time to tests of his progress and receiving, without scruple or diffidence, such wages of good fortune or adversity as unseen Providences may know to be his due.

The inmost sanctuary he will find closely guarded. Nothing unclean can enter or approach that holy place. Hence in the biblical description of the symbolic Temple one finds that, in the forecourt, stood the great laver of water for the cleansing of pollutions, and the altar of fire for the sacrificial burning up of one's impurities. The sword of the G., directed to those unqualified to enter the Lodge, is the Masonic way of inculcating that peril exists to those who are not properly prepared to approach the Centre or who would rush in where angels fear to tread; it corresponds with the sword of the Cherubim in Genesis, which turned every way to keep the way to the Tree of Life from the approaches of the unfit.

Mental as well as physical purity is indispensable to real Initiation, but is far more difficult of the two to acquire. Modern psychology discloses not only how fractional a part of our entire mentality functions above the threshold of our normal awareness, but also what knots and twists, what mental lumber, what latent horrors and accumulations of inner foulness, lie stored in the sub-consciousness of even those living ordinarily clean lives. They are the deposits of the mind's past activities; forgotten often by the conscious mind itself, yet automatically registered upon our impalpable mind-stuff by the recording pencil (mentioned among the Third Degree working-tools) which at every moment of our lives posts up entries of our thoughts, words, and actions. For at the centre of ourselves is the all-observant Eye; so that we ourselves constitute our own Judgment Book, wherein each of us unwittingly inscribes his own history and formulates his own destiny, and its pages we have each to read ourselves.

With these mental deposits and consolidations those skilled in Initiation science are well familiar. The modern psychologist calls them "complexes." In the old treatises on the subject they are termed foul ethers, congelations of impure mental matter. They are the "base metals" of Masonry. Each of us has been an artificer of those metals and worked them into all manners of grotesque designs in his mental nature, and hence the conferment upon the candidate, at a certain stage, of a name attributed to the first of such artificers and signifying him to be still incompletely purged of worldly possessions of this kind. These "base metals" require to be discharged from the system by a long process of corrective purifying thought and aspiration and to be transmuted into gold, or pure mind-stuff, before real Initiation is possible. No inward fog must intervene between the outer and innermost organs of consciousness when the time comes for these to be unified. The light of Truth cannot penetrate a mind crammed with pernicious thought and with opinions to which it clings tenaciously. It must empty itself of all pre-acquired knowledge and prejudices, and then rise on the wings of its own genius into the realm of independent Thought and there learn Truth at first hand by directly beholding it.

The incident of attaining light and self-knowledge is dramatically emphasised in Masonic ceremonial. It is represented by that important moment in the ritual of the Third Degree when darkness suddenly gives way to bewildering light, in which light the candidate gazes back for the first time upon the remains of his own past and beholds the emblems of his own mortality. He has now (at least in ceremony) surmounted the great transitional crisis involved in becoming raised from a natural to a higher order of humanity. He perceives his temporal organism to have been the "tomb of transformation," in which the great change has been wrought. He has risen from that tomb, and for him the old grave of the natural body has lost its sting, and that spiritual unconsciousness, which is termed "death," has been swallowed up in the victory won at last by his higher eternal principle over his lower temporal one. The mystical sprig of acacia has bloomed at the head of his grave, by the efflorescence of the Vital and Immortal Principle in his purified mind and neural system.

Thus is portrayed for us, in Masonic ceremony, the moment of attainment of knowledge of one's true self. The incident, let it be emphasised, does not involve the physical death of the body and its faculties, for to "the companions of his former toils" the purified mind will thereafter be reunited. But thenceforth they will be his docile, plastic, obedient servants, and no longer his master. He will continue to live in the world for the remainder of his appointed span, no longer for his own sake, but for the uplifting and advancement of his fellowmen to his own high degree. His expansion of consciousness and wisdom will become part of his equipment for practical work in the world. His own spiritual evolution is complete, so far as the educative experience of this world can take it; he lives now to help on that of humanity.

A great and good Brother, reviewing his long connection with Masonic sanctuaries more than a century ago, wrote thus about Initiation:

> "*The only initiation which I preach and seek with all the ardour of my soul is that by which we may enter into the heart of God and make God's heart enter into us, there to form an indissoluble marriage which will make us the friend, brother and spouse of our Divine Redeemer.*"

This attainment is the self-knowledge pointed to by the Craft teaching, and to which that teaching seeks to guide the reflections of every Mason. Masonic Initiation has no other end than this conscious union between the individual soul and the Universal Divine Spirit.

Ok Louis Claude de Saint-Martin, *Theosophic Correspondence* with Baron Kirchberger; a work of great value and disclosing the nature of Masonic work in French Lodges prior to the Revolution of 1789.

This union is symbolised by the familiar conjunction of the square and the compasses. The square is the emblem of the soul; the compasses of the Spirit which indwells in that soul. At first the Mason sees the points of the compasses concealed behind the square, and, as he progresses, their points emerge from that concealment until both become superimposed upon the square. Thus is indicated the progressive subordination of the soul and the corresponding coming forward of the ultimate Spirit into personal consciousness, so that the Mason can "work with both those points," thus becoming an efficient builder in the spirit and rendering the circle of his own being complete by attaining conscious alliance with his ultimate and only true self.

THE "G"

Centrally, in the ceiling of each Lodge, is exhibited this striking symbol. It is the emblem of the Divine Presence in the Lodge; it is also the emblem of that Presence at the spiritual centre of the individual Mason. Its correspondence in the Christian Church is the perpetual light burning before the high altar.

In the First and Second Craft Degrees, the symbol is visible in the heavens of the Lodge. In the Third Degree, it has become invisible, but its presence is still manifested, being reflected in the small light in the East which, in correspondence with the Divine Presence, is, as every Mason knows, inextinguishable even in one's darkest moments. In the Royal Arch Degree, it again becomes visible, but in another form and in another position—on the floor of the Temple and at its centre, and in the form of a cubical altar, a white stone, bearing the Sacred Name. In the course of the Degrees, therefore, it has come down from heaven to earth; Spirit has descended to the plane of purified Matter; the Divine and the human have been brought together and made one. God has become Man; Man has been unified with God, and has found the Divine Name written upon the altar of his own heart.

In the significance of this symbol and its transpositions during the four Degrees may, therefore, be discerned the whole purpose and end of Initiation, the union of the personal soul with its Divine Principle. Masonry has no other objective than this; all other matters of interest connected with it are but details subsidiary to this supreme achievement.

When the Lodge is opened, the mind and heart of every Brother composing it should be deemed as also being opened to the "G" and all that it implies, to the intent that those implications may eventually become realised facts of experience. When the Lodge is closed, the memory of the "G" symbol and its implications should be the chief one to be retained and pondered over in the repository of the heart.

Further, great significance lies in the centrality of the "G." The Lodge is grouped around it, not assembled immediately below it. It is as though this Blazing Star or Glory in the centre burned with too fierce a light for anything less pure and bright than itself to withstand the descent of its direct rays; and, accordingly, the floor of the Lodge is left open and unoccupied; and only at its extremities do the assembled Brethren sit, removed from its direct rays. Directly beneath it lies the chequer-work floor; the symbol of the manifested creation, where the one White light from above becomes differentiated into perpetual duality and opposites of light and darkness, good and evil, positive and negative, male and female, as evidenced by the black and white squares, yet the whole held together in a unity as is denoted by the symbolic skirt-work around the same.

The "G" therefore denotes the Universal Spirit of God, permeating and unifying all things. It is a substitute for the Hebrew letter Yod, the tenth letter of the Hebrew alphabet, and out of which all the other letters of that alphabet are constructed in correspondence with the truth that all created things are modifications of the one primal Spirit. In the Instruction-lecture of a Degree outside our present constitutions, the "G" is explained as having a three-fold reference: (1) the Glory of God, or glory in the centre; (2) Grandeur, or the greatness of perfection to which man may become raised by initiation into union with God at his centre; (3) Gom-El, a Hebrew word of praise for the Divine power and goodness in designing that perfection and that union between the Creator and the creature. There is also a Hebrew tradition that Gom-El was the word uttered by Adam on first beholding the beauty of Eve and perceiving the ultimate destiny of humanity.

The "G" had its equivalent in the Egyptian Mysteries in the solar symbol of Ra, the spiritual Sun. In the great temple of the Greek Mysteries at Delphi, where the Eleusinian initiations took place for seventeen centuries, it was represented by the fifth letter of the Greek alphabet, the E (or Eta); five being a numerical symbol of man in the Pythagorean system, as evidenced by his five senses, the five-fold extension of his hands and feet, and in accordance with considerations of a more abstruse nature. Hence the five-pointed star (or pentagram) is also a symbol of man, and expresses a variety of truths concerning him. In the rituals in the *Book of the Dead* the candidate is described as a "keeper of five"; Operative fellow-craft Masons worked in batches of five, and a Speculative fellow-craft Lodge today consists of five brethren; all these allusions having a deeper significance than can be explained here, but bearing upon the present state of human evolutional development.

Plutarch records that the "E" was regarded as a symbol of the greatest importance and instructiveness and was exhibited in three forms (corresponding with our three Degrees), first in wood, afterwards in bronze, and finally in gold. The progression signified a corresponding advance of the candidate's moral and spiritual nature under the discipline of Initiation. He is likened at first to soft, perishable wood; hardening into the durability of bronze, which impure, alloyed metal finally becomes sublimated into gold—the symbol of the attainment of purity, wisdom, and perfection to which Initiation leads.

Beyond this, however, the central symbol had another deep meaning. The great Initiation-temples of antiquity, as also certain Christian Churches of historic interest (such as those of Iona and Glastonbury, from which Britain became Christianised), were erected at certain focal points of the earth's surface known to the Initiates of the time as being magnetic centres or nodal points of spiritual force peculiarly favourable for the influx into this world of currents of Divine Power and for their irradiation thence to surrounding regions. Each such place was called an Omphalos, a navel, or mystical centre; and the Temple at Delphi is related to have been built where it was under divine guidance and for that purpose; and we know that it became the centre of light and religion to the then civilised Western world for seventeen centuries.

This historical fact and this occult principle are now reproduced in Masonry. Every Lodge, every place of Initiation, is in theory—though not nowadays in practice—held at a centre or physical focus point selected as being favourable both to the initiation of those who enter it and to the spiritual advancement of the uninitiated popular world resident in its vicinity. "A city set on a hill cannot be hid." A Temple or Lodge of Brethren intelligently performing its work is not only engaged in a work of spiritual building as regards its own members; it is, though perhaps unconsciously, at the same time, generating and throwing off vibrations of spiritual energy to all around it; its occult influence extends, and its radiations are of efficacy, to a greater range than one dreams of.

If, then, the Lodge be a spiritual focus-point, the centre of the Lodge, where the "G" is exhibited, is its most vital and sacred point; the point at which Divine Energy may be thought of as concentrated and specially powerful. And the reason will become clear for placing the candidate at that point at a certain moment in the Ceremony.

Why is he then placed in the centre? Previously he has been placed, not there, but in certain more removed places in the Lodge; in the N.E. or the S.E. corners where the intensity of the central light is theoretically less powerful, where it is tempered and adjusted to his as yet unperfected organism, and where charges and instruction appropriate to his then state of advancement are imparted to him. But when directed to be placed in the Lodge-centre, he is called upon to stand, as it were, in direct alignment with the descending ray of the Supernal light and to bear the stress of its full current.

The intensity of that current can only be borne and withstood by one who is perfect in all his parts and in whom the sensual, emotional, and mental natures have been purified, rectified and brought into harmony and to an alignment corresponding with the physical and moral erectness of a just and upright man; an unpurified man would run the peril of having his organism injured or shattered by a current of that fiery Power, by which every soul must sooner or later be tested, but which consumes everything not assimilable with itself. The three Hebrew "children" (i.e., initiates) who withstood unscathed the fiery furnace into which they were plunged, typify the truth here testified to.

When, therefore, a candidate is placed in the centre of the Lodge, beneath the "G" symbol, let those assembled around him try to realise the intention of what is thereby implied. Let them reflect that at that important moment, more perhaps than at any other in the ceremonies, it is possible for the celestial light to descend upon the duly prepared candidate, to flood his heart and expand his mind, and so to open his understanding to the instruction then communicated to him that he may realise the spirit as well as hear the letter of it, whilst standing in that sacred position. And let them at that moment silently and earnestly invoke the light of the centre, that it may then consciously arise in both him and them, so that what is done ceremonially may become for them both a great fact of spiritual experience.

The point is emphasised here with earnestness, because the Masonic procedure of placing the candidate in the centre of the Lodge at an important stage of his progress not only perpetuates a traditional and purposeful ancient practice, but also accords with what occurs in Initiations of a much more advanced and real character than it is possible to speak of here, as those who become duly qualified will one day come to find. By understanding and being faithful in the small things of even an elementary and ceremonial system, one becomes educated for and prepared to be entrusted with greater ones when the time for acquiring them arrives.

THE LADDER

A most important part of the curriculum of the Ancient Mysteries was instruction in Cosmology, the science of the Universe. The intention of that instruction was to disclose to candidates the physical and meta-physical constitution of the world and the place and destiny of man in it. They were shown how the complex human organism reproduces the great World and summarises it in small, so that man may see himself to be a microcosm or miniature copy of it. They were enlightened not only upon the external visible aspect, but also upon the physically unseen and impalpable aspect, both of the Universe and themselves. They learned truths concerning the material and the ultra-material sides of the world and were taught that corresponding features were present in themselves.

They learned of the continual flux of matter, of the transiency of bodily forms, and of the abiding permanence of the one Life or Spirit which has descended and embodied itself in matter, and has there distributed and clothed itself in an endless but progressive variety of forms from the mineral up to the human, with the purpose of generating eventually a finished perfected product as the result of the mighty process. There was demonstrated to them the dual cosmic method of Involution and Evolution, by which the universally diffused Life-force involves and circumscribes itself within material limitations and physical conditions, and thence evolves and arises out of them, enriched by the experience.

They were taught of the different levels and graduations of the Universe—some of them material and some ethereal—the planes and sub-planes of it, upon which the great scheme is being carried out; which levels and planes, all progressively linked together, constitute as it were one vast ladder of many rounds, staves, or rungs; a ladder which Tennyson once well described as:

> *"The world's great altar-stairs*
> *Which slope through darkness up to God."*

Candidates in the old systems were instructed in these matters before being admitted to Initiation. The knowledge served to explain to them their own nature and constitution and their place in the World system. It demonstrated to them their own evolutionary possibilities and made clear to them why Initiation-science had been instituted, and how Initiation itself was an intensive means of accelerating the spiritual evolution of individuals who were ripe for it, and capable of intelligently co-operating with and expediting the cosmic process. With this knowledge they were then free either to proceed to actual Initiation and undertake its obligations, sacrifices and discipline, or to stand down and go no farther if they found themselves unwilling, or without the courage, to undertake the arduous task involved. Freedom of the personal will in this momentous choice was always essential to admission to Initiation, and the same absence of constraint still attaches to admission to modern Masonry.

The modern Mason, however, is left entirely without any cosmologic instruction and to such hazy notions on the subject as he may happen to hold. It becomes difficult, therefore, in regard to this and many other matters of Masonic moment, to speak of the *disciplina arcani* to those who may be either not interested in it or who would treat the information with incredulity as something about which nothing certain is known or perhaps knowable. Skepticism, freedom and independence of thought about matters of a more or less occult nature have their undoubted place and value in the outer ways of the world. But they are foreign to and inconsistent with the mental attitude appropriate to those who, on entering a hall of Initiation, are supposed to tyle the door to the outside world and its conceptions, and, divesting themselves of all ideas there preacquired, to offer themselves as humble teachable pupils of a new and authoritative order of knowledge. Where everyone claims to be already possessed of a sufficiently satisfactory explanation of the Universe and his place in it, or is content to get along without one, and in either case prefers his private judgment to any other that may be offered him, the soil for making Initiates in any real sense is distinctly unfavourable. For such, however, these pages are not written. They are offered only to the minority of Brethren eager to learn what Masonry has to teach them upon matters in which they earnestly seek knowledge and guidance.

Masonry, then, in exhibiting to them a simple ladder offers them a symbol the significance of which is calculated to open widely the eyes of their imagination. It is true that in the Instruction lecture the ladder is expressly referred to that of Jacob in the familiar biblical episode, and that that ladder is then given a moral significance and made to suggest the way by which man may ascend from earth to heaven by climbing its symbolic rungs, and especially by utilising its three chief ones representing the virtues Faith, Hope and Charity. This moral interpretation is warranted and salutary. But it is far from exhaustive, and conceals rather than reveals what "Jacob's ladder" was really intended to convey to the perspicuous when the compilers of our system gave it the prominence they did. We may be assured they had a much deeper purpose than merely reminding us of the Pauline triad of theological virtues.

The ladder, then, covertly emphasises the old cosmological teaching before referred to. It is a symbol of the Universe and of its succession of step-like planes reaching from the heights to the depths. It is written elsewhere that the Father's House has many mansions; many levels and resting places for His creatures in their different conditions and degrees of progress. It is these levels, these planes and sub-planes, that are denoted by the rungs and staves of the ladder. And of these there are, for us in our present state of evolutionary unfoldment, three principal ones; the physical plane, the plane of desire and emotion, and the mental plane or that of the abstract intelligence which links up to the still higher plane of the spirit. These three levels of the world are reproduced in man. The first corresponds with his material physique, his sense-body; the second with his desire and emotional nature, which is a mixed element resulting from the interaction of his physical senses and his ultra-physical mind; the third with his mentality, which is still farther removed from his physical nature and forms the link between the latter and his spiritual being.

The ladder, and its three principal staves, may be seen everywhere in Nature. It appears in the septenary scale of musical sound with its three dominants; in the prismatic scale of light with its three primary colours; in our seven-day scale of weekly time, in the septenary physiological changes of our bodily organism, and the similar periodicities known to physics and indeed to every branch of science. The perfect Lodge has seven members, including three principal Officers. The advancement of the Third Degree candidate to the East is by seven steps, the first three of which, it will be remembered, are given special significance.

Thus the Universe and man himself are constructed ladder-wise, in an orderly organised sequence of steps. The one universal substance composing the differentiated parts of the Universe "descends" from a state of the utmost ethereality by successive steps of increasing densification until gross materialisation is reached; and thence "ascends" through a similarly ordered gradation of planes to its original place, but enriched by the experience gained by its activities during the process.

It was this cosmic process which was the subject of the dream or vision of Jacob and which accounts for "Jacob's ladder" being given prominence in our symbolism. What was "dreamed" or beheld by him with super-sensual vision, is equally perceptible to-day by anyone whose inner eyes have been opened. Every real Initiate is one who has attained an expansion of consciousness and faculty enabling him to behold the ethereal worlds revealed to the Hebrew patriarch, as easily as the uninitiated man beholds the phenomenal world with his outer eyes. The Initiate is able to "see the angels of God ascending and descending"; that is, he can directly behold the great stairway of the Universe and watch the intricate but orderly mechanism of involution, differentiation, evolution, and re-synthesis, constituting the Life-process.

He can witness the descent of human essences or souls through planes of increasing density and decreasing vibratory rate, gathering around them as they come veils of matter from each, until finally this lowest level of complete materialisation is reached, where the great struggle for supremacy between the inner and the outer man, between the spirit and the flesh, between the real self and the unreal selves and veils built around it, has to be fought out on the chequer-work floor of our present existence, among the black and white opposites of good and evil, light and darkness, prosperity and adversity. And he can watch the upward return of those who conquer in the strife and, attaining their regeneration and casting off or transmuting the "worldly possessions" acquired during their descent, ascend to their Source, pure and unpolluted from the stains of this imperfect world.

But to no man comes such vision as this unless he too be a Jacob who flees from the clash and hurly of secular activities into the solitude of his own soul, and in that barren wilderness interrogates himself and struggles agonisingly to penetrate the mystery of his existence, to read its purpose, and tear out the last secret of his own being. So, perchance, he may fall asleep, his head at last quietly pillowed upon that hard stone, against which hitherto he has been blindly dashing it. And then by the surrender of his own will and mental activities, and in the silence and quietude of the senses, his own inmost great light may break, and from that newfound centre he will see and know and find the answer to all his needs.

For, in the words of an ancient record of Initiation, "the sleep of the body becomes the awaking of the soul, and the closing of the eyes true vision, and silence becomes impregnated with God. This happened to me when I received the supreme authentic Word. I became God-inspired. I arrived at Truth. Wherefore I give from my soul and whole strength, blessing to the Father." (*Hermes, Poemandres,* I. 30).

Jacob's vision and ladder, therefore, exemplify the attainment of Initiation, the expansion of consciousness that comes when the light of the centre is found, and the cosmic vision that then becomes possible. The same truth is taught in a little treatise, of great instructiveness to every Mason, written by the initiate philosopher Porphyry in the third century and entitled *On the Cave of the Nymphs*. It is an exposition of a passage in Homer's *Odyssey*, which he shows likewise to be a veiled story of the soul's wanderings, of its crossing the rough seas of life and enduring the tempests and trials of this world, and finally perfecting itself and escaping into the haven of peace.

The passage describes a certain dark cave, above which grew an olive-tree, and into which certain nymphs entered at one end and became busy in weaving purple garments for themselves; and it was not possible to leave the cave save by a gate at the other end and after having ceased to be satisfied with the pleasure of inhabiting that agreeable but benighted place and sought a way of escape. Porphyry thus explains the allegory: The dark cave is that of the body into which the soul (a "nymph" or spiritual being) enters and weaves around itself a garment of flesh and blood, and indulges in sense-gratification alien to its real nature. The nymph-soul has descended through the planes of the Cosmos until it has entered this cave by the "gate of man" (i.e., by evolving to human status), and it can only leave it by passing out through the opposite gate, the "gate of the gods" (i.e., by becoming perfected and divinised). This it cannot do save with the help of oil from the olive planted at the top of the cavern; the oil of Wisdom which shall initiate the soul and guide it to the way out to the higher worlds and the regions of the blessed.

Porphyry's exposition continues thus:

> *"In this cave, therefore, says Homer, all external worldly possessions must be deposited. Here, naked and as a suppliant, afflicted in body, casting aside everything superfluous, and renouncing all sensual energies, one must sit at the foot of the olive and consult with Minerva (Wisdom) by what means we may effectually destroy that hostile rout of passions which lurk insidiously in the secret recesses of the soul. It will not be a simple task to become liberated from this sensible life; but he who dares to do this must transmute himself, so that, being at length divested of the torn garments by which his true self is concealed, he may recover the ruined empire of his soul."*

The Mason who reads this parable will not fail to see in it the allusion to the preparation of candidates for initiation, or to recognise that the cave and the olive-tree growing above it correspond precisely with the grave of Hiram Abiff and the sprig of acacia planted at its head. Both of these allude, of course, to the human body in which the true spiritual self of man lies buried and imprisoned, and from the bondage of which it can only be freed by cultivating and lighting the oil of wisdom (or, alternatively, by causing the sprig of acacia to blossom) which will enlarge his consciousness and reveal to him his path through the Universe.

We have each descended into this world by the steps of Jacob's ladder; we have each to ascend from it by the same steps. In some Masonic diagrams and tracing boards, upon the ladder is exhibited a small cross in a tilted, unstable position as if ascending it. That cross represents all who are engaged in mounting the ladder to the heights, and who

> *"Rise by stepping-stones*
> *From their dead selves to higher things."*

Each carries his cross, his own cruciform body, as he ascends; the material vesture whose tendencies are ever at cross-purposes with the desire of his spirit and militate against the ascent. Thus weighted, each must climb, and climb alone; yet reaching out—as the secret tradition teaches and the arms of the tilted cross signify—one hand to invisible helpers above, and the other to assist the ascent of feebler brethren below. For as the sides and separate rungs of the ladder constitute a unity, so all life and all lives are fundamentally one, and none lives to himself alone.

Indeed, Life, and the ladder it climbs, are one and indissociable. The summit of both reaches to and disappears out of ken into the heavens; the base of both rests upon the earth; but these two terminals —that of spirit and that of matter—are but opposite poles of a single reality which cannot be known as a unity or otherwise than in its differentiated aspects of many planes, many mansions, many rounds or staves, except by him who has unified them in himself and become able to ascend and descend upon the ladder at will. But this is the privilege only of the Initiate skilled in that science of life which teaches how to mount the *Scala Perfectionis*, as a famous classical work of the 15th century terms the ladder of initiation, known to Masons under the glyph of "Jacob's Ladder."

THE SUPERSTRUCTURE

The novitiate Mason is taught to regard his normal, natural personality as but a foundation-stone upon which he is recommended to erect a superstructure, perfect in all its parts and honourable to the builder.

To how many does this instruction mean anything more than a general pious counsel to become merely a man of strong moral character and virtue? It is something, of course, to fulfil that elementary standard, which needs, however, no membership of a Secret Order for its accomplishment; but the recommendation implies a very different meaning from that, as a little reflection will show. It is not a recommendation merely to improve the condition of the already existing foundation-stone (the personality), but to erect upon that foundation something which previously did not exist, something which will transcend and outrange it, although built upon it.

For the reader who is unversed in the deeper side of Masonic significance, and is unaware of the hidden nature of it as thoroughly known to the original exponents of the science, the subject may prove difficult. It must therefore be explained at the outset that the superstructure to be erected is the organisation of an ethereal or spiritual body in which the skilled Mason can function in independence of his physical body and natural personality.

The theory of Masonry presupposes that man is a fallen creature; that his natural personality is a transient and unreal expression of his true self as conceived in the Divine Mind; and that, under appropriate tuition and self-discipline, he may become rebuilt and reorganised into the original condition from which he has fallen. The present natural personality, however, is the basis or foundation-stone out of which that reorganisation can proceed, and within it already exists, though in a condition of chaos and disorder, all the material requisite to the purpose.

Building a superstructure upon one's present self involves much more than merely improving one's moral character. It is not a novice's task, although the advice to perform it is rightly given in the Apprentice-stage. It is a work of occult science, only to be undertaken by those educated and skilled in that science. It is the science to which the Christian Master referred in the words:

> "*Which of you, intending to build a tower, sitteth not down first and counteth the cost, whether he have sufficient to finish it? Lest, after he hath laid the foundation and is not able to finish it, all that behold begin to mock, saying, 'This man began to build but was not able to finish!'*"

Accordingly, the Mason desirous of building a tower or superstructure should "sit down first and count the cost" by acquiring a thorough understanding of what is involved; and before he is able even to begin the erection of such a building, he will find a good deal of rough labourer's work has first to be done upon himself in clearing the ground for the intended structure.

There is an old Masonic Degree, not comprised in our present Constitutions, devoted specially to this subject. It is called the Degree of Grand Architect, and throws great light on the intention of those who, well understanding the secret science, made reference in our Ritual to the building of a superstructure.

In that Degree, the reference is to "building structures in the air," and it is taught that this is the work only of grand architects, "being too great for inferior craftsmen, who only know by admiring them at a distance when done."

"Structures in the air!" All structures, save subterranean ones, rise into the air—the average reader will say; yet not buildings of brick or stone are here meant. Again, building castles in the air is a familiar term for indulgence in day-dreaming and fanciful speculation; but, whilst all thought energy is constructive and creates objective form upon the plane of mind, we may be assured that the sages who perpetuated Masonic science were innocent of recommending the practice of anything so futile and unpractical.

The airy structure to which they allude is the formation of a superphysical ethereal body, a "body of mist" as Hesiod and other Greek classics describe it, in which the adept Mason may consciously function in the finer planes of life and apart from his gross physical organism, and in which he will continue to live when the latter has become permanently discarded.

It is spoken of by Origen, the Christian Father of the second century, as follows "Another body, a spiritual and ethereal one, is promised us; a body not subject to physical touch, nor seen by physical eyes, nor burdened with weight, and which shall be metamorphosed according to the different regions in which it shall be. In that spiritual body, the whole of it will be an eye, the whole of it an ear, the whole serve as hands, the whole as feet"; implying that all the now distributed faculties will be unified in that body into one, as was the case with man before the fall and descent into matter and multiplicity.

Let us justify these observations by some pertinent references to the subject in the great text-book of Initiation-Science, the Volume of the Sacred Law; though they might be abundantly supplemented from other sources. Like the famous Orphic Hymns of the Pythagorean and Eleusinian Schools of the Mysteries, the Psalms of our Bible are an anthology of hymns of the Hebrew Initiates and are full of Masonic allusion and instructiveness.

In the 48th Psalm, the disciple of spiritual science is directed to take a walk round the symbolic City of Jerusalem; he was told to mark well its bulwarks, to observe its palaces, and particularly to pay attention to the great tower of the Temple, which, like a modern cathedral spire, rose into the air above all other buildings, so that he might not only himself appreciate the symbolism of what he saw, but might be in a position to interpret its significance to "them that come after"; that is, to junior students of the science.

He thus received a striking object-lesson in the analogy of material buildings to spiritual ones. In the massive defensive walls of the city, he was to recognise the strength, permanence and resisting power of the spiritual organism or "holy city" which he must build for himself in exchange for, but upon the foundation of, the frail perishable temporal body. In the palaces of the mighty, with their gorgeous interiors and stores of costly furnishings and precious objects of art, he was to perceive that his own interior must become correspondingly beautified and enriched with spiritual treasures.

But in the great heaven-pointing tower, to which his attention was specially directed, he was to see the symbol of a structure as far transcending his present temporal organism as the Temple-spire outranged the adjacent buildings at its feet. From this, he was to deduce the necessity of building and projecting upwards from his lower organisation a "tower," a superior spiritual body, rising into and capable of functioning in the "air" or more tenuous and ethereal worlds than this physical one.

This is the "structure in the air" which only "Grand Architects" are competent to raise; this is the "superstructure" which our Entered Apprentices are enjoined to aspire to building.

Let us turn next to the further pertinent information on the subject given by the Apostle-Initiate to his Corinthian pupils. He instructs them on this subject of superstructures. How is it possible to rear them? "How are the dead raised up, and with what body do they come?" (He is not speaking of the physically defunct, but of that condition of atrophied spiritual consciousness do the normal animal man, which is always described as a state of "death" in the biblical and other writings on the subject).

He proceeds to explain that the physical body itself cannot be raised, since corruption cannot inherit incorruption, but that nevertheless there can be a "resurrection from the dead" through a sublimation of its vital essences, which can be reorganised and reconstituted into a new body of subtle matter on a supra-physical level. First comes the natural body we all wear to begin with; but out of it can be evolved a psychical body. The former is an entirely earthy vesture exhibiting an illusory unreal self to the world; the latter is the body of our true spiritual self (or "lord from heaven") which hitherto has remained masked and buried within that temporal vesture; "sown" in it as a seed, but capable of bursting its sheath and being raised from its former impotence to "power" (activity and conscious function).

He properly speaks of it as one of the secrets and mysteries of Initiation, and his familiar words may thus be paraphrased:

"I am expounding to you a mystery, one of the arcana of Initiation. We are not designed to remain always asleep in this drugged, deadened state of consciousness in which we are plunged, where we suffer the illusion that we are really alive, but are not. In the course of our evolution the due time comes for each of us to awake out of that sleep, and to become changed, transmuted; for our consciousness to be transposed to a higher level. We have borne the earthly human image; we have now to exchange it for an ethereal one of finer texture and purer quality."

The change, the transposition of consciousness from the old to the new centre, comes suddenly (though it may take long to prepare and purify ourselves for its coming). When it occurs it comes with an inwardly heard crash, like a trumpet-blast, as the nervous system and brain-structures react to the stress upon them involved in the transition.

(It must be explained that the "trumpet" and "last trumpet" are technical terms among Initiates for the spiral, trumpet-shaped, whorls or vortices occurring in subtle matter under stresses, audible to those in whom the change occurs. The reference to the "sound of the last trumpet" stands for a physiological experience as the last fine physical strands of the old nature are, as it were, snapped and the nervous system re-electrified. In the East, this experience is called the "end of the world," since for the Initiate it means the termination of his old worldly consciousness and its replacement by one of a much more vivid and intense quality.)

The Apostle further explains that for this newly evolved Ego or conscious centre there is an appropriate body, for there are celestial as well as terrestrial bodies. There cannot be consciousness apart from a formal vehicle for it, and as the old earthy body has served (and will so continue to serve) for ordinary mundane purposes, so will the newly evolved consciousness possess its own separate appropriate psychic or spiritual body for function upon supraphysical levels.

The Initiate of this high degree, therefore, will possess a twofold organisation; his ordinary physical one (the "companion of his former toils") and his supra-physical one, and will be able to utilise and function in each. He will have built his "tower"; his "superstructure in the air."

The superstructure must be perfect in all its parts and so be honourable to the builder. What are its parts?

Man, even in his natural, unregenerate, imperfectly evolved state, is a highly composite creature. Blended with his purely physical frame are three other supra-physical, but quasi-physical, bodies; his etheric body (the "double" or wraith), his emotional or desire body, and his mental organisation or body; whilst over and beyond these, and not necessarily, in functional alignment with them, exists his ultimate spiritual self which distinguishes him from the sub-human creatures. These are his "parts," and they are but too often extremely ill-organised, uncoordinated and unbalanced.

If they be imperfectly organised in the lower natural man, how can they be expected to be able to contribute requisite sublimations of themselves for the up-building of a body upon a higher level? All bodily and mental disease and infirmity originates in disorder in these inner bodies, which disorder thereupon becomes reflected forwards and manifested in the physical husk. Unless the inner natures be disciplined and organised before the gross mortal vesture is shed at physical death, how can one enter the ethereal kingdoms otherwise than "maimed," without a "wedding-garment," and in a distorted shape, not perfect in all its parts, and anything but honourable to the builder?

But, as we have long since seen, the first duty of every spiritual Craftsman is the purification and discipline of these bodies, and the elimination from himself of all base metals therein of which he has himself been an artificer. Only in proportion to the achievement of this arduous task can he hope to bring these "parts" into order, into subjection to his will, and into coordinated function and alignment, and so in the fullest sense stand erect, a just and upright man and Mason.

He need not trouble to know how his superstructure will develop or to what extent or measure of perfection he may have built it. For it will become automatically built in his heights proportionately as he schools himself in his depths and tests his work by the continual application to it of the cross (which is the square, level and plumb-rule in combination). When the time comes for his consciousness to be raised to that superior level and he hears the call "Friend, come up higher!" he will find the superstructure he has been building in the darkness below, perfect in all its parts and honourable to himself.

He will have climbed a section of the life-ladder; he will himself have built, dedicated and consecrated King Solomon's Temple; and, through the result of his own labour upon himself, that resplendent body will appear to him more like the work of the Great Architect of the Universe than that of human hands.

There are, however, farther sections of the infinite ladder to be climbed, even when this high level has been won. From thence there remains still further building to be done, a body to be fabricated manifesting still loftier wisdom, strength and beauty . For was not the first symbolic Temple to be destroyed and become replaced by a second, of which it is written that "the glory of the former house is not to be compared with that of the latter ?"

But this still loftier work need not now be treated of. Let it suffice if what has already been said assists any reader to the building of his first superstructure! Temple.

THE CABLE-TOW

These expositions are being offered in their present order with a purpose. That purpose is to outline, as nearly and systematically as may be, the due sequence and progressive stages of the work of spiritual Craftsmanship or self-building. We have traced that work from its inception in the heart's desire to pass from darkness to light and attain a higher order of life and mode of being, through its stages of the outer and inward purification essential to that attainment, and through the crisis of a deeper gloom, a voluntary abnegation of and dying to all the attributes that go to constitute the natural personality, until the aspirant who endures all these to the end is finally rewarded by receiving his "crown of life," as the biblical metaphor very fittingly terms that exalted order of conscious being which marks the fulfilment of human spiritual evolution. And we have shown how, in winning that high degree of consciousness, he has simultaneously built for himself out of the sublimations of his original nature a new superstructure! body appropriate to it and in which it can function. In the abounding wealth of the symbols and veiled verbal references in our rituals and instruction lectures to the details of this truly scientific work, there remain, however, many others needing explanation, some of which can now be considered more advantageously than at our earlier stage and with better chance of being understood.

One of these is the cable-tow. In my previous book it was explained that its use in the E. A. Degree taught the beginner the useful lesson that he who has once felt within him the impulses of the central light and been moved to seek it should never recede from his quest and, indeed, cannot do so without doing violence to the highest within him, a violence equivalent to moral suicide. At the same time, he is also enjoined not to be unduly precipitate, not ignorantly and rashly to rush forward in an unprepared inward state to grasp the secrets of his own being, in which case peril of another kind threatens him; but to proceed humbly, meekly, cautiously and under instructed guidance. The ancient maxim "Know thyself," was coupled with another, Ne quid nimis, "Nothing in excess"; for the science can only be learned and applied gradually. It will unfold itself more and more as it is diligently studied and pursued.

The foregoing explanation of the cable-tow is but a very partial one, and inculcates a salutary, but purely moral, piece of advice. The deeper significance is a psycho-physiological one, and has to do with the mysteries of the human organism. It should not be overlooked that the cable-tow is given prominence not only in the First Degree. It is again mentioned in the obligation in the Third Degree, whilst it appears under another guise in that working-tool of the Master-Mason which acts upon a centre-pin. And finally it reappears in the Royal Arch Degree as a cord or life-line. It is requisite to understand what is involved in something to which such recurring prominence is given.

Let us first recall what has been already stated about the human organism being a composite structure of several natures or bodies (physical, etheric, emotional, and mental), fixated in a unity or synthesis; each of such bodies being constituted of gross or subtle matter, of differing density and vibratory rate, and the whole coordinated by the central divine Principle (which may or may not yet have come forward into the formal conscious mind, although there are few in whose awareness it is not lurkingly present and more or less active as "conscience").

Thus the human constitution may be likened to a number of glass tumblers placed one within the other and with, say, a night-light (representing the central Principle) inserted in the inmost one. The glass of the tumblers may be imagined as of progressive thickness and coarseness, from within outwards, and some of them as coloured, dirty, or not closely fitting in with the others. The coarser, dirtier, and more opaque the glasses, the less able will be the central light to shine through them; a single glass may be so opaque as to prevent the passage of the light through all the rest. Here, then, is an object lesson in the need for the inward purification of our various constituent sheaths, and for becoming "perfect in all our parts." As William Blake said very truly: "If the gates of human perception were thoroughly cleansed, we should perceive everything as it is—infinite; but man has closed himself up till he sees all things only through the narrow chinks of his own cavern."

Another illustration. Human compositeness may be compared with the concentric skins or sheaths of a vegetable bulb (an onion, or hyacinth). Here the sheaths are all equally pure and coordinated; and because the bulb is perfect in all its parts or sheaths, and, when planted, fulfils the whole law of its nature, its life-force bursts its natural bonds, throws up a self-built superstructure into the air, and there effloresces into the bloom which is its "crown of life" or fullness of development. Man should do this, and, as we have shown, this is what the Mason is taught to do. But man having (what the bulb has not), freedom of will to fulfil or to violate, the law of his nature, has chosen the latter course, and consequently by indulgence in perverse desire and wrongly directed thought, has fouled and disorganised his sheaths. Hence his spiritual darkness and his liability to all forms of disease. The central Principle cannot shine through his opacity, lighting up his mind and governing his desires and actions. It remains imprisoned within him. He sees, thinks and knows only from his self-darkened outer sheaths, and is misguided and illuded accordingly.

For a final example, let us turn to the instructive familiar episode in the Gospels of the storm overtaking a boat containing a number of men, of whom the Chief was "asleep in the hinder part of the boat." The boat typifies the human organism; its occupants, its various parts and faculties, including the as yet unawakened Master-Principle resident in its depths or "hinder part." An emotional upheaval occurs; the rough waves of passion threaten to wreck the whole party. A brain-storm arises; intemperate gusts of fright, wrong-headedness, and mental un-control, make the position still worse. The extremity is sufficiently acute to awaken the Master-Principle into activity whose beneficent power is able instantly to still those unruly winds, and waves, which suddenly are reduced to a great peace.

Every Master-Mason, who is a real and not merely a titular one, is able to perform this "miracle" in himself; perhaps in others also. There is nothing super-natural about it to him. It is possible to him because he "has the Mason Word and second sight"; he both understands the composite structure of the human organism, can visually discern the disordered part or parts, and can apply healing, harmonising, vibratory power from his own corresponding part to the seat of mischief, saying to this disordered mental part or that unruly emotional sheath, "Peace, be still!" Every Master-Mason is therefore also a Master-Physician, able to benefit patients in a medical sense, and also to visualise the inner condition of those who look to him for instruction and initiation in a Masonic sense, to advise upon their interior needs and moral ailments, and help them to purify and align their disordered natures. But this is not possible save to one who himself has become pure and rectified in all his parts; the physician must first heal himself before he can communicate either physical or moral health to others.

This promise about the compositeness of the human structure and the existence in us of a series of independent, yet coordinated "parts" or sheaths, has been necessary before we can speak directly of the cable-tow. What is it that connects these parts? And are these parts dissociable from one another?

We know that they are normally in close association and to this association applies the enjoinder that what God hath joined, man shall not put asunder. What the age-long process of evolution has built up with infinite patience and care is not to be tampered with for improper purposes, or even by well-meaning but, as yet, unenlightened experiment in the supposed interests of science; a point upon which the old Masters and teachers of our science are specially insistent, for reasons which now need not be entered upon.

Nevertheless, a measure of dissociation does occur naturally in even the most healthy and well-organised people (and of cases of abnormal psychic looseness of constitution we need not speak). It occurs in sleep, when the consciousness may be vividly active, whether in an orderly or disorderly manner; people "travel" in their sleep. It occurs at times of illness or violent shock. It may be induced by alcohol or drugs; the "anaesthetic revelation" is a well-recognised phenomenon. Under any of these conditions there may be a complete ec-stasis, or conscious standing out or away of the Ego from the physical body. Apparitions and even action at a distance are well-accredited facts.

Such phenomena are explicable only upon the suppositions of the existence of a subtler vehicle than the gross body, of the fact that consciousness becomes temporarily transferred from the latter to the former, and that the two are capable of conjoint function in complete independence of the physical brain and body.

What preserves the connection between the two "parts" thus disjoined, and makes possible their subsequent re-coalescence, is the "cable-tow." It is a connective thread of matter of extreme tenuousness and elasticity issuing from the physical abdominal region and maintaining the same kind of connection with the extended subtle body as the string with which a boy flies a kite. As the boy can pull in the kite by the string, so does the extruded subtle body become drawn back to its physical base. Were the kite-string severed during the kite's flight, the kite would collapse or be blown away. Similarly, were the human "cable-tow" permanently severed, death would ensue and each of the severed parts go to its own place.

Biblically this human "cable-tow" is called the "silver cord" in the well-known passage, "or ever the silver cord is loosed and the golden bowl is broken; then shall the body return to the earth and the spirit to God who gave it." "Silver" is the technical esoteric term for psychical substance, as gold is for spiritual, and iron or brass for physical. Its physiological correspondence is the umbilical cord connecting the child with its mother. Its analogue in ecclesiastical vestments is the girdle worn by the high-priests of the Hebrew and by the priests and monastics of the Christian Church.

Everyone unconsciously possesses the cable-tow, and it comes into use during sleep, when a less or greater measure of involuntary dissociation of our parts occurs. A Master, however, is one who has outgrown the incapacities to which the undeveloped average man is subject. Unlike the latter, he is in full knowledge and control of all his parts; whether his physical body be awake or wrapped in sleep, he maintains unbroken consciousness. He is able at will to shut off consciousness of temporal affairs and apply it to supra-physical ones. He can thus function at a distance from his physical body, whether upon the mundane or upon higher planes of the cosmic ladder.

His cable-tow, of infinite expansiveness, unwinds from his centre-pin and, stretching like the kite-string, enables him to travel where he will in his subtle body and to rejoin and reanimate his physical one at will. Hence it is that the Master-Mason is pledged to answer and obey all signs and summonses from any Master-Mason's lodge if within the reach of his cable-tow; and such assemblies, it should be remembered, are contemplated therefore as taking place not at any physical location, but upon an ethereal plane.

For corroboration of what is possible in this respect to a Master, one should reflect upon the instances of bi-location, passing through closed walls, and manifesting at a distance, recorded of the Great Exemplar in the Gospels. These are representative of what is feasible to anyone attaining Mastership.

The cable-tow, therefore, is given prominence to the reflective Craftsman as a help towards understanding his own constitution, and to foreshadow to him work that lies before him when he is fitted to undertake it—work which now may seem to him impossible and incredible. For as the skirret (which is the cable-tow in another form) is intended for the skilful architect to draw forth a line to mark out the ground for the intended structure, so the competent builder of the spiritual body will unwind his own "silver cord" when he learns how to function consciously on the ascending ladder of supraphysical planes, and to perceive the nature of the superstructure he himself is intended to construct.

Further importance attaches to the significance of the cable-tow from the fact testified to at the admission to our Order of every new candidate for ceremonial initiation. For all real Initiation involves the use of the actual "silver cord" or life-line; since such Initiation always occurs when the physical body is in a state of trance or sleep, and when the temporarily liberated consciousness has been transferred to a higher level. Thence it subsequently is brought back to the physical organism, the cerebral and nerve centres of which become illumined, revitalised, and raised to a higher pitch of faculty than was previously possible. The perspicacious Royal Arch Mason will not fail to perceive how this truth is dramatically exemplified in that Degree.

This subject might be considerably extended, for whilst in a ceremonial system like the Masonic, only one initiation is portrayed (or, rather where initiation only occurs once), yet in the actual experience of soul-architecture Initiation succeeds Initiation upon increasingly higher levels of the ladder as the individual becomes correspondingly ripe for them, able to bear their strain and to assimilate their revelations. What the Craft teaching and symbols inculcate is a principle common to every degree of real Initiation that one may prove worthy to attain. For each upward step the candidate for the heights must be prepared as he is in the E. A. Degree; at each, there will be the same peril in turning back, and at each the same menace directed against rashly rushing forward.

THE APRON

So much was said in my former volume, *The Meaning of Masonry*, in explanation of the Masonic Apron, that it seems needless to speak at length of it again. Yet, to maintain continuity of thought, it seems desirable once more to refer to its symbolism at this point, since we have been closely considering the manner in which consciousness becomes expanded and enveloped in bodies or vehicles appropriate to that expansion; and we have been dealing with the arcanum or "mystery" propounded by St. Paul as to how the "dead" (the as yet uninitiated and spiritually unquickened) are raised up to a new order of life and the new kind of embodiment they take on, or automatically fabricate, in the process.

Consciousness cannot exist without body. "To every seed (or conscious unit) its own body," says the Apostle-Initiate; or, as we Masons may paraphrase it, to every Degree of life is allotted the appropriate Apron, proclaiming the wearer's spiritual rank. As no one can enter the Lodge unclothed with the Apron, so no one can enter any of the unseen worlds without wearing a body appropriate. There are bodies terrestrial, adapted to use on the lower planes of life; and bodies celestial or ethereal, adapted to functioning on higher ones. Man is a composite of many bodies, one within the other; though ordinarily he is unaware of it and has not yet organised them and come to know them separately, as the Initiate is expected to do.

The physical body is but one, and the grossest, of the terrestrial bodies; it is but a plaster of organised chemical particles, within and around which his subtler bodies exist, and for which it forms a nexus or fixation-point. When totally discarded at death, it disintegrates; when partially abandoned in sleep or anaesthesia, its energies persist passively, and connection with it is kept by the cabletow or "silver cord." In each case, the Ego, whether aware of it or not, stands minus its physical sheath and enclosed in its remaining ones. And a similar divesting of each successive body may take place until only the ultimate Ego remains.

That Ego, the ultimate Divine Principle in man, is represented by the triangular flap of the Masonic Apron. The triangle (or pyramid form) is the geometrical symbol for Spirit or Fire, and the ultimate Spirit of man may be likened to a pointed flame or tongue of fire. (The word "pyramid" derives from the Greek word *pur*, fire.)

The body or form (or rather the succession of bodies or forms) which that Ego assumes on descending into manifestation through the ladder-like planes of the Universe, aggregating to itself and organising around itself material from each, is represented by the lower quadrangular part of the Apron. The quadrangle, square, or superficies, is the geometrical symbol for Body, Form, Physicalisation. The quadrangle is further appropriate because (1) all Body is constituted of four elements, earth, water, air, fire; (2) because the human organism is fourfold, a complex of four distinct departments, physical, etheric, emotional, and mental; and (3) because in man the three sub-human kingdoms (mineral, vegetable, and animal) are unified into the human synthesis.

The candidate's first investiture with the Apron is symbolic therefore of his Ego's entrance into this world, and becoming clothed with form or body. He is meant to realise himself as a sevenfold being, perfectly constituted originally in the Divine Mind; his triangle of Spirit combining with the quadrangle of materialised form to make up the perfect number seven. He is meant to realise that he has descended to a condition of embodiment and limitation of consciousness for the purpose of acquiring experience in those conditions, and of performing certain work upon himself which shall raise him to full realisation of his own ultimate nature and of the Divine purpose in him, and that though his present state or form is one of restrictedness and humiliation, it will never disgrace him if he never disgraces it.

In the First Degree, the triangular flap of the Apron is kept erect. In the Second, it is lowered. Thereby is denoted the physiological truth that the Ego or human Spirit on entering this world at birth does not immediately attain full embodiment, but at first is, as it were, an overhovering presence, organically connected with the body, but only gradually taking possession of it. We recognise this truth in practical life. Moral and legal responsibility is never attributed to a child under seven years of age, for the moral sense has not yet developed. Important physiological changes connected with puberty occur at the age of fourteen. Civic responsibility is denied until twenty-one is reached. The basic reason for all this is the occult truth that the Ego does not attain its maximum of incarnation until twenty-one. Accordingly, it is not until this age is reached that a man is presumed competent to enter the Craft and undertake the science of himself.

As the Ego immerses itself in its body and works upon it, it creates changes in it, whether for good or evil. It either organises or disorganises its vehicles according to its will and desires. It becomes an artificer in metals, whether base or precious; it either stores itself with ornaments and jewels and the invaluable furniture of self-knowledge, or with useless trumperies and grotesque contrivances of which sooner or later it must get rid. Assuming its activities to have been wisely directed, they are evidenced in the Apron by the blue rosettes imposed upon it in the Second Degree; if they are persisted in and the Spirit more and more subjugates and controls the Form, that increasing domination and the further progress made in the science are testified to by the additional elaborations found in the Apron in the Third Degree. Still more advanced progress is evidenced by further changes and beautification of the Apron in the Royal Arch Degrees, and in the Grand Lodges of provinces, and of the nation.

The Tau displayed upon the Apron worn by those of Master rank is a form of the Cross, and also of the Hammer of Thor, of Scandinavian religion. It is displayed triply, to signify that the wearer has brought his three lower natures (physical, emotional, and mental) under complete control; that he has crucified them and keeps them repressed by the hammer of a strong will.

The further important point should be noticed that the Apron covers the creative, generative organ of the body; and it is especially to these that the significance of the Tau attaches. Spiritual self-building and the erection of the "superstructure" are dependent upon the supply of creative energy available from the generative nervous centre, the "power-house" of the human organism. Thence that energy passes upwards through other ganglionic "transformers" and, reaching the brain, becomes finally sublimated and transformed to consciousness. Conservation of that energy is therefore indispensable both for generating consciousness and providing the material for the finer vehicle or "superstructure" in which that consciousness may function; the life-energy is always creative, either in the direction of physical propagation or in that of super-physical up-building; hence the importance attached in religious spheres to celibacy.

It should also be noted that in the three Craft Degrees, the investiture with the Apron is made in the West; and not by the Master, but by his principal officer who is deputed to bestow it. The meaning behind this important detail is that while the human Ego is resident in this temporal world ("the West"), Nature, as the chief officer and deputy of Providence, supplies it with bodies of her own material and temporal substance. But in all cases beyond those three, the investiture takes place in the "East," the realm of spirit, and from the hands of the Master himself. For the progressed soul receives a clothing beyond Nature's power to supply; and, without intermediate hands, "God giveth it a body as it pleaseth Him," and to every such soul its own body, according to its measure of progress and consciousness.

THE WIND

The Instruction Lectures of the First Degree (unfortunately not used in some Lodges), contain a curious reference to the blowing of the wind, which must puzzle a good many minds. What has the wind to do with Masonic work, and why should it be particularly favourable to that work when blowing from East to West or vice versa?

Again we must look below the letter of the reference. The subject has not been introduced without purpose and instructiveness, to discern which will once more reveal the wisdom of the compilers and the crypticism with which they purposely shielded it when preparing our system for more or less promiscuous use.

The wind referred to is not the atmospheric breeze. It is that Wind (*Pneuma*) which "bloweth where it listeth"; the Wind of the Spirit; the currents of Divine Energy. The "East" and the "West" are not our ordinary geographical directions of space. In Initiate and Biblical language, as in the quarters of the Lodge, the East is the realm of Spirit and light; the West that of Matter and Darkness, the place of the disappearing sun. Man partakes of both; he is polarised east-west, as Spirit-Matter in one.

When, mystically, the wind blows east-west, a current of Divine Energy has set in towards the west, stimulating, vitalising and enlightening it. When it blows west-east, man has himself directed a current of aspiration from his own spirit eastwards to God.

The wind is therefore said to be specially favourable to Masonic work when blowing from either of those points of the mystical compass. When the Mason sends up his aspirations to the heights, as he should perpetually be doing, he is as a dynamo generating and transmitting an electric current upwards; that is, eastwards. When the Divine Fire descends upon himself, a similar current has set in westwards. It is written elsewhere and in the same sense, "As the lightning shineth from the east unto the west, so is the coming of the Son of Man" into the personal consciousness.

Prayer, upward aspiration in the above sense, is a practical scientific necessity for the work of the spiritual Craftsman. He himself is but as the leaden weight swinging at the lower end of the string of the plumb-rule. The string itself is as the connecting wire between that weight and the top of the plumb rule, a wire through which a current may pass up or down. Until that instrument is held erect, and the leaden weight brought to stillness and steadiness, it is ineffective for any form of work. So long as man is spiritually unaligned and out of plumb with his spiritual pole, directness of current between them is impossible. When that current is established, the lead of darkness and ignorance may become transmuted into the gold of conscious light and wisdom by the alchemy of the Spirit.

Real Initiates have always known there to be both special times and seasons, and special localities favourable to inducing the flow of currents of Divine Energy; but of these the modern Mason has not yet come to learn, though there are references to them in his system. The two solstices and equinoxes are such times, and others are known in the greater Churches whose calendar of feasts and fasts have been based upon this principle. The Festivals of the two Masonic patron-saints, St. John Baptist at midsummer, and St. John the Divine at mid-winter, have special bearing upon favourable times for spiritual Craftsmanship, but the former is now ignored, and the latter profaned. The matter may be left to the reflection of Brethren. When the Craft comes better to realise its purpose and science, these times and seasons will be taken advantage of for the furtherance of both individual and collective Masonic work.

The teaching in the Instruction Lecture upon the wind is supplemented by a reference to the escape of the Israelites from Egyptian bondage under their Master Moses, who caused a mighty east wind to blow, dividing the waters of the Red Sea to permit of their safe passage, which waters then rolled back and overwhelmed Pharaoh and his pursuing army. Again, the bearing of this episode is lost upon the average Brother, who for want of a key fails to see its relevance to any form of Masonry. And, indeed, it carries us into much deeper water than the average mind bathes in, although to those versed in Initiation science, the striking biblical incident masks and prefigures an equally momentous one in the individual life of everyone who seeks to fulfil his own spiritual evolution.

The allusion is to the important crisis which occurs when the personal soul of the aspirant ardently aspires for complete liberation from the tyranny of the flesh. It is then possible, in proper cases—and this was part of the office of the old Mysteries—for one who is a real Master so to act upon and separate his disciple's interior organic structures as to effect a permanent liberation of the latter's consciousness from sensual bondage. The "waters" that are then "divided" are what have previously been explained as those of the fluidic subtle body of desire and emotion, which normally constitute an untraversable barrier between the highest and the lowest elements in our nature. "Wretched man that I am, who shall deliver me from this body of death?" exclaimed one who afterwards attained delivery. For the "body of death" is made up of all those lower natures in us which inhibit consciousness in the spirit; and, as we have elsewhere stated, it is dissociable by a competent adept Master, who holds the keys of life and death (i.e., consciousness and unconsciousness in the spirit).

The higher nature of the disciple is then liberated from the bondage of the lower; his waters are divided; he passes through them into permanent safety from the Pharaoh-like tyranny of his material vesture; the still pursuing tendencies of which are checked, overwhelmed and shut off when the temporarily held-up waters are permitted to roll back to their former channel, to the extreme joy of the now liberated disciple.

This is an incident of real Initiation, and it is achievable only under the guidance of the equivalent of a Moses, a real Master. To those unversed in the deeper aspects of Initiation science, what cannot here be more than briefly explained may appear incredible, as would much more that lies concealed beneath the symbols and the text of the Masonic system. But those responsible for compiling or inspiring that system were clearly deeply versed in much that they permitted themselves to do no more than hint at, and it remains for reflective Masons to penetrate their disguises by their own research, intuition, and perspicacity.

SEEKING A MASTER

The junior Brother learns that, as a Mason, his duty is to seek a Master and from him gain instruction, and usually supposes that by making acquaintance with the W.M. of his Lodge, and learning by rote the rituals and lectures, he is fulfilling that duty. If he desires nothing more than ceremonial Masonry, he is doubtless doing all that need be expected of him. But if he be in earnest quest of that to which ceremonial Masonry is but an entrance-portal, he may be interested in the following considerations.

It is axiomatic in the traditional secret wisdom that real Initiation is not to be looked for save at the hands of one who has himself experienced it. And it is equally axiomatic that "when the disciple is ready, the Master will be found waiting." The modern Masonic student will be well advised to accept both these axioms as being as valid to-day as they have ever been in the past.

A Master is not easily found. But neither is he often properly sought. "Ask, seek, knock," are simple words to say with the tongue. Their putting into effective operation is a task involving persistent and concentrated will. Under no circumstances does a Master ever proclaim himself as such; he must be sought, must be clearly recognised and wholeheartedly accepted as one; and you may have grave doubts of his status and your own judgment about him before according him that confidence. You might live in close contact with a Master for years without suspecting the fact. Recognition being due to spiritual rapport, to vibratory harmony and to intuitional certainty; until you possess these a Master's physical personality will convey no more to you than any other man's. But of one thing be assured; the Master will know you through and through long before you recognise him, or perhaps even realise that you are seeking him.

Exoterically, in the operative mason's trade, the youth proposing to enter a Building Guild had first to find a Master Mason who would accept him as his apprentice and to whom he became bound for seven years, the Master making himself responsible for his maintenance and training. In spiritual Craftsmanship precisely the same method applies. The Master has first to be sought and found, and, if the disciple be accepted, he must be served and implicitly obeyed for a similar probationary period, the Master assuming a real (not a nominal) spiritual sponsorship for the pupil. The association not being for any temporal advantage but for purely selfless spiritual advancement, the intimacy is of the closest, as the responsibility is of the gravest, character. For the apprentice is to become spiritually integrated with the Master. To use the beautiful touching simile of the greatest of Masters, as a hen gathers her chickens under her wing, so is the pupil to become gathered and built into the very being of his teacher. The real Initiation (or rather sequence of Initiations) the pupil hopes in due course to attain cannot be achieved until this intimate relationship exists.

In the days of the Ancient Mysteries, Masters were to be found resident in the seclusion of the Temples, for Initiation science was then an organised institution, publicly recognised. In the Orient, no such formal organisation has obtained, but the practice, both in the past and to-day, is for the aspirant to seek and find his appropriate Master, the onus of searching being upon the former, and serving as a test of his earnestness and perspicuity. The Master is there termed a Guru (defined as "one who removes the veil of darkness from the spiritual eyes of the pupil"), and the accepted pupil a Chela or spiritual child, in the same sense that St. John addresses his pupils as "little children."

The ancient Sanskrit word Guru passed from India to Asia Minor and Greece, and reappears in the latter part of the name of such ancient Initiates as Protagoras, Anaxagoras, Pythagoras. The last-mentioned of these literally means the Pitta (or Pater) Guru, the Master or Father-Teacher, as in fact he was in his day; and the continuity of both the science and of the title Guru is further evidenced by the fact that that title is preserved both in Hebrew and in Masonry in the name of Hiram Abiff (spelt also in the Scriptures as

Huram and Churam Abiff). Hiram Abiff has precisely the same meaning as Pythagoras, the Father-Teacher, or alternatively the Teacher from the Father. The Egyptian form of the name Hiram is Hermes, the teacher of the secret or "hermetic" science and wisdom, and the student is strongly urged to study those two important ancient treatises of Initiation-science, *The Divine Pymander of Hermes* and *The Shepherd of Hermes*.

("Shepherd" is the ancient and biblical word signifying "Initiator" or "Hierophant." Hence "the Good Shepherd," "the Great Shepherd of the sheep," "The Lord is my Shepherd." The "Shepherds watching their flocks" at the time of the Nativity were not rustics or farmers, but spiritual adepts in charge of groups of initiate pupils.)

A Master, while rejoiced to find a suitable pupil, does not accept him without subjecting him to severe preliminary tests. He "knows what is in man." No hypocrisy deceives him. He discerns the thoughts and desires of the heart of the intending candidate and sees whether the latter is properly prepared there, and really anxious and ready for the work involved. Of this, an example came to my knowledge, which it may be useful to record, and to remember in connection with the acceptance of Masonic candidates. It was as follows:

A young man in India sought out a venerable Master there and asked to be accepted as a pupil and trained for initiation; he professed to want to find the light, to know God at first hand. The old sage, after a searching glance into the aspirant's inward condition, discerned that the latter, while not insincere, was still a long way from readiness, and far from being sufficiently detached in desire for worldly possessions and sensual enjoyments; and, explaining this, he firmly but kindly sent him away to exhaust or merge himself of these attractions, but with the suggestion that he might present himself again in two years' time. After two years, the young man returned, found the old Master bathing in the river at the foot of his garden, and from the river-bank renewed his application.

Again the old man read his visitor's heart to its depths and perceived how divided it still was between the claims of the outer and the inner life; but, calling him down into the river, he laid his hand upon the young one's head and gently pressed and held it below the surface of the water. Presently the young man forced it above the surface. "Why did you do that?" he was asked. "I was obliged to do so to find breath." Then came the Master's answer: "When you want God and the inward light as badly as you just now wanted breath, you may come back to me and you shall have your desire. But for the present you want other things as much, and you can't have both." Like the other young man in the Gospels, the applicant went away sorrowful; but he had found his eventual Master and gained from him the instruction suitable to him at the moment.

How, where, is one to seek one's Master, if he be so secluded, so hard to find? He may be sought both without and within oneself. He should first be sought in every event of the daily life, in the person of everyone you meet. Finding him depends on the intensity of your search. "Seek and ye shall find" is not a vain promise. Look not to meet immediately with some learned or impressive personality capable of giving you all truth in tabloid form in a few hours. Final truth cannot be communicated at all from one person to another orally; it exists already within yourself and needs only to be dug out and liberated. Socrates—himself a Master, though the son of a poor midwife—used to joke that he had inherited something of his mother's profession in that his task was to help others to bring truth to birth out of themselves; and in the same sense the medieval teachers speak of using "the obstetric hand" in eliciting truth from their pupils rather than of instilling it into them.

For the pupil has first to learn to clear away his own falsities and unrealities, so that what is already central in himself may no longer be obscured, but shine out, in its own self-conscious light.

When the time is ripe and the pupil in a deep sense ready, he may come to meet a Master literally and in personal wise. But a Master, being one who has evolved in his spirit, is no longer to be thought of as a separate independent person, although displaying a separate personality and presence to the world. He is integrated with others of the same rank; he is part of a group, all the members of which are conscious on the plane of Spirit. And Spirit is universal, not fettered by place, time, or space. What the group perceives, each of its parts sees, and vice versa. Remember the All-seeing Eye, the universal Watchman, that perceives you and knows the quality of your spirit, though you yourself know nothing of it.

Until, then, a Master is met with personally, the search should persist in confidence that he will be found. Responses, justifying your confidence and demonstrating that the Eye is watching you, will come in unsuspected ways to the earnest seeker; perhaps from a chance passage in an apparently quite irrelevant book you may be led to pick up; perhaps from a casual meeting with a stranger, an offhand remark, the conversation of a friend who speaks more wisely and pointedly to you than he himself realises. Through such and other ways may the veiled Master look or speak to you, and proportionately to the ardor of your search will you find evidences of his presence and watchfulness. A saintly woman, a great British poetess, so keenly sought a Master in the details of daily life that she would pick up torn scraps of paper in the street on the chance that they might reveal his name or yield some evidence of him. Another seeker traveled across the world in blind faith that somewhere the unknown Master would be found. One day in the street of a foreign city the recognition came suddenly; before a stranger in the crowd the seeker stopped, saying "Master, teach me!" and the search was ended.

"The Master" to be sought, then, is a comprehensive term—abstract and mystical if you will, but standing for a reality embracing many personal Masters integrated in it. In seeking a personal Master, one seeks also the group of which he is a member; in seeking the impersonal Master one may be brought into personal contact with one of that group. Life in the realm of Spirit is a unity, not a diversity, and for Masonic seekers the wide world over, of whatever nation or creed, there is but one Grand Master and Hierophant, but He can manifest and deputise through divers channels. As in the Craft Lodge there is but one Master, yet many of equal rank capable of representing him and doing his work, so has the world's Grand Master in the heights His associates and deputies here in its dark depths.

So far we have spoken only of seeking exteriorly, for an outward personal Master. But the search can and should also be made interiorly, within oneself; for what is sought subjectively and spiritually can then more readily come to be realised and found objectively. The great Indian manual of Initiation (the Bhagavad-Gita) therefore teaches:

There lives a Master in the hearts of men
Who makes their deeds, by subtle-pulling strings,
Dance to what time He will. With all thy soul
Trust Him, and take Him for thy succour.
So shalt thou gain,
By grace of Him, the uttermost repose,
The Eternal Peace

Seek therefore to realise the Master in the heart. Conceive him imaginatively. Build up in your constant thought a mental image of him, invested with the nature and qualities of that master-soul to whom you look to raise you from your present deadness, to remove the stone from your sepulcher, and to utter to your inmost self that vibrant word of liberating power, "Lazarus, come forth!" For until you have in yourself something in common with him, points of fellowship with him—be it but a bare desire for resemblance—how shall you expect to be raised into fullness of identic relationship with him, to be "gathered as a chicken under his wing?"

Our Science in its universality limits our conception of the Master to no one exemplar. Take, it says, the nearest and most familiar to you, the one under whose aegis you were racially born and who therefore may serve you best; for each is able to bring you to the centre, though each may have his separate method. To the Jewish Brother it says, take the Father of the faithful, and realise what being gathered to his bosom means. To the Christian Brother, it points to Him upon whose breast lay the beloved disciple, and urges him to reflect upon what that implies. To the Hindu Brother it points to Krishna, who came and rode in the same chariot with Arjuna, and bids him look to a similar intimate union. To the Buddhist it points to the Maitreya of universal compassion, and bids him reflect upon him till he become drawn beneath his bo-tree; and to the Moslem it points to his Prophet, and the significance of being clothed with the latter's mantle.

Let the earnest Craftsman, then, seek a Master where and how he will. He cannot—*experto crede*—fail to find. Failure to find will be due to his having failed, rightly, and from his heart, to seek.

WAGES

Initiates of the secret science in the past ("our ancient Brethren") are said to have been paid wages. The wages, we are told, were paid in the porchway of the Temple; and, much or little, they were accepted without demur, because of the recipients' complete confidence in their employers and the recognition that only so much would be received as their work was actually worth. The Masonic tradition asserts that the wages were not paid in cash—cash was of no use to those who had already learned to do without money and metals—but in corn, wine, and oil. (Note the threefold form of the wages.)

Wages of the same kind are still paid to real Craftsmen in the same place, and in the same mode. The porchway of the Temple figures the outer natural life which forms a portal to an inner supernatural life at the central sanctuary which we have not yet consciously reached, but to which we labour to ascend by an in-winding stairway, gradually rebuilding body and mind on the way with a view to acquiring a new reconstituted organism appropriate and adapted to that sublime degree of life.

Such a new body and mind require sustenance to build them, and the food we consume becomes built into our organism. What we eat, we become. Corn goes to body-building, the fashioning of substantiality and structural form. Wine goes to the vitalising and stimulating of the mind, strengthening the intellect, deepening the inner vision. Oil is a lubricant for the system, enabling its parts to run smoothly and without friction.

In their higher symbolism, Corn (or Bread) and Wine relate to those of the Altar, and were Eucharistic elements in the Mysteries long before the Christian Master in a certain "upper room" (or higher level of application) took over and gave a new application to the wheat of Ceres and the wine of Bacchus-Dionysos; while Oil, the crushed out and refined product of the olive, refers to that Wisdom which is the ultimate essence of experience and knowledge, and which has been associated, in the different Mystery teachings, with Minerva, with Solomon, and with the Mount of Olives.

The spiritual Craftsman not only earns his own wages proportionately to his work; his own labours automatically supply them. God, as his employer, has already lodged them within him in advance; he has only to appropriate them as he becomes justly entitled to them by his own labours, as the sons of Jacob found their money restored to them in their corn-sacks.

The Mason is himself likened to an ear of corn, nourished by a fall of the Water of Life. In virtue of the animal element in his nature he is himself "the ox that treadeth out the corn," separating his own golden grain from the stalk that bore it. He is himself the "threshing floor of Araunah," winnowing his own chaff from his own wheat. He treads his own wine-press alone; in singleness of effort and in the solitude of his own thought distilling his own vintage, until the cup of his mind runs over with the wine of a new order of intelligence. He is his own oil-press, and out of his own experience and self-realisation extracts wisdom—that oil which anoints him with a joy and an ability above his fellows, and that runs down to the "skirts of his clothing," manifesting itself in his personality and in all his activities.

Corn, wine, and oil, are therefore laid upon the altar at the consecration of every Masonic Lodge; they are the emblems of a Craftsman's wages. Upon the collar of Grand Lodge Officers are displayed ears of wheat and sprays of olive, the symbolic indication that those who arrive at the summit of their profession possess that which they exhibit, and are able to minister bread and wine and oil to those below them in the Order.

There are less agreeable forms of wages, however, but such as also are to be received without scruple or mistrust, for they are both disciplinary and signs of progress. A man cannot set up to reform his old nature and readjust his interior constitution without feeling it, or without unsettling the fabric of his emotional and mental sheaths. Accordingly, it is a common experience with those who take themselves seriously in hand in the task of self re-building that unexpected obstacles suddenly arise; the wages that come to them are those of adversity in temporal affairs, sickness, the turning away of former friends, and the like. There is good reason for this. Within ourselves are sown the seeds of all our past activities and emotional tendencies, good or evil. Within ourselves are stored all our old mind-forms and fabrications of base metal. To try to disturb the former or to divest ourselves of the latter, promotes immediate reaction from them.

He who deliberately invokes the light upon himself, as the earnest Masonic aspirant does, *ipso facto* utters, with corresponding intensity, a challenge to his own bad past, his own unreal self. And if his invocation be effective, the light streaming into him from his own dormer-window, whilst giving him illumination, will also play upon and stimulate in him all that is undesirable, as sunlight stirs to activity the unpleasant insects dwelling in darkness beneath a stone that is suddenly removed from an old position. light impartially affects both the good and evil in oneself, as the sunshine causes a rose to bloom, and a lump of carrion by its side to putrefy. It induces new growth in a spiritual sense, but it also, and at the same time, accelerates the germination of seeds implanted in us, which, but for it, would continue to lie dormant and unmatured until a more favourable time.

Under the discipline of Initiation, the seeds or compressed results of one's own past, the potential reactions from one's own former actions and inaction, all that goes to make up a man's fate and that, if unchecked, will shape his future destiny, are brought to a sudden head and crisis; the normal slower development they would have undergone, if not so interfered with, becomes interrupted, expedited. It is often as though vials of undeserved wrath break upon the devoted head of him who at last has struck the road to salvation, and is resolved at all costs to follow it. And yet these are the wages he receives for his laudable enterprise! Lacking self-knowledge as yet, ignorant of what is latent in him, not realising that the path of Initiation is one of intensive culture and accelerated evolution, he may become dismayed from further pursuing his quest, unless he be made aware that these wages are actually due to him, that they represent his past earnings, that he is justly entitled to them, and that the sooner the debit and credit sides of his own self-written judgment-ledger are balanced, the freer will he be to proceed with his newly undertaken building-work.

"The wages of sin are death"—death in the sense of being spiritually unconscious, however vigorously alive in other ways. "Sin" in all or any of its forms is, in its final analysis, disharmony induced by the assertion of the unreal personal self in unalignment with the impersonal Universal Self, the Holy Spirit. But the Path of Initiation involves the obliteration of all sense of the personal self. The just and perfect man and Mason is therefore one who is utterly selfless; being selfless he is sinless; and being sinless he stands in, consciously shares, and becomes the instrument of, the divine Kingdom, Power and Glory.

THE LAW OF THE MOUNT

In Masonry, as in the Scriptures and every other ancient expression of mystical teaching, there is frequent allusion to mountains and hills, and to the work of Lodges and Chapters being conducted upon them.

Let it be understood at once that in no case is the allusion to any physical mountain or geographical position, but to the spiritual elevation of the work undertaken by some particular group or school of Initiates. Spiritual science has nothing to do with material things or places, save in so far as the latter serve as a foundation-stone or point of departure for achieving spiritual results.

From immemorial time the Vedists of India have spoken of their sacred Mount Meru, which, later in history, becomes reproduced among the Hebrews as Mount Moriah. The Greeks had their Mounts Olympus and Parnassus, on the summits of which dwelt the Gods. The Israelites obtained their law from Divine hands on Mount Sinai; the Christians theirs from the Mount of Olives. The woodwork for Solomon's Temple came from the Mountains of Lebanon. The Gospels tell of the "exceeding high mountain" of Temptation and of the Mount of Transfiguration. Prometheus was immolated upon a mountain of the Caucasus (or Ko-Kajon, i.e., "ethereal space"), and Christ upon the Hill Calvary. Medieval Christian mystical tradition tells of the hidden sanctuary of the mysteries and the holy Grail built upon Mont Salvatch (the mount of safety or salvation) in the Pyrenees (which is another form of "Parnassus").

None of these mountains are situate in this world, in time or place. The names are mystical names associated with super-physical heights to which man in his spiritual consciousness may ascend. Mountains bearing those names, or some of them, do exist on the map, but their names and the ideas they connote existed long before they were given a local association for symbolic purposes.

There is scarcely a country without its sacred mountain that reminds its inhabitants of the heavenly heights and to which sacred traditions are not attached. The snow-clad Himalayas have always typified the eternal heavens to the East; Fujiyama is the sacred mountain of Japan, as Snowdon is of Britain; and if such places have been, as indeed they have, the scenes of religious practices, their sanctity derives less from what has occurred there than from the ideas that resulted in those practices. The names of these sacred mountains are drawn almost always from ideas representative of the religion of the district, and constitute a sort of spiritual geography which nations of great spiritual genius, such as the Indians, the Greeks, and the Hebrews, have been faithful in preserving.

Subsequently, the materialising tendencies of the human mind literalise and localise what originally existed as a purely spiritual idea.

When Initiates of the past are said to have held Lodges and performed their work upon this or that hill or mountain, the meaning is that they were engaged in work of a high spiritual order and efficacy—work entirely beyond the conception of the average modern and merely ceremonial Mason. The actual place at which they met for such work may or may not have been upon a physical eminence. Often it was not, as abundant evidence might be brought to show.

The entirely super-physical nature of their work may be deduced from an old Scottish Degree of advanced Masonry, which speaks, with a dry humour that to the inexpert eye will seem grotesque and irreverent, of their Lodge having originally been held upon a hill in the North of Scotland, a place "where a cock never crowed, a lion never roared, and a woman never tattled." Now in traditional esoteric terminology, as also in the Bible, the "North" signifies that which is spiritual and ever unmanifested, as the other three cardinal points of space indicate varying degrees of spiritual manifestation.

The allusion to cock-crow is to the guilty conscience of Peter, which could only exist in the world of time and in one who is spiritually imperfect. The allusion to the lion is to the Evil One "going about as a roaring lion" in the lower world, but unable to enter the Paradisal world; whilst the third reference is to the contemplative silence of the soul (the "woman") upon that high plane of life of which the Psalmist says that "there is neither speech nor language but their voices are heard among them." In the *Odyssey*, Homer testifies to the same truth when Ulysses is told in regard to certain mysteries, "Be silent; repress your intellect, and do not speak; such is the method of the Gods upon Olympus."

It must be left to the reader's own research and reflection to deduce the nature of the spiritual work undertaken by real Initiates; he will discover that it is work that is not performed in the physical body or with that body's faculties, but upon the ethereal planes and with a higher order of faculty than the average man of to-day has learned to cultivate. For a striking instance of the kind of work implied, reference can be made to the narrative contained in the 19th and 24th chapters of Exodus, describing a Lodge of the elders or Adept-Initiates of Israel upon "Mount Sinai"; though for the instructed reader many other passages of like information are to be found in both sections of the Sacred Law, as also elsewhere.

To pass to a less abstruse and more elementary point, those who seek to become real Initiates and aspire to the work upon the mountain-tops that is feasible only to such, must first conform themselves to the Law of the Mount. That law may be so called because it involves a loftier teaching and a totally different order of conduct from those to which the uninitiated popular world conforms. We have a reference to this in the direction that a Mason's conduct ought to be such as will "distinguish and set him above the ranks of other men," and not merely leave him at their level. Hence the instruction given by the Great Master to his initiate disciples, which is called the "Sermon on the Mount," and is popularly supposed to have been delivered upon a hill-side. There exist, however, many great pieces of Initiation-teaching going by that name, notably the great and eloquent discourses known as *The Divine of Hermes*; and all of them are called "sermons on the mount," not because of having necessarily been delivered upon any actual mountain, but because they relate to spiritualities and to the loftier plane of thought and action upon which every Initiate must live. The "Mount" is that of Initiation, where alone, in the silence of the senses, the spirit of man can learn the things of the spirit.

That the standard of thought and conduct for Initiates is always beyond the capacity of the popular world is evidenced by the fact that society, however advanced in civilisation, find itself quite unable to act up to it. Even the Churches find the Sermon on the Mount impracticable doctrine for general social observance. It is regarded as a counsel of perfection, and eminent clerics are found declaring that it was never meant to apply to the unforeseen, complex social conditions of to-day, and declare that, whilst sound as a theoretic ideal, it must be compromised with in practice. From their low level of outlook they are right. The popular world is truly quite unable to act up to the terms of the Law of the Mount. But it is overlooked that that high doctrine was not meant for the popular world nor addressed to it. It was delivered to, and intended for, those few who have outgrown and renounced the ideals of the outer world and who seek initiation into a new and higher order of life which contradicts the wisdom of that world at every point.

But the real Initiate must observe it at all cost and conflict to himself, and is told that unless his righteousness exceeds that of popular orthodoxy and convention, he cannot hope to realise the goal at which he aims. The whole life of the real Initiate, and of those aiming to become such, will be at cross purposes with the standards and methods of the rest of the world, which will be as it were in conspiracy against him for not conforming to its ways; and, as with Hiram Abiff, at every attempt to leave the gates of his temple and come into contact with the outer world, he will find himself opposed by persecuting "ruffians," by objections to his refusal to fall in with popular conventions, and by demands to know the secrets of his superiority to them. Hence one of the reasons for the silence and obscurity of real Initiates, as also for Masonic secrecy, is self-protection, which the Christian Master gave as a justification for not casting pearls before those incapable of appreciating them "lest they turn and rend you."

The way of the natural uninitiated man is that of self-assertion and material acquisitiveness; he is bent upon securing all he can get from this world; and wisdom, knowledge, and power, are what seem to be such in his own eyes. He is not wrong or blameworthy; he is simply fulfilling the law of his present nature, which is the only law he as yet knows; he is merely ignorant and self-blinded to any higher nature and law. The initiated man is one to whom a higher nature and law have become revealed, and who, conscious of their compulsion upon himself, has abjured all the ideals of his less advanced fellows. He lives upon the Mount and fulfils the law of the Mount; and therefore to him come wisdom, grace and power transcending anything his uninitiated fellowmen can as yet conceive. Initiates were termed by the Great Master the "salt of the earth," for, without their leavening presence in it, the world would descend to greater corruption than it at present suffers. "Ten just men (i.e., Initiates) shall save the city," as was said of those "cities of the plain" which are a figure of civilisation at large.

It is not, however, for his personal aggrandisement or salvation that a man seeks, or should seek, Initiation into the higher order of life, or should aspire for the wisdom and power that therewith come. To do so from this motive would be merely to imitate the ways of the outer world, apart from the fact that it would neutralise the whole purpose of Initiation. His real purpose is to help on the world's advancement, to become one of its saviours, at the sacrifice of himself. For the real Initiate is self-less; he has abandoned all personal claims and the "rights" to which lesser men claim to be entitled; and, having crucified his own personality, is able to look upon human life impersonally and to offer himself as an instrument for its redemption. When wisdom and power come to him, they are not for his own use but for the help of the whole race; he is a Master among men, because he is a universal servant; he is the most effective spokesman in the world, because of his utter silence.

Masonic secrecy and silence are inculcated for this very reason; for all spiritual power is generated in silence. In silence the aspirant must concentrate his own energies and climb from his own earth into his own heavens, rendering to the Caesar of the outer world the things that are his, but in other respects fulfilling the law of the Mount in a way that will "distinguish and set him above the ranks of other men" who are not yet ready or prepared to follow him. If the Masonic Brotherhood has not yet risen to full appreciation of the meaning of its own system, it nevertheless stands provided with all the information needful to lead it to Initiation in the high sense indicated throughout these pages, to which each of its members may aspire if he follow the Ancient Sage in Tennyson's poem and:

Leave the hot swamp of voluptuousness,
A cloud between the Nameless and thyself;
And lay thine uphill shoulder to the wheel
And climb the Mount of Blessing; whence, if thou
Look higher, then perchance thou mays't—beyond
A hundred ever-rising mountain-lines,
And past the range of Night and Shadow—see
The high-heaven dawn of more than mortal day
Strike on the Mount of Vision!

"FROM LABOUR TO REFRESHMENT"

The Masonic reader who recognises that every reference in Speculative Masonry is figurative and carries a symbolic significance behind the literal sense of the words, will at once dismiss from his mind any suggestion that the formula of adjourning the Lodge from labour to refreshment, and of recalling it from refreshment to labour, relates to the customary practice of passing from the formal work of the Lodge to the informalities of the dining-table.

The familiar formula of dismissing the Lodge after seeing that every Brother has received his due, no doubt came over into the present system from Operative usage when Guild-masons periodically received their material wages. But it has now become the *Ite, Missa est!* of spiritual Masonry, and carries a sacramental meaning. We have to consider what labour, refreshment, and dues, are in their higher and concealed sense.

First as to Labour. The allusion is less to the temporary ceremonial work of the Lodge than to the work the earnest light-seeker is continually to be engaged upon in his task of self-perfecting. Let it be realised that this is labour indeed, to be undertaken with earnestness and vigour, "*Hic labor; hoc opus est,*" wrote Virgil of it. "The Gods sell their arts only to those who sweat for them" runs another ancient adage of the science. Purification of the bodily senses and reformation of personal defects are but part, the simpler and grosser part, of the work; the redirection of one's mind and will to the ideal involved, the requisite research and study conducing to that end, and the necessary control and concentration of thought and desire upon the end in view, are not child's-play nor matters of casual, superficial interest.

Intellectual and spiritual labour necessitate rest and refreshment, equally with physical, that the harvest of that labour may be assimilated. Wise activity (*Boaz*) must be balanced with an equally wise passivity (*Jachin*) if one is to become established in immortal strength and to stand firm, spiritually consolidated and perfect in all one's parts. Nor is it a work to be hurried; those build most surely who build slowly. *Festina lente!*—hasten slowly, is an old maxim of the work addressed to those who would "lay great bases for eternity." "*Ne quid nimis!*" is another; "let nothing be done in excess."

Now it is not easy to combine work of this nature with that which the exigencies of one's normal duties and responsibilities entail. But to those who are in earnest, the co-adaptation and harmonising of all one's duties will form part of the work itself; one's present position and avocation will be discerned to be precisely those suited to making advancement, and to provide opportunities for doing so. Doubtless difficulty and opposition will be encountered in abundance; but these again are parts of the process and tests of fidelity. No growth is possible without resistance to draw out latent power. The aspirant must steadily and conscientiously persevere along the path to what he seeks, just as each candidate engages himself to do so in respect of its ceremonial portrayal; and every Brother may be assured of receiving his exact dues for the labour he expends.

"There is a time to work and a time to sleep." Respite from labour is as contributive an element to progress as labour itself, for the mind must digest, and the whole nature assimilate, what it absorbs. More may be learned from the Teacher in the heart than from what is gathered by the head, when that Teacher—the principle at the Centre—is once awakened. Meditation and reflection are of greater instructiveness than book-reading and information acquired from without oneself.

Think'st thou among the mighty sum
Of things for ever speaking,
That nothing of itself will come,
That we must still be seeking?

FOR THE CARE AND NOURISHMENT OF THE OUTER BODY

For the care and nourishment of the outer body, Nature provides a passive, sympathetic system, which arranges digestion, distributes energy, builds up the body, and discharges its functions for us without interference with our formal consciousness. In like manner, in our higher being resides a corresponding principle which winnows out thought, clarifies and arranges ideas, and settles problems and difficulties for us, in entire independence of our formal awareness. It is this higher principle that must be found, trusted, and relied upon to participate in the work of interior up-building.

The old writers call it the Archaeus, or the hidden Mercury, which ingathers and utilises the fruit of our conscious efforts, building them up into a "super-structure" or subtle-body. As ages have gone to the organisation of the physical body, so also long periods are requisite for that of the super-physical structure, the building of which is true Masonry; but the process can be expedited by those who possess the science of it, as Masons are presumed to do. The process itself is the real Masonic "labour"; and, as we have shown, it has its active and its passive aspects.

This is a difficult subject to treat of briefly. Its nature is merely indicated here, and its fuller study must be left to individual research and, where possible, to personal tuition; for this work is precisely that about which a Master-Mason is presumed to be able to give private instruction to Brethren in the inferior degrees.

Let the reader reflect that Masonic "labour" involves the making of his being whole and perfect; that it is intended to "render the circle of it complete." His complete being is likened, in geometrical terms, to a circle—the symbol of wholeness, entirety, self-containedness. But let him remember that as he knows himself at present, he is not a circle, but a square, which is but the fourth part of a circle. Where are the other three-fourths of himself?—for until he knows these as well as the fourth part which he does know, he can never make the circle of his being complete, nor truly know himself.

This is the point at which Masonry becomes mystical Geometry, the important science of which Plato affirmed that no one should enter the Academy where true philosophy and ontology were to be learned, until he already was well versed in that science. For in former times these deeper problems of being were the subject of geometrical expression, and echoes of the science remain to us in our references to squares, triangles, and circles, and particularly in the 47th problem of the first book of Euclid, which is now the distinctive emblem of those who have won to Mastership. How many of those who now wear that emblem, one wonders, have any conception of its significance?

It is a mathematical symbol representing, for those who can read it, the highest measure of human attainment in the science of reconstructing the human soul into the Divine image from which it has fallen away. No wonder the great Initiate who composed this symbol was raised to an ecstasy of joy on realising in his own being all that it implies, depicts, and demonstrates, and that upon that fortunate occasion he "sacrificed a hecatomb of oxen"—an expression the meaning of which, like the symbol itself, must be left to the reader's reflection, for these matters cannot be summarily or superficially explained. Pythagoras himself is said to have refused to explain them to his own pupils until they had undergone five years' silence and meditation upon them. Those five years represent the period that is still theoretically allotted to the work of the Fellow-Craft Degree, in regard to which the modern Mason is instructed to devote himself to reflecting upon the secrets of nature (i.e., his own nature) and the principles of intellectual truth, until they gradually disclose themselves to his view and reveal his own affiliation to the Deity.

In declining to explain these geometrical truths to students until they had familiarised themselves with them for five years, the meaning of the great teacher of Crotona was that, by that time, the earnest disciple would have discerned their import, and gone far to realise it, for himself.

Labour, understood in the sense here defined, and Refreshment after it, constitute a rhythm of activity and passivity; a rhythm similar to that which we daily experience in respect of waking and sleeping, working and resting. To speak of Refreshment, however, in the deeper sense implied in Masonry is even more difficult than to speak of the philosophic Labour; for it involves a subject to which few devote deep thought—the subjective side of the soul's life as distinct from the objective side which, for most men, is the only one at present known to them. In that deeper sense, Refreshment implies what Spenser speaks of in the lines:

Sleep after toil, port after stormy seas,
Ease after war, death after life, doth greatly please.

To the wise, the study of the subjective half of life is as important as that of the objective half, and without it he cannot make the circle of his self-knowledge complete. Even the observant Masonic student is made aware by the formula used at Lodge closing, that by some great Warden of life and death each soul is called into this objective world to labour upon itself, and is in due course summoned from it to rest from its labours and enter into subjective celestial refreshment, until once again it is recalled to labour. For each the "day," the opportunity for work at self-perfecting, is duly given; for each the "night" cometh when no man can work at that task; which morning and evening constitute but one creative day of the soul's life, each portion of that day being a necessary complement to the other. Perfect man has to unify these opposites in himself; so that for him, as for his Maker, the darkness and the light become both alike.

The world-old secret teaching upon this subject, common to the whole of the East, to Egypt, the Pythagoreans and Platonists, and every College of the Mysteries, is to be found summed up as clearly and tersely as one could wish in the *Phaedo* of Plato, to which the Masonic seeker is referred as one of the most instructive of treatises upon the deeper side of the science. It testifies to the great rhythm of life and death above spoken of, and demonstrates how that the soul in the course of its career weaves and wears out many bodies and is continually migrating between objective and subjective conditions, passing from labour to refreshment and back again many times in its great task of self-fulfilment.

And if Plato was, as was once truly said of him, but Moses speaking Attic Greek, we shall not be surprised at finding the same initiate-teaching disclosed in the words of Moses himself. Does not the familiar Psalm of Moses declare that man is continually "brought to destruction," that subsequently a voice goes forth saying "Come again, ye children of men!" and that the subjective spiritual world is his refuge from one objective manifestation to another? What else than a paraphrase of this great word of comfort is the Masonic pronouncement that, in the course of its task of self-perfecting, the soul is periodically summoned to alternating periods of labour and refreshment? It must labour, and it must rest from its labours; its works will follow it, and in the subjective world every Brother's soul will receive its due for its work in the objective one, until such time as its work is completed and it is "made a pillar in the House of God and no more goes out" as a journeyman-builder into this sublunary workshop.

"Did I not agree with thee for a penny?" said the Great Master parabolically. Now the round disc of the coin was meant to be an emblem of that completeness, wholeness, and self-containedness which is denoted by the Circle, and which every Mason is enjoined to effect in himself. When the Mason has made the circle of his own being complete, he will not only have earned his penny and received his dues; the circle of his then glorious being will be as the sun shining in his strength, and he will be able to say with the Initiates of Egypt, as they contemplated the sun ascending from the desert into the heavens: "I am Ra in his rising!"

THE GRAND LODGE ABOVE

Express reference is made in the Order rituals to the existence of a Grand Lodge Above, having its Grand Master and Officers. Doubtless the allusion is often regarded as but a pious sentiment expressing the belief that, after their death, worthy Masons combine to constitute such a Lodge or assembly in the heavens.

With such a belief no one would wish to interfere, but there are good grounds for suggesting that the reference was intended to carry a quite different meaning. It is meant to testify to the fact, which forms part of the long stream of esoteric tradition throughout the ages, that a supernal Masonic Assembly not only exists, but that it preceded, in point of time and constitution, the Masonic Order on earth. Had it not so existed and preceded the terrestrial Order, that Order itself would not have existed; for the hypothesis is that the latter is the shadow and projection upon the physical world of a corresponding hierarchical Order in the super-physical.

In other words, the Masonic Order on earth is the reflex and effect, not the generating cause, of the Grand Lodge Above. The latter is not necessarily recruited from the former, since death of the body does not constitute *per se* a title to admission to the Grand Lodge Above, which, according to the tradition, possesses its own qualifications and passports for admission; but neither, according to the same tradition, does life in the earthly body preclude the duly qualified Mason from reception into, and conscious co-operation with, the Supernal Lodge, while he is still in the flesh.

A certain resemblance will be noticed between this doctrine and the corresponding theological one of the complementary relations between the Church Militant on earth and the Church Triumphant in the heavens, the doctrine of the Communion possible between all Saints upon whichever side of the veil. Neither in the case of the Church nor of Masonry does the claim imply, what is obviously not the fact, that every member of either community has actual knowledge or first-hand experience of the truth of this doctrine. But it does imply that there have been, and still are, members possessing it.

Farther on in these pages more will be said of the Grand Lodge Above, and in a way which perhaps will suggest to the reflective reader a fuller idea than one can convey upon such a subject than by expository methods. It is a theme deserving of larger consideration than the Craft accords it, and one about which no little literary evidence is available for those with sufficient interest to look for it. One such important piece of evidence shall be mentioned here.

It consists of a remarkable series of communications of the highest spiritual value and instructiveness to every Brother seeking to realise the spiritual essence of the Masonic system, issued by a saintly man and advanced initiate, Karl von Eckartshausen, to a group of pupils in the secret science in Germany, at roughly about the same period as that in which the English Masonic Order was becoming established. The synchronism is not without significance and, in conjunction with other evidences (which exigencies of space prevent being now adduced) of spiritual activity at work at that time behind the events of public history, points to efforts to put forward a great movement for human enlightenment; a movement conceived from behind the veil by the Grand Lodge Above, and projected into the world through some of its members in the flesh.

The communications or letters deal with the subject of the need for human regeneration and the rationale of Initiation. In the first of them, the author asserts that "the great and true work of building the Temple consists solely in destroying this miserable Adamic hut and in erecting in its place a divine temple; this means, in other words, to develop in us the interior sensorium or the organ to receive God. After this process, the metaphysical and incorruptible principle rules over the terrestrial, and man begins to live, not any longer in the principle of self-love, but in the spirit and in the truth, of which he is the Temple. The most exalted aim of religion is the intimate union of man with God; this union is possible here below, but it can only take place by the opening of our inner sensorium, which enables our hearts to become receptive of God. Therein are those great mysteries of which human philosophy does not dream, the key to which is not to be found in scholastic science."

He then proceeds to state that "a more advanced school has always existed to which the deposition of all spiritual science has been confided, which has continued from the first day of creation to the present time. Its members are scattered all over the world, but they have always been united by one spirit and one truth. They have had but one science, a single source of truth, one Lord, one Doctor, one Master, in whom resides substantially the whole Divine plentitude, who also alone initiates them into the high mysteries of Nature and the Spiritual World."

In the second letter it is explained (I compress the substance) that: "This community possesses a school in which all who thirst for knowledge are instructed by the Spirit of Wisdom itself, and all the mysteries of God and of Nature are preserved therein for the children of light. It is thence that all truths penetrate into the world. It is the most hidden of communities; it possesses members gathered from many Orders. From all time there has been an exterior school based on this interior one, of which it is but the outer expression. The community has been engaged from the earliest ages in building the grand Temple for the regeneration of humanity, by which the kingdom of God will become manifest. It consists in the communion of those who have most capacity for light. It has three Degrees, and these are conferred on suitable candidates still in the flesh. The first is inspirationally imparted. The second opens up the human rational intellectuality and understanding, and ensures interior illumination. The third and highest is the entire opening of the inner sensorium, by which the inner man attains objective vision of real and metaphysical verities."

The instruction goes on to explain that this Society does not resemble temporal organisations that meet at certain times and elect their own officers. It knows none of these formalities, but proceeds in other ways. The Divine Power is always present. The Master of it himself does not invariably know all the members, but the moment a member's presence or services are needed he can be found. If a member is called to office, he presents himself among the others without presumption, and is received by them without jealousy. If it be necessary that members should meet, they find and recognise each other with perfect certainty. No disguise, hypocrisy, or dissimulation, can hide their true characteristics. No one member can choose another; unanimous choice is required. All men are called to join this hidden community; the called may be chosen, if they become ripe for entrance. Anyone can look for entrance; any man who is within can teach another to seek it, but only he who is ripe can arrive inside. Worldly intelligence seeks this Sanctuary in vain; all is undecipherable to the unprepared; he can see nothing, read nothing, in its interior. He who is ripe is joined to the chain, perhaps often where he thought least likely, and at a point of which he knew nothing himself.

Seeking to become ripe should be the effort of him who loves wisdom. But there are methods by which ripeness is attained, for in this holy communion is the primitive storehouse of the most ancient and original science of the human race, with the primitive mysteries also of all science. It is the unique and illuminated Community which possesses the key to all mystery, which knows the centre and source of nature and creation. It unites superior power to its own, and includes members from more than one world. It is the Society whose members form a theocratic republic, which one day will be the Regent Mother of the whole world.

Upon this description of the Grand Lodge Above, by one who, even in the days of his flesh, claims to have been a member of it, it is not proposed here to descant. That it may provoke surprise and doubt as to its veraciousness in those to whom such ideas may now come for the first time, is probable. This must be hazarded in giving voice to those ideas here, and the subject left to such responsiveness as may come from the heart of the individual reader; for obviously no proof can either here be offered or given to even the most sympathetic querist upon a matter which in its nature is incapable of verification otherwise than by direct personal experience.

But with an earnest counsel to accept its accuracy and to seek confirmation of it in the only way in which such confirmation is possible, it must be left to the deep and protracted reflection of those to whom the idea of the existence of a Grand Lodge in the heavens, watching over the Masonic Israel on earth and superintending its development, is at least a matter of probability and a subject for faith. They will at least perceive in the description of it given above, that the Masonic Order faithfully reproduces, in point of form and hierarchical progression, its alleged supernal prototype; and if they recognise that invisible things are in some measure knowable by perceiving things that are made, the contemplation of their own three-graded Order, with its ascending sequence of Grand Lodges of districts, provinces, and finally of the nation, will perhaps help them on to the conception of an unseen Grander Lodge beyond all these, —one to membership of which any duly qualified Brother may hope to be called to take progressive Initiations no longer ceremonial and symbolic, but as facts of spiritual experience—at the hands of the Universal Master and Initiator, whose officers are still Brethren of our own, though risen to the stature of holy angels.

REFLECTION: THE LUMINOUS SPIRAL

A PILGRIMAGE TO THE MIDDLE CHAMBER

MYSTICAL PATH OF INITIATION: CULTIVATING LIGHT WITHIN

Freemasonry's mystical path of initiation transcends the boundaries of mere ceremonial practice, presenting a profound invitation to journey inward. It calls each of us to undertake the transformative work of self-discovery and spiritual refinement. As this section outlines, initiation is not a singular event but an evolving process—a gradual ascent toward wisdom and enlightenment. This journey aligns Freemasonry with ancient mystery traditions, such as the Eleusinian Mysteries and the teachings of Pythagoras, both of which serve as archetypes of self-transmutation.

In the sanctuaries of Eleusis, initiation was a sacred rite of passage, demanding preparation, purification, and perseverance. Aspirants faced trials and symbolic deaths, emerging with an awakened understanding of life, death, and rebirth. Similarly, Pythagoras's school challenged its initiates to align their lives with the cosmos. Numbers, for Pythagoras, were not abstract symbols but living truths, reflecting the harmony of the universe. His teachings emphasised a life of balance—combining intellectual rigour, moral discipline, and spiritual insight. These ancient traditions remind us that initiation is not the end of a journey but the beginning of profound self-transmutation, where the aspirant reshapes their inner nature to mirror universal harmony.

The mystical path outlined in Freemasonry echoes these traditions, presenting initiation as a process of inner refinement. From the moment we symbolically step out of darkness into light, we are challenged to confront our limitations and align ourselves with universal truths. This gradual enlightenment mirrors the classical notion that true wisdom comes not from external knowledge but from an internal awakening. As we ascend the symbolic staircase of the Craft, each step reveals new insights, reminding us that personal growth requires deliberate effort, humility, and the courage to face and transform our imperfections.

In today's world, the principles of initiation are more relevant than ever. Modern life often emphasises external success, speed, and immediacy, leaving little room for contemplation or inner growth. The mystical path stands as a counterbalance, encouraging us to resist the allure of superficial embellishments and instead embrace the enduring work of self-transmutation. This perspective shifts our focus from the external—the material, the measurable—to the internal, where true enlightenment resides.

As emphasised by Wilmshurst, meditation's role is central to this journey. Whether practised personally or collectively, meditation opens a window to the inner self, allowing light to stream into our understanding. As the Bhagavad Gita suggests, "There lives a Master in the hearts of men who makes their deeds, by subtle-pulling strings, dance to what time He will." This divine presence, often symbolised as a point of light within the heart, grows as we nurture it daily. Through meditation, reflection, and self-discipline, we refine this inner light, aligning our lives with the principles of the Craft and gradually transmuting our base tendencies into higher virtues.

Freemasonry's working tools serve as practical guides on this transformative path. The compasses, for instance, teach us to set boundaries for our desires, while the square reminds us to act with integrity and fairness. When internalised, these tools become more than symbols; they are alchemical instruments, enabling us to transmute our lives into something nobler. Each tool offers a lesson, a step toward building the "superstructure" of the soul—a Temple that reflects the divine order and the aspirant's evolving mastery over self.

The parallels between Freemasonry and the Hero's Journey, as articulated by Joseph Campbell, further illuminate the initiatory path. Like the mythological hero, the Mason embarks on an inner adventure, facing trials and emerging transformed. This journey is not without challenges, as we are called to confront our shadows, integrate our flaws, and refine our virtues. Yet, as Campbell notes, "The cave you fear to enter holds the treasure you seek." In Masonry, this treasure is self-knowledge, the wisdom to navigate life, and the alignment of our lives with higher principles. It is an alchemical process where the base elements of our personality are purified and elevated through deliberate inner work.

As we navigate the complexities of contemporary life, Freemasonry offers a framework for integrating spiritual and material pursuits. The lessons of the Lodge extend beyond its walls, encouraging us to approach every interaction, challenge, and decision as an opportunity for growth. The principles of the Craft—patience, perseverance, and reflection—guide us in creating a life of purpose and harmony. These moments of application are the crucibles where our character is tested and refined, each experience forging us into truer expressions of our potential.

Ultimately, the mystical path of initiation is a lifelong journey that challenges us to see each step as sacred, each trial as transformative, and each moment as an opportunity to transmute our nature. By embracing this perspective, we honour Freemasonry's timeless ideals and ensure its light continues illuminating the way forward. In doing so, we refine ourselves and contribute to the collective ascent of humanity, carrying the Craft's legacy into the future.

THE SPIRITUAL SCAFFOLD: UNVEILING THE MEANING BEHIND THE MASON'S TEMPLE

Freemasonry's Temple is a living symbol of humanity's potential to construct a self that reflects divine order and unity. This sacred metaphor extends an invitation to Masons, urging them to craft their lives as holy architecture—thoughtfully, intentionally, and harmoniously aligned with the virtues of the Craft. Within the Temple's timeless design lies a blueprint for self-transmutation and spiritual growth, reminding us that each chisel stroke in the quarry of life shapes the superstructure of our inner being.

From antiquity, the Temple has represented the nexus of the divine and the human, where the material meets the spiritual. Solomon's Temple, central to Masonic teachings, embodies this sacred intersection. Its meticulous, deliberate, and purposeful construction symbolises the aspirant's internal journey of shaping a life imbued with virtue, balance, and wisdom. Every stone of the Temple represents a thought, word, or action that contributes to the soul's tower, with the Craft's tools guiding this sacred labour. The square, level, and plumb rule transcend their operative origins to become spiritual instruments. The square encourages fairness and integrity, calling us to ensure that our thoughts and actions align with moral principles. The level emphasises equality, reminding us that we share a common foundation with all of humanity. At the same time, the plumb rule insists upon uprightness, urging us to remain steadfast and true in our dealings. These tools are not merely symbolic but active guides, shaping how we engage with the world and ourselves.

Through this allegory, Freemasonry invites us to see the construction of the Temple as more than a task—it is an act of devotion. The aspirant, like a master builder, must harmonise their inner and outer lives, ensuring that every facet of their character reflects the sacred geometry of the universe. This harmony resonates with Nietzsche's concept of the Übermensch, the individual who transcends base instincts and societal constraints to create a life of higher purpose and authenticity. Just as the Übermensch redefines values and shapes existence, the Masonic aspirant constructs an internal superstructure reflecting the divine and inspiring transformation.

The Temple's allegory parallels psychological frameworks like Maslow's hierarchy of needs, where personal growth begins with foundational stability and ascends toward self-actualisation. However, Freemasonry's vision goes beyond psychological models, integrating spiritual dimensions into this ascent. While Maslow emphasises the fulfilment of individual potential, the Temple's message extends outward, urging Masons to consider how their self-improvement contributes to the collective good. Each aspirant's inner work becomes a stone in the greater edifice of humanity, a reminder that the Craft's teachings are both personal and universal. Ancient temples were designed to reflect cosmic order, their architecture aligning earthly forms with divine harmony.

Similarly, the Masonic Temple serves as a metaphor for aligning our lives with universal truths. With its intricate carvings and precise measurements, Solomon's Temple embodies the principle that divinity resides in the details. Every small act of integrity and reflection becomes part of this sacred construction. Through deliberate effort, we create a structure capable of housing the light of divine wisdom.

The Temple is not built alone. Just as operative builders collaborated to raise monumental structures, so too does the spiritual Temple thrive on the shared labour of the Lodge. Each Mason's contribution strengthens the whole, reflecting the unity and harmony at the heart of the Craft. In an age increasingly marked by individualism and fragmentation, the Temple serves as a counterpoint, reminding us that our collective efforts create something greater than the sum of its parts. This collective vision extends beyond the Lodge, inspiring Masons to act as builders of community and understanding in the broader world. By embodying the principles of the Craft, we contribute to a shared spiritual superstructure that reflects humanity's highest ideals. The Temple challenges us to balance the outer demands of daily life with the inner pursuit of wisdom and virtue, offering a framework that transcends time and place. It invites Masons to integrate their actions with their aspirations, ensuring that their lives resonate with the values of the Craft.

For the individual Mason, the Temple is an intimate and transformative symbol. It calls us to approach life as sacred architecture, where every decision shapes the soul's superstructure. As Wilmshurst wrote, "The Temple must be raised in the air, on higher planes of consciousness, and in spiritual light." This lofty aspiration invites us to treat each moment as an opportunity for refinement and alignment, building a life that mirrors the order and beauty of the divine. In modern contexts, the Temple's symbolism offers a timeless anchor amid the turbulence of daily existence. The demands of contemporary life often distract from the inner work required for self-transmutation. Yet, Freemasonry reminds us that true fulfilment comes not from external success but from the quiet harmony of a well-constructed life. The Temple teaches us to integrate our actions with our aspirations, ensuring that every stone we lay contributes to a structure of enduring value.

The legacy of the Temple is not confined to the past; it is a living testament to the power of intention, artistry, and connection. Every act of service, every moment of humility, brings the Temple to life, beaming with unity and purpose. By embracing this allegory, Freemasonry reveals its enduring mission: to construct lives of integrity, wisdom, and light, ensuring that the Craft remains a guiding force for future generations. The Temple challenges us to see our lives as sacred endeavours, where each thought, word, and deed contributes to the universal harmony we seek to embody. It reminds us that we are all builders—not only of our destinies but of a shared vision that unites us as Brethren. Through the Temple, Freemasonry calls us to live with purpose, construct with care, and build a legacy reflecting the divine order we strive to honour.

THE LIGHT WITHIN: A REFLECTION OF THE COSMIC SOURCE

The pursuit of "light" in Freemasonry is a profound metaphor, signifying the aspirant's journey toward knowledge, wisdom, and spiritual clarity. Rooted in ancient mystical traditions, the quest for light transcends cultural and temporal boundaries, offering Masons a timeless framework for personal growth. This section's emphasis on stages of illumination mirrors the progressive nature of initiation, encouraging Brethren to see their Masonic path as a series of transformative awakenings.

In other traditions, light is equally central to the spiritual journey. In Kabbalah, the Tree of Life symbolises a structured ascent through realms of understanding, where the seeker progresses from material awareness (Malkuth) to divine insight (Keter). Each stage corresponds to deeper layers of enlightenment, like the Masonic journey through the degrees. Similarly, in Buddhist practice, the path to enlightenment involves shedding ignorance through disciplined meditation and ethical living, culminating in the attainment of nirvana—a state of ultimate clarity and peace.

However, in today's world, the disciplined pursuit of light faces unique challenges. Modern life's constant disruptions and emphasis on immediate dopamine driven reward systems can obscure the patient and deliberate search for deeper understanding. For Freemasonry, this presents both a challenge and an opportunity: How can Lodges adapt to these conditions while preserving the depth and integrity of their teachings?

One solution lies in fostering environments that prioritise intellectual curiosity and spiritual growth. Lodges can encourage deeper engagement with Masonic symbols and philosophies through structured discussions, study groups, or meditative practices. Revisiting the ritualistic emphasis on seeking light as a call to lifelong learning can reinvigorate the Craft, reminding Brethren that the pursuit of wisdom is not confined to the Lodge room but extends into every aspect of their lives.

Freemasonry also offers a unique antidote to the superficiality of modern culture: a space where reflective dialogue and meaningful exploration are celebrated. The Craft's timeless lessons on light remind us that true knowledge cannot be commodified or rushed; it must be sought with patience and humility, and the pursuit of light in Freemasonry serves as a profound metaphor, signifying the aspirant's journey toward knowledge, wisdom, and spiritual clarity. Rooted in ancient mystical traditions, the quest for light transcends cultural and temporal boundaries, offering Masons a timeless framework for personal growth. This section's emphasis on stages of illumination mirrors the progressive nature of initiation, encouraging Brethren to see their Masonic path as a series of transformative awakenings.

Freemasonry's metaphor of light aligns with the Kabbalistic concept of the "point in the heart," which represents an innate desire for spirituality and connection with the Divine. According to Kabbalist teachings, this point is the embryonic state of the soul, distinct from worldly desires. It is a unique yearning to reveal and unite with the Creator. Rav Michael Laitman, PhD, explains that this point emerges as the central spark within the heart—the origin of all desires—and marks the beginning of a person's spiritual journey. The cultivation of this point is gradual and deliberate, involving daily efforts to expand spiritual awareness and align personal intentions with higher charitable goals.

In a contemporary context, the pursuit of light is particularly relevant as modern life bombards us with social media, consumer culture, and the frenetic pace of daily existence often pull us away from the reflective practices that foster enlightenment. Freemasonry offers a vital antidote, providing a structured framework for introspection and cultivating virtues. The call to "seek light" challenges us to move beyond superficiality and embrace the patient work of personal and spiritual transformation.

The metaphor of light in Freemasonry serves as a symbol of intellectual curiosity and a guide to cultivating the point within the heart. This inner spark becomes the foundation for profound personal change when carefully nurtured. Like the ancient mystery schools, Freemasonry and Kabbalah teach that the journey inward is as critical as any outward accomplishment. Rituals, symbols, and meditative practices become tools for rediscovering the virtues of patience, humility, and dedication.

Moreover, Freemasonry's emphasis on light reminds us of the universal nature of this quest. In other traditions, such as Buddhism, the shedding of ignorance through disciplined living and meditation culminates in enlightenment, much like the Masonic journey through degrees. The parallels are striking: the Tree of Life in Kabbalah and the Buddhist path to nirvana represent structured ascents toward higher understanding. These shared frameworks highlight the interconnectedness of human spiritual endeavour, placing Freemasonry within a broader tapestry of traditions seeking to illuminate life's ultimate truths.

One of Freemasonry's greatest strengths is its ability to offer timeless lessons through the metaphor of light. By focusing on nurturing the aspirant's connection to divine wisdom—the point within the heart—Masons are reminded of their role as seekers of truth in a world often clouded by material preoccupations. Each Lodge meeting, ritual, and moment of reflection becomes an opportunity to realign with this higher purpose.

For modern Masons, the pursuit of light is an invitation to navigate the complexities of contemporary life with intention and clarity. It calls to rediscover the profound wisdom embedded in the Craft and apply it to harmonise their internal and external lives. As we cultivate the light within, we honour the Craft's legacy and contribute to a brighter, more spiritually aware world. This enduring journey reminds us that the light we seek outwardly resides within us, waiting to be revealed through deliberate effort and unwavering dedication. The quest for light is as much about rediscovering these virtues as it is about uncovering hidden truths.

By embracing this metaphor as a guide, Freemasons today can navigate the complexities of contemporary life with purpose and clarity, drawing upon the wisdom of the Craft to illuminate their path. In doing so, they honour the enduring legacy of the pursuit of light while adapting its lessons to meet the needs of a rapidly changing world. Each Lodge meeting, ritual, and moment of reflection becomes an opportunity to realign with this higher purpose.

BEARER OF THE FLAME: THE MASTER AS A BRIDGE TO HIGHER UNDERSTANDING

The Master's role in Freemasonry is of profound influence and significance, echoing the enduring traditions of mentorship across spiritual and philosophical systems. Unlike mere instructors, Masters are catalysts for transformation, embodying the ideals of the Craft and nurturing the aspirant's growth through wisdom, guidance, and example. This relationship is a microcosm of Freemasonry's greater purpose: the shared pursuit of light through individual and collective progress.

Throughout history, the archetype of the Master has been revered as both a teacher and a spiritual compass. In Sufism, the murshid leads the murid through sacred teachings and the labyrinth of the self, dissolving the ego and revealing unity with the Divine. Similarly, the Zen Master's use of paradox and koans transcends logic, encouraging the aspirant to access direct, intuitive insight. These traditions illustrate that the Master's role is not to dictate answers but to guide the aspirant in uncovering their inner truths, reflecting the Masonic ideal of building one's spiritual superstructure from within.

Within Freemasonry, the relationship between Master and aspirant is defined by the interplay of instruction, reflection, and inspiration. The rituals of the Craft symbolically highlight this dynamic, particularly in the role of the Worshipful Master, who leads with both authority and humility. Yet, the impact of this role extends far beyond ritual, offering a template for real-world mentorship. Through their example, Masters demonstrate how Masonic principles such as justice, integrity, and self-discipline can manifest daily, bridging the esoteric with the practical.

However, modernity presents unique challenges to this traditional relationship. In an era characterised by the democratisation of knowledge, aspirants have access to abundant information about Freemasonry, often before setting foot in a Lodge. While this accessibility can empower, it risks diminishing the experiential and relational aspects of the Craft. A Master's personal guidance, nuanced understanding, and ability to contextualise the teachings are irreplaceable, offering what texts and online resources cannot: lived wisdom and a tangible connection to the fraternity's lineage.

To adapt, contemporary Lodges must reimagine the Master's role while preserving its essence. Structured mentorship programs can provide a formal framework, pairing experienced Brethren with newer members to ensure continuity of knowledge and support. These programs should emphasise Freemasonry's ritualistic and historical dimensions and its philosophical and ethical implications, encouraging Brethren to apply Masonic values to their personal and professional lives.

Equally important is fostering an environment of mutual learning. Today's aspirants often seek collaborative mentorship rather than hierarchical instruction, valuing open dialogue and shared exploration. Masters who embrace this ethos can deepen engagement, making mentorship a reciprocal process that enriches both teacher and student. This approach aligns with the principles of equality and fraternity, demonstrating that leadership in the Craft is rooted in service and inclusivity.

The Master's role also invites reflection on the evolving nature of authority in Freemasonry. While tradition imbues the Worshipful Master with a degree of hierarchical significance, their true power lies in moral authority—the ability to inspire through action and example. A Master's wisdom is not measured by their ability to command but by their capacity to foster growth, embody virtue, and uplift the Lodge as a whole.

In this light, the Master becomes a living symbol of Freemasonry's transformative potential. Their influence is not confined to the Lodge but extends into the wider world, as they exemplify the Craft's principles in action. By mentoring with humility, wisdom, and compassion, they remind us that the journey of the aspirant is also the journey of the Master, for both are engaged in the shared pursuit of light.

The modern Mason who seeks a Master finds more than a guide; they find a partner in the ongoing work of self-improvement and enlightenment. Together, aspirant and Master uphold the Craft's timeless ideals, proving that the path to mastery is not solitary but shared—a collective effort to build a better self, Lodge, and ultimately, a better world.

BEYOND MATERIAL GAIN: THE SOUL'S WAGES IN THE CRAFT

The concept of wages in Freemasonry transcends material remuneration, embodying the profound spiritual rewards that come from diligent inner work and self-transformation. In a world that often equates success with wealth, power, and status, the symbolic wages of corn, wine, and oil remind us of deeper, enduring values that nourish the soul and sustain our higher purpose. These metaphors, rich with historical and spiritual significance, invite modern Masons to reflect on how they measure achievement and fulfilment in their lives.

CORN: THE FOUNDATION OF GROWTH

As the sustainer of physical life, corn represents the foundational work of self-discipline and character-building. Just as corn provides the nourishment necessary for survival, the foundational virtues of Freemasonry—integrity, temperance, and diligence—are essential for spiritual growth. In the modern context, corn serves as a metaphor for grounding oneself in values that withstand the test of time. Amid the noise and complexities of contemporary life, this symbolism reminds us that success is rooted in the steady cultivation of our moral and ethical foundations.

Corn also connects to the universal theme of labour. The Masonic call to earn one's wages resonates with the principle that personal growth requires effort, patience, and consistency. This labour is not merely physical or transactional but deeply introspective—a call to refine the rough ashlar of the self into a perfected stone fit for the spiritual edifice. For today's Mason, corn becomes a symbol of the daily disciplines—acts of kindness, self-reflection, or commitments to lifelong learning—that build the foundation of a virtuous life.

WINE: THE ELIXIR OF JOY AND INSIGHT

Traditionally associated with celebration and vitality, wine symbolises the emotional and intellectual nourishment of self-discovery and growth. It represents the invigorating effects of spiritual enlightenment, which bring clarity, creativity, and a profound connection to the world around us. Freemasonry reminds us that the pursuit of wisdom is not a solemn or joyless task but one that should bring inner fulfilment and a zest for life.

In the modern world, where stress and emotional discord often take centre stage, the symbolism of wine offers a powerful lesson in resilience. It challenges Masons to seek a balance between life's challenges and joys, reminding us that intellectual curiosity and emotional depth are essential components of the human experience. Just as wine can elevate the spirit, the inner work of the Craft fosters a sense of purpose and optimism that allows us to face life's difficulties with grace and wisdom.

OIL: THE ESSENCE OF REFINEMENT

Oil, with its properties of lubrication and illumination, symbolises the aspirant's pursuit of wisdom and spiritual enlightenment. Just as oil reduces friction and facilitates smooth motion, the insights gained through reflection and experience help us navigate life's complexities more easily. In the Masonic context, oil signifies the refinement of character and the acquisition of wisdom—qualities that benefit the individual and contribute to the harmony of the Lodge and the broader community.

In today's often contentious and fragmented world, the lesson of oil is particularly poignant. It reminds Masons of their role as peacemakers, who were called to bring light and unity when there was discord. The pursuit of wisdom is not a solitary endeavour but one that radiates outward, influencing the lives of others and fostering a collective sense of purpose. Oil serves as a call to cultivate qualities such as patience, understanding, and compassion, ensuring that the spiritual rewards of the Craft extend beyond the self.

THE CURRENCY OF VIRTUE: REIMAGINING SUCCESS THROUGH MASONIC WAGES

The Masonic concept of wages invites a profound reevaluation of what it means to succeed. In contrast to the materialistic values of modern society, Freemasonry challenges its adherents to seek rewards that enrich the soul rather than the bank account. Corn, wine, and oil are not just symbols; they guide living a life that balances the material and the spiritual, reminding us that the ultimate wages align with our higher purpose.

This teaching also invites reflection on balancing external pursuits with internal values. In the digital age the Craft provides a timeless framework for grounding our efforts in enduring principles. The true wages of the Craft are paid not in coins or accolades but in the currency of self-knowledge, moral clarity, and service to others.

As Masons engage with the symbols of corn, wine, and oil, they are reminded that their labours contribute to the construction of an internal superstructure—a Temple not built with hands but with the virtues and insights that define a meaningful life. This allegory challenges us to reflect on how our daily actions shape the foundation and structure of our inner Temple, urging us to prioritise spiritual sustenance over material gain.

Ultimately, the wages of the Craft call us to align our efforts with our values, ensuring that our labours serve not only ourselves but also the greater good. By embracing these symbolic rewards, Masons can navigate the complexities of modern life with purpose and clarity, honouring the timeless lessons of the Craft while adapting them to the needs of a rapidly changing world. Through this lens, Freemasonry remains a powerful guide for those seeking to build lives of integrity, wisdom, and service.

THE INNER ASCENT: REACHING FOR LIGHT

The "Law of the Mount" encapsulates the timeless pursuit of spiritual elevation, drawing upon the universal imagery of mountains as symbols of humanity's ascent toward higher consciousness. Across cultures and traditions, mountains have long represented the meeting place between the earthly and the divine, their peaks touching the heavens. From Mount Sinai, where Moses received divine law, to Mount Olympus, home of the Greek gods, sacred geography reflects an enduring truth: true wisdom and transformation require rising above the mundane to reach the transcendent. For Freemasonry, this imagery is a profound metaphor for the inner journey, urging Brethren to ascend the heights of moral and spiritual understanding.

Mountains, in this allegorical sense, are not just physical landmarks but thresholds of transformation. In biblical tradition, Mount Sinai symbolises the sacred space where divine revelations are given, and human frailty is tested against the weight of universal truths. Similarly, Mount Olympus evokes the aspirational climb to the realms of the gods, reserved for those who transcend the limits of the human condition. Freemasonry draws deeply from this reservoir of symbolism, positioning the Lodge as a metaphorical mountain. In this sanctuary, the aspirant ascends through degrees of enlightenment, striving to align themself more closely with the divine principles underpinning the Craft.

The call to ascend is not merely an abstract concept but a challenge to Masons to elevate their conduct and character beyond the ordinary. The "Law of the Mount" does not advocate superiority; rather, it asks each Brother to embody virtues that "distinguish and set them above the ranks of other men." This elevation is rooted in humility, compassion, and an unwavering commitment to the collective good. The teachings of the Sermon on the Mount find resonance here, offering a blueprint for living a life of higher ideals. In a world so often consumed by self-interest and material pursuits, these principles invite Masons to adopt a broader perspective and act with integrity and charity.

This ascent is far from effortless, often requiring a confrontation with internal and external challenges. The ruffians of doubt, distraction, and fear stand ready to obstruct the path. Yet through such trials, the Initiate's true essence is refined. As the aspirant climbs, they must shed the burdens of ego and embrace the discipline of self-mastery, learning to navigate the steep terrain of their consciousness. This journey is deeply personal, yet its implications extend outward, urging the aspirant to lead by example and inspire others to undertake their own ascent.

In a contemporary context, the "Law of the Mount" profoundly reminds us of the importance of perspective. Just as scaling a mountain provides a panoramic view of the world below, pursuing higher consciousness enables the aspirant to see beyond immediate concerns and align their actions with enduring truths. This expanded perspective is especially vital today, where quick fixes and short-term gains often overshadow the deeper values that sustain personal and collective growth. By cultivating this elevated awareness, Masons are better equipped to navigate the complexities of modern life with clarity and purpose.

The inner ascent is also a collective endeavour. Just as no physical mountain is climbed alone, the spiritual ascent described in Freemasonry emphasises the importance of community. Brethren support one another on the path, their shared efforts building a legacy that transcends individual achievements. The Lodge becomes not just a place of ritual but a gathering point for those committed to elevating themselves and their communities, reflecting the interconnected nature of the Craft's teachings.

Ultimately, the "Law of the Mount" challenges Masons to live with intention and integrity, embracing the ascent as a personal and collective journey. It is a call to transcend the trivial and temporary, to strive for the enduring light that lies at the summit of human potential. As we climb this metaphorical mountain, we are reminded that each step upward brings us closer to the divine, ensuring that the timeless wisdom of Freemasonry continues to illuminate the path for future generations. Through this ascent, the Craft fulfils its sacred purpose: to inspire and transform, one soul at a time, in the shared pursuit of light.

TRIALS AND ORDEALS: FORGING THE MASONIC SOUL

The trials and ordeals we encounter on the Masonic path are not mere ritualistic performances but profound symbols of the inner challenges we must face to grow and transform. The Craft teaches us a timeless truth through these allegories: growth is forged through struggle. Just as iron must endure the fire to become steel, we are shaped and refined by the adversities we confront. These trials are not punishments but opportunities—sacred invitations to confront our limitations, integrate our shadow selves, and emerge stronger, wiser, and more attuned to the light. As Wilmshurst eloquently puts it, "The ordeals are not imposed from without, but arise out of the aspirant's own nature, which is stirred into activity by his conscious and deliberate invocation of light upon himself."

Joseph Campbell's archetype of the *Hero's Journey* offers a powerful parallel. In myths and legends, the hero's trials are universal metaphors for human experience. Whether it is Odysseus navigating the sirens and the Cyclops or Persephone's descent into the Underworld, these stories resonate because they reflect our own journey. Each trial tests courage, wisdom, and perseverance, forcing the hero to shed their former self and embrace transformation. The path is rarely easy. Freemasonry's symbolic trials remind us that life's adversities are not barriers but stepping stones, guiding us toward self-mastery and greater understanding.

Indigenous traditions offer further illumination. Across cultures, initiation often involves rituals of profound challenge designed to strip away the ego and prepare the individual for new responsibilities. In the rites of passage for Indigenous peoples, initiates might endure fasting, isolation, or physical endurance to symbolise their transition from one stage of life to another. These ordeals reflect the aspirant's symbolic death to their old identity and rebirth into a new, elevated state. Similarly, our Masonic rituals are designed to lead us from ignorance to enlightenment, urging us to confront the unknown with trust in the Craft and ourselves. As the Lakota phrase reminds us, "We must die to the person we have been to be born as the one we are becoming."

Today, the symbolic trials of Freemasonry are just as relevant as they were for our ancient Brethren. Life continually presents us with challenges—our own symbolic “ruffians”—that test our character and resolve. Whether it is the loss of certainty, internal doubts, or external hardships, these moments demand that we draw upon the teachings of the Craft. As Masons, we are reminded that such trials are not meant to defeat us but to strengthen us, transforming adversity into signposts along our journey to becoming more complete, enlightened individuals. Marcus Aurelius, the Stoic philosopher, reflects a similar principle, stating, "The impediment to action advances action. What stands in the way becomes the way." Freemasonry calls upon us to turn these impediments into opportunities for growth and transformation.

What makes these trials particularly profound is their communal nature. Though we must walk our own path, the Lodge surrounds us as a sanctuary of collective support. The shared intention of the Brethren strengthens the aspirant during their most vulnerable moments. Just as the Master and the Lodge guide us through symbolic darkness, our Brethren stand ready to offer guidance and encouragement as we confront life's challenges. This collective strength underscores one of the greatest lessons of Freemasonry: while growth is deeply personal, it flourishes in embracing a community committed to our success. In this sense, the Lodge becomes a place of fellowship and a living embodiment of the alchemical crucible—a space where we are tested, refined, and ultimately transformed.

The trials we endure also offer us perspective. They challenge us to step beyond the superficial and to seek deeper meaning in our struggles. Confucius reminds us, "The gem cannot be polished without friction, nor man perfected without trials." Each difficulty we face serves as a mirror, reflecting our strengths and the areas where we must grow. The lessons of Freemasonry remind us that adversity can shape us into instruments of service, wisdom, and compassion—not through avoidance but perseverance.

Moreover, the trials within the Craft are not confined to symbolic actions within the Lodge. They echo into our daily lives, reminding us that every challenge we face is an opportunity to apply Masonic principles. For example, when confronted with discord or ethical dilemmas, we are called to remember the values of Brotherly Love, Relief, and Truth. These moments become the proving grounds for our Masonic commitment, inviting us to live out the teachings of the Craft in real and meaningful ways.

As we navigate life's symbolic and literal trials, let us remember that these challenges are not solitary endeavours. As a fraternity, we form a sacred circle of intention, a collective will that empowers us to rise above our hardships. Rumi's words resonate here: "Be like a tree and let the dead leaves drop." Through our trials, we shed what no longer serves us, creating new growth and greater clarity.

The symbolic trials of Freemasonry challenge us to embrace the unknown with courage and resolve, viewing each hardship as a stepping stone toward the light. They remind us that transformation is a journey, not a destination, and the path is illuminated by our willingness to persevere. By facing these trials with the collective support of our Brethren and the guiding principles of the Craft, we honour the timeless wisdom of Freemasonry and move ever closer to our highest potential.

SILENCE AND SECRECY

Silence and secrecy are revered in Freemasonry, not as tools of exclusion but as profound disciplines that foster introspection and sacredness. These principles align with practices in spiritual traditions worldwide, where silence is a pathway to clarity, and secrecy safeguards the sanctity of shared wisdom.

In monastic traditions, the vow of silence is a cornerstone of spiritual practice. Monks and nuns embrace silence to quiet the mind and attune themselves to higher truths. Similarly, in Freemasonry, silence serves as a means to cultivate inner stillness, allowing the aspirant to reflect on the teachings of the Craft. In a world filled with constant noise and distraction, this discipline is more relevant than ever, reminding Masons of the value of listening and contemplation.

Secrecy, often misunderstood, is equally significant. In ancient mystery schools, the veil of secrecy protected esoteric knowledge, ensuring that it was revealed only to those prepared to receive it. This practice was not about withholding information but about honouring its sacredness. For today's Masons, secrecy can be reimagined as a commitment to discretion and humility, preserving the sanctity of the Craft's teachings and fostering trust within the Lodge.

The bond of secrecy within the Lodge also serves a practical purpose: it creates an environment where Brethren can share freely, knowing their words will remain in confidence. This practice nurtures deeper connections and a sense of mutual respect. In today's digital age, where privacy is often compromised, the Masonic emphasis on discretion offers a refreshing counterbalance, reminding us of the importance of safeguarding what is sacred.

Silence and secrecy also encourage personal accountability. By refraining from boasting about their knowledge or achievements, Masons are reminded that the true work of the Craft is inward and ongoing. This discipline cultivates humility, an increasingly valuable trait in a society that often prioritises outward displays of success over genuine self-improvement.

Finally, these principles invite Masons to approach their practice with reverence. The Lodge is not merely a meeting place; it is a sacred space where timeless truths are explored. Silence and secrecy help preserve this sanctity, allowing the teachings of the

Craft to resonate more deeply with those who engage with them sincerely.

In embracing silence and secrecy, modern Masons can reconnect with the profound wisdom of the Craft. These principles remind us that self-discovery requires patience, humility, and a willingness to honour the sacred. By cultivating these disciplines, we deepen our understanding and strengthen the bonds that unite us as Brethren.

THE ETERNAL PURSUIT: MASTERY AS SELF-TRANSCENDENCE AND SERVICE

The journey toward mastery in Freemasonry is not a finite accomplishment but a lifelong pursuit of self-perfection, embodying spiritual and moral alignment with the Divine. This ideal reflects the profound purpose of the Craft: to inspire Masons to continually refine their inner lives and contribute meaningfully to the world around them. The concept of mastery invites introspection into the nature of leadership, personal growth, and service, both within the Lodge and in society.

Wilmshurst's framing of mastery as alignment with the Divine finds echoes in philosophical traditions such as Stoicism. The Stoic ideal of the sophos, or sage, mirrors the Masonic Master—an individual who acts with wisdom, temperance, and virtue, irrespective of external circumstances. Similarly, Eastern traditions like Zen Buddhism emphasise lifelong practice and mindfulness as the means to enlightenment. Both frameworks underscore the shared human aspiration toward self-transcendence, reminding us that mastery is not a destination but a disciplined way of being.

In a contemporary context, the Masonic journey toward mastery gains new relevance. In a world often focused on external achievements and material success, Freemasonry offers an antidote—a path that prioritises inner transformation and the cultivation of character. The lessons of the Master Mason degree, for example, challenge

Brethren to confront mortality, transcend ego, and dedicate themselves to higher principles. These teachings provide a timeless framework for navigating the complexities of modern life with integrity and purpose.

Modern Lodges play a pivotal role in supporting this journey. Mentorship can be a cornerstone of this effort, pairing seasoned Brethren with newer members to foster mutual growth and understanding. Education, too, is vital: lectures, workshops, and study groups can deepen members' engagement with Masonic philosophy and its practical applications. Ritual remains central, both as a reminder of the Craft's ideals and a tool for personal reflection.

Freemasonry's emphasis on mastery as a lifelong endeavour also calls for a reimagining of success. In a demanding world, the patient, steady work of self-improvement may seem countercultural, but precisely, this quality makes the Craft indispensable. Lodges can encourage this perspective by celebrating personal growth highlights and creating spaces where Brethren feel empowered to share their insights and challenges.

The ultimate goal of mastery is to align one's actions with universal truths, contributing to both individual fulfilment and collective harmony. This aspiration finds its ultimate expression in the Masonic tenet of service: the Master is not one who commands but serves, embodying the principles of humility, wisdom, and compassion. By striving toward this ideal, Masons affirm the enduring relevance of their Craft in a world that is often in search of deeper meaning and connection.

Through mentorship, education, and ritual, Lodges can support their members in embodying the Masonic ideal of mastery. In doing so, they ensure that the Craft remains a repository of ancient wisdom and a living tradition that continues to inspire, challenge, and transform those who seek its light.

THE ETERNAL ASCENT: FREEMASONRY'S PATH TO UNIVERSAL TRUTHS

As this chapter has explored, a Mason's journey is not a simple progression through degrees or the mere acquisition of ritual knowledge. It is an intricate, transformative process to master the self and align with universal truths. From the earliest steps of initiation to the profound ideals of mastery, Freemasonry provides a timeless framework for personal and spiritual growth.

In our modern world, the principles of the Craft offer both a sanctuary and a challenge. They call us to slow down, reflect deeply, and commit ourselves to intentional self-improvement. The lessons imparted by symbols, rituals, and mentorship must remain living tools that guide us in navigating the complexities of today's life.

As we strive toward mastery, we also carry forward the responsibility to uphold the ideals of Freemasonry for future generations. Each step on this path contributes to the greater whole—a reaffirmation that the light we seek within ourselves can illuminate the world around us.

In the words of Wilmshurst, "The just and perfect man and Mason... consciously shares and becomes the instrument of the divine Kingdom, Power, and Glory." May we, as Masons, take this charge to heart, continually ascending the symbolic mountain and finding inspiration and purpose in the journey itself.

CHAPTER THREE - THE MASONIC INITIATION

FULLNESS OF LIGHT: OBSERVATIONS AND EXAMPLES

The light of the body is the eye. When thine eye is single, thy whole body also is full of light. Take heed, therefore, that the light in thee be not darkness."
—(Luke xi., 34-5)

Now will I open unto thee—whose heart
Rejects not—that last lore, deepest concealed,
That farthest secret of My heavens and earths,
Which but to know shall set thee free from ills;
A royal lore, a kingly mystery;
Yea, for the soul such light as purgeth it
From every sin; a light of holiness
With inmost splendour shining.
—(The Song Celestial, ix.).

We have shown that Initiation, in its real and not merely ceremonial sense, effects in him who undergoes it a permanent enlargement of consciousness to a level and of a quality never previously known to him. The expansion may be small or great; indeed, the Science contemplates successive degrees of Initiation and ever-widening expansions to which no limit can be set.

The reader will ask himself, "What are the nature and characteristics of this new order of consciousness when attained? How will it differ from my present normal consciousness?" To answering this question, the present paper is devoted, and it shall be dealt with first in some general observations, and subsequently in a more illustrative manner.

Even normally, and without deliberately sought Initiation, human consciousness becomes enlarged as the result merely of progressive life-experience. For what is life itself but a slow, gradual Initiation process, with the world as a Temple in which it is conferred? The consciousness and resultant sagacity of experienced age exceed those of raw youth, even if the change be of an intellectual rather than of a spiritual kind, and involve merely increased *savoir faire* and mundane wiliness rather than growth in unworldly wisdom. Still, enlargement has occurred, and it adumbrates what is possible with the spiritual consciousness when it becomes awakened.

Nature, indeed, exhibits nothing but consciousness in process of expansion through her fourfold series of kingdoms from the mineral upwards. The outward forms of life, even of the mineral, are but the objective bodies of a subjective life-activity resident in that body. The Earth-planet itself, as also each of the stellar bodies, is, the Ancients rightly taught, not dead matter, but a *Zoon*, a living Animal, conscious as a whole, conscious (though differingly) in each of its parts however materialised or tenuous, and girdled round with a Zodiac of other mutually interacting "living creatures," the separate consciousnesses of all the parts of the complex mechanism blending in the synthetic Omniscience, God.

Life is fundamentally one, a unity, though distributed into many separated lives and divided into separate self-contained kingdoms, as compartments of a ship are divided by decks and bulkheads. It is "an ever-rolling stream," a stream that pours through those kingdoms in a continuous flow which is never more than momentarily checked by the forms (or bodies) it flows through, which are as it were but little eddies and vortices in the stream; and these forms, from the lowest to the most highly evolved, are devised and adjusted to raising consciousness to progressively higher levels.

Nature, in a word, is a system of restricted consciousness in perishable bodies, leading up to unrestricted consciousness in an ultra-natural immortal body.

Each successive kingdom of Nature assumes into itself the sublimated characteristics of the one below it, but becomes endued with an additional principle and takes on a new and appropriate bodily form. Thus, as the scale is ascended, the sensitive, the emotional, the intellectual, and the spiritual principles are successively added and built into the evolving structure. When the Life-essence specialised in the mineral passes on into the vegetable kingdom, it, as it were, takes a degree of Initiation; a fresh start is made, a new form or body is given to it as "a mark of its progress." It takes similar and higher grades of initiation, and acquires appropriate new bodies, as it passes on to the animal and thence to the human kingdoms.

It is not here implied that mineral forms directly evolve into vegetable, thence to animal and so on, at some point which the biologist has sought for but failed to trace. This is not the case. The kingdoms of Nature are closed compartments without intercommunicating doors on the phenomenal plane, and do not there change into one another. The transition takes place on a super-physical noumenal plane, beyond the range of now current science.

Man, as at his present evolutional stage, is, in his lower nature, but a summary and synthesis of the three sub-human kingdoms; his embryo recapitulates, and his physique incorporates, the kingdoms he has traversed in the long ascent; but superimposed and dovetailed into it is now an additional, a spiritual divine principle, distinguishing and setting him above the lower kingdoms. To them he stands as a god; a high initiate, conscious in a way inconceivable to them. Similarly a plant is a god, an initiate, relatively to the soil it grows in; and an animal a god to the plant.

Yet in virtue of the new spiritual principle grafted upon his highly evolved bodily structure, man is capable of rising to still loftier conscious levels; he awaits still further initiation. Before him lies the prospect of outgrowing the kingdom of merely animal man and of entering the higher one of spiritual Man. Four kingdoms—mineral, vegetable, animal human—he has known and built into his organism. He has now to rise to a fifth kingdom, that of Spirit, of which already he is a member potentially, but without having yet developed and realised his potencies.

The secret Science therefore shows him a five-pointed Star as an emblem of himself and invests him with the five-pointed Apron as a symbol in which he may visualise himself, read his own past, and deduce his present possibilities.

The important fact must be emphasised that, on each transition from a lower to a higher kingdom, on each initiation into a new order of life, a death to, a complete break-away from and abandonment of, the old form and method of life, is involved. Natural man must, therefore, die to himself, must abnegate and put off his old nature, before he can hope to pass into the fifth kingdom as spiritual Man. This death, we have shown, is signified by the Masonic Third Degree, which ceremonially dramatises what the individual must pass through before attaining an order of life and consciousness he has never before experienced or been able to experience.

The death in question is not a physical death; the physical organism is still retained by its former wearer. He has merely effaced and died to his old self and its natural tendencies, and suffered them to become superseded by a new self, functioning not from his former constricted mind, but from a new centre of illimitable conscious capacity; a capacity not displaced by the resumed use of his physical body for the residue of its natural duration, but one that enables him thenceforward to use that body as a much more effective instrument for furthering the cosmic purpose.

How is that newly-won consciousness to be described? It is, of course, indescribable. As sight is indescribable to the man born blind, as consciousness in this world would be unexplainable to the unborn babe, so that of the Initiate is incapable of description to those as yet unborn in the kingdom of Spirit. To be known it must be experienced. It belongs to the Greater Mysteries which always remain ineffable and incommunicable, whatever instruction may be imparted about the Lesser ones. Yet something may be said about it to help the imagination.

In my former volume, it was explained that the moment of restoration to light in the Third Degree, and also the corresponding moment in the Royal Arch Degree, are both of them attempts—the former a simple, the latter a more elaborate one—to dramatise the enlarged conscious state into which the candidate passes in actual Initiation. A very fine and wonderful literary description of expanded consciousness effected by Initiation is to be found in the eleventh section of the great Indian manual of initiation-science, the *Bhagavad Gita* (most accessible to English readers in Sir Edwin Arnold's fine poetic translation, *The Song Celestial*). Dante's vision in the *Paradiso* is an example, as also that recorded in the biblical book of *Revelation* by the seer who was "in the spirit in the Lord's day."

Keats imagined it accurately when, in *Hyperion*, he wrote of it:

Knowledge enormous makes a god of me.
Names, deeds, grey legends, dire events, rebellions,
Majesties, sovran voices, agonies,
Creations and destroyings—all, at once,
Pour into the wide hollows of my brain
And deify me; as if some blithe wine,
A bright elixir peerless, I had drunk
And so become immortal.

A large collection of evidence and records of personal experiences has been brought together in recent years testifying to the fact of such conscious expansions. One such compilation is that entitled *Cosmic Consciousness*, by Dr. R. M. Bucke, a member of the Craft in America and an exponent of the mystical nature of Masonry. The subject has even been investigated experimentally by the late eminent psychologist Professor William James and others, and although such artificially induced heightening of consciousness are strongly to be dissuaded from as perilous to those who undertake them—and Professor James confessed that to himself it brought with it a painful reaction and penalty—he has left an able, vivid description of what is known as "the Anaesthetic Revelation," which may be quoted; it could not better have expressed the truth had it been written by one who had attained Initiation legitimately and in the natural development of the life of sanctity and contemplation, instead of by one who was merely intoxicating himself with nitrous oxide gas. He writes:

> "*In this intense metaphysical illumination, Truth lies open to the view in depth beneath depth of almost blinding evidence. The mind sees all the logical relations of being with an apparent subtlety and instantaneity to which its normal consciousness offers no parallel. The centre and periphery of things seem to come together. The Ego and its objects, the meum and the tuum, are one. Its first result was to make peal through me with unutterable power the conviction that the deepest convictions of my intellect hitherto were wrong. Whatever idea or representation occurred to the mind was seized by the same logical forceps and served to illustrate the same truth; and that truth was that every opposition, among whatsoever things, vanishes in a higher unity in which it is based; that all contradictions, so called, are but differences; that all differences are of degree; that all degrees are of a common kind; that unbroken continuity is the essence of being; and that we are literally in the*

midst of an Infinite. It is impossible to convey an idea of the torrential character of the identification of opposites as it streams through the mind in this experience."
—(The Will to Believe, *by W. James, p. 294).*

With this statement, let us compare one by a real Initiate describing the opening up of the light at his centre:

"My whole spirit seemed to break through the gates of hell and be taken up into the arms and heart of God. I can compare it to nothing but the resurrection at the last day. For then, with all reverence I say it, with the eyes of my spirit I saw God. I saw both what God is, and how God is what He is. The gate of the Divine Mystery was sometimes so opened in me that in one quarter of an hour I saw and knew more than if I had been many years at a university. I saw and knew the Being of all Beings; the Byss and the Abyss; the generation of the Son and the procession of the Spirit. I saw the descent and original of this world also, and of all its creatures. I saw in their order and outcome the Divine World, the Angelical World, Paradise, and then this fallen dark world of our own. I saw the beginning of the good and of the evil, the true origin and existence of each of them. For twelve years this went on in me. Sometimes the truth would hit me like a sudden smiting storm of rain, and then there would be the clear sunshine after the rain."

The writer of this statement was the poor, uneducated cobbler, Jacob Boehme, who lived near Dresden and died, aged 49, in 1624. He has been described by a disciple and competent judge—Louis Claude de Saint Martin ("Le Philosophe Inconnu"); himself a Freemason and advanced illuminate—as "the greatest light that has come into the world since Him who was Himself the light of the world." The fuller record of his illuminations and profound metaphysical insight can be found in his series of lengthy but difficult and obscure works, from the study of which Sir Isaac Newton, a deep student of them, drew the information from which he became able to formulate the principles of gravitation and planetary motion, and other laws now known to regulate physical phenomena.

Instances might be multiplied indefinitely of cases in which the inner being of persons ripening for Initiation expands towards all sides from an infinitely deep central point in themselves, so that they acquire a totally different outlook upon life, a larger deeper envisaging of the world, than others. Three outstanding features characterise such cases:

- The fact that objects, whether those of nature or one's fellow beings, cease to be seen singly, as separate objects and beings, but as partial expressions of a single, sublying, inexpressible unity.
- The fact that for such percipients all ordinary values become changed; what the average man supposes important shrinks to worthlessness, and what he thinks negligible assumes prime importance.
- The fact that the five senses, distributed in the ordinary man as distinct, unrelated channels of perception, remain no longer separate and diffused, but become unified and co-functional in one comprehensive faculty, so that to see is also to hear; to touch, even with blindfold eyes, is to visualise.

As a Brother in the Craft, known to me, writes of his own experience of this enrichment of consciousness: "You know everything and understand the stars and the hills and the old songs. They are all within you, and you are all light. But the light is music, and the music is violet wine in a great cup of gold, and the wine in the golden cup is the scent of a June night."

The brilliant young German, Novalis, an advanced illuminate, though he died at 29 over a century ago, tells of his Master, Werner (a professor of mineralogy at Freyburg), as one who "was aware of the inter-relation of all things, of conjunctions, coincidences. He saw nothing singly. The perceptions of his senses thronged together; he heard, saw, felt, simultaneously. Sometimes the stars became man to him, men as stars; stones as animals, clouds as plants. He sported with forces and phenomena. He knew where and how to find and bring to light this or that. What came to him more than this he does not tell us. But he tells us that we ourselves, led on by him and by our own desire, may discover what happened to him."

"Led on by our own desire." In desire lies the secret of it all! All Initiation presupposes concentration and intensity of desire for it, and is impossible without that indispensable prerequisite. Desire turned outward, squandered upon exterior attractions, wastes the soul's forces, distributes its energies through the five channels of sense. Turned inward, focused upon interior possibilities, desire ingathers those forces, unifies those senses, and is the heat which, gathering in intensity, finds its ultimate fruition in a burst of conscious flame. *"If thine eye be single thy whole body is full of light."*

Here is an example. In a small lone isle of the Hebrides lived a young fisherman-crofter, one of the few natives of a place necessarily poor and with such scanty social and educational advantages that a mind of any power and depth is thrown back upon itself; a place where almost the only book is that of Nature, the only place of worship the Temple of earth and sky and sea. Such conditions, however uninviting to most people, are particularly favourable to self-realisation and initiation; since they ensure that poverty, that simplicity and unsophistication of the mind which are so difficult to acquire in crowded places and amid the tyrannies, artificialities and strife of current so-called civilisation. So they were to the man in question. With something of the old primitive passion of Demeter-worship, he loved the island and the sea, his soul straining continually to know directly and at first hand the Living Beauty which he knew resided beneath its manifested veil.

One golden day, in a moment of concentrated adoring contemplation, he threw himself on the ground, kissing the hot, sweet heather, plunging his hands and arms in it, sobbing the while with a vague strange yearning, and lying there nerveless, with closed eyes. His posture at that moment resembled, unwittingly yet surely, that of one who with blinded eyes and with his hands upon the Sacred Law declares that the supreme light is the paramount desire of his heart and asks to be accorded it. And then came the moment when his longing was satisfied, when the veil was torn from his eyes and he received his initiation into light.

Suddenly—for, whatever its nature to the cold-blooded inquisition of the scientist, thus he translated the psychopathic experience he then underwent—two little hands rose up through the spires of heather and anointed his forehead and eyes with something soft and fragrant.

Thereafter he was the same, yet not the same, man; the place he lived in was the old familiar place, yet had become new, glorified. The Eternal Beauty had entered into him, and nothing that others saw as ugly or dreary was otherwise than perpetually invested with it. Waste, desolate spots became to him passing fair, radiant with lovely light. When, later, he went away to great towns and passed among their squalor and sordid hideousness, amid slums, factory smoke and grime, he saw all that others see, yet only as vanishing shadows, beneath which everything and everyone was lovely, beautiful with strange glory, and the faces of men and women sweet and pure, and their souls white.

Such was this man's involuntary Initiation, unsought, or rather not knowingly sought, yet bringing him the fruits of the travail of his soul and leaving him permanently enlightened and transformed. *(The incident is referred to in the works of the late Fiona Ma)*. He came to be known among those with whom he dwelt as "the Anointed Man." In their Greek original, the words "Christ" and "Christian" bore just that significance—an anointed, "baptised," or initiated man.

Actual Initiation, then, regarded, as it may be, as "baptism," is of two classes: a lesser and a greater. The lesser (scripturally described as the "baptism of water") is one affecting the lower nature—the mind, the intelligence, the psychic nature and sensibilities. The mentality becomes expanded and illuminated; there is a quickening and hyper-aesthesia of the senses, a growth of psychic faculty and perception; for the soul (or psyche) is now beginning to exercise its hitherto dormant, atrophied powers.

The greater form of Initiation, the "baptism of fire," is the awakening of the Spirit, the innermost essence, the "Vital and Immortal Principle" centrally resident in the soul, as the soul is resident in the sense-body. Numbers of people attain the lesser baptism in the ordinary development of life, often without awareness of the fact. The greater baptism is of rarer occurrence, and to experience it is a crisis that cannot be mistaken, or pass unnoticed or forgotten.

To attain either form, Initiation of a formal character is not an indispensable requirement, for the growth of the soul and Divine dealings with the soul are not dependent upon human formalities. But formal Initiation has always been, and is today, an opportunity and means of grace for attaining interior advancement which otherwise might not be secured. For this reason, the Masonic Initiation, though only a ceremonial one at present, assumes such great importance and is capable of being put to uses so much higher and farther-reaching than the Craft has hitherto dreamed of.

Life itself, we repeat, serves for thousands as an initiating-process, without any supplementary formality. Numbers of people attain, in less or greater measure, the lesser baptism of water in the expanded consciousness associated with the poetic, artistic, musical, or mystical types;—our Wordsworths, Shelleys, Tennysons, and the like are natural initiates in whose lives formal initiation has played no part, and numberless unknown people exist about us who, in silence and obscurity, have developed their deeper nature and could assert of themselves:

> *"We have built a house that is not for Time's o'er-throwing,*
> *We have gained a peace unshaken by pain for ever."*

Many there are who are conscious of the "mystic tie" that binds not merely all men into brotherhood but all the elements of the Universe into unity; who have lost the sense of separateness and divided interests that characterise the average sensual man, whose consciousness and desires extend no farther than his own carnal affections; who, still incarcerated in the mortal body, can evade its prison-walls and laugh at its iron window-bars, escaping into the world of soul, exploring its wonders, mingling in conscious communion with other similarly liberated souls, and there:

> *"Spend in pure converse their eternal day,*
> *Think each in each, immediately wise,*
> *Learn all they lacked before; hear, know, and say*
> *What this tumultuous body now denies;*
> *And feel, who have laid their groping hands away;*
> *And see, no longer blinded by their eyes."*
> *—(Rupert Brooke).*

But those who know the "baptism of fire," the Initiation of, and into, central Spirit, are few. To help form a conception of such cases, one may refer to recorded instances where the Blazing Star at the human centre has so fully opened itself, so habitually brought its fire forward into the purified carnal body and formal mind, that the light has become visibly perceptible—not merely as a flesh-transmuting grace that beautifies and glorifies the personality, but as a radiant aura emanating from the face and person, casting off an actual quasi-physical glow.

The traditional depictions of saints and angels with aureoles, halos, and garments of flame are a testament to this heightened state. It is credibly recorded of such Initiates as Columba and Ruysbroeck that their persons were seen bathed in a self-radiated luminosity, illuminating their chambers or the surrounding space over a significant radius. If the Central light can manifest in such an observable way, it may inspire the imagination to consider the intensity and depth of subjective consciousness experienced by those in whom it so brightly burns. These instances of "fullness of light" exemplify the symbol of the completed Temple of Solomon, into which the Divine Presence descended, filling the entire house with glory *(2 Chronicles 7:1-3)*.

Now, setting aside these broader observations, let us move forward with an imaginative exploration of how light in its full magnitude might be encountered and, with Divine guidance, intentionally invoked through methods of actual—rather than purely ceremonial—Initiation.

APOCALYPSIS—AN ALLEGORY OF INITIATION

> *"At the time of the end shall be vision."* (Dan. viii, 17)
>
> "*O truly sacred Mysteries! O pure light! I am led by the light of the torch to the view of heaven and of God. I am made whole by Initiation. The Lord Himself is the hierophant who, leading the candidate for initiation to the light, sends him and presents him to the Father to be preserved for ever. These are the orgies of my Mysteries. If thou wilt, come and be thou also initiated, and thou shalt join in the dance with the angels around the uncreated, imperishable, only true God, the Word of God joining in the strain!*" (Clemens Alexandrinus)

"APOCALYPSIS" is a Greek word meaning an unveiling, a removal of the veils that obstruct our perception of Absolute Truth. Hence, our biblical word "Revelation" or "Apocalypse." The Initiate-Apostle Paul speaks of attaining the exalted state of beholding the Divine Glory with an unveiled face, reflecting it as a mirror, and becoming transformed into it to an ever-increasing degree *(2 Corinthians 3:18)*.

Whoever would thus behold and reflect naked, unveiled, living Truth must himself stand forth in his own bare spirit, stripped of all veils of sense, emotion, desire, and thought that obscure clarity. He must be, as the biblical Apocalyptist describes, "in the spirit" on the "Lord's day"—"day" symbolising conscious awareness in the spirit (the "Lord") as opposed to "night," which represents the inherent limitations of any lower level of conscious faculty (the "servant").

In the Ancient Mysteries, this power of spiritual perception was called Epopteia, and those seers who attained it were termed Epopts. This state of complete illumination, this direct encounter between the unadorned human spirit and the unveiled universal Holy Spirit, was achieved only by high Initiates; it was the ultimate matured fruit of Initiation. "If thine eye be single, thy whole body shall be full of light."

What now follows is a descriptive example of the path leading to that attainment, as I seek to convey to my Brethren—even if faintly—an idea of what real, as distinct from merely ceremonial, Initiation entails and ultimately leads to, and this is the most fitting approach by which I can achieve that aim.

Greatly daring, I therefore venture to follow—however distantly—the example of the Initiate poet Virgil in the sixth *Aeneid*, where, in veiled terms, he depicts the quest of the human soul for its "Father," or Divine Paternal Principle. This journey, as he shows it, is pursued from the dark cave of earthly life into the bright Elysian Fields of the Universal Spirit. Likewise, similar portrayals of Initiation and Epopteia are found in the biblical book of *Revelation*, and in *Parsifal* by Wolfram von Eschenbach and Richard Wagner.

Although written in the first person, I ask that my description be viewed impersonally regarding the writer. However, I also hope that the reader will look forward earnestly to such an experience becoming true for themselves one day; not necessarily in this exact form, but in its essential qualities. For the Spirit bloweth where and how it listeth, and those who are taught by it may receive their lesson in varied forms, yet reach similar outcomes.

To what extent the following is allegorical, a work of creative imagination drawing on prior knowledge, or a reflection of personal intuition and spiritual experience, need not be stated; it contains elements of each. The only important aspect is that it faithfully portrays truth. Those who have journeyed with me so far, finding any resonance of verity in prior sections, will understand my aim here is solely to speak with good intent and sincerity, in terms reflecting utmost sincerity. Whether these words bear truth, let him that hath understanding and inward hearing discern and judge.

I.

Being of an inquiring disposition, hearing that in the Brotherhood called Masonic there were to be known certain valuable arcana and secrets of life not learnable elsewhere, and imagining it to be desirable from other motives which, whilst not mercenary, were perhaps of little better character, I followed a fashion of the time and the example of some friends, and associated myself with a community from which I looked to become possessed of some special but undefined wisdom within a brief space of time.

Looking back now across the years, my conduct at that time strikes me as not a little unworthy. I was looking for something for nothing. I was expecting to acquire valuable knowledge without paying or working for it; to get without giving. Nor had I considered to what use I should put the acquisition when I had secured it. But I was young, inexperienced, unreflecting, and knew no better.

My presumption soon received its appropriate penalty, for on being formally and with a most cordial welcome received into the community and solemnly undertaking to conform to its regulations, I was promptly cornered and humiliated. Instead of being given what my rashness had expected, I was asked what I was prepared to give for the benefit of any of the brotherhood who might need it. I felt trapped, but it would have been impolite to say so.

It was as obvious to them as it was painfully conscious to myself that my financial and intellectual poverty was such that I had nothing whatever to give. I was impelled, however, to mutter the perhaps scarcely sincere reply that had I been a person of any means I would have gladly contributed accordingly; an answer which, to my surprise, satisfied them, and they generously proceeded to tell me that, though I could offer them nothing, they would proceed to give me something, but upon the understanding that if I ever met anyone as poor as myself I must remember the present occasion, be as good as my word, and treat him liberally.

The incident impressed me, and is of importance in view of later developments; for I am now trying to fulfil that old promise.

In my novel, flurried position, I had but a hazy notion of what then occurred or of what they gave me. I remember some talk about a stone, a foundation-stone, and of identifying myself with that stone and putting it to some good use or other. I did not recall any stone changing hands or passing into my possession; but then, if I were already identified with it, it would not change hands; I already possessed it and was merely made aware of something of which I was previously unconscious.

Be that as it may, on returning home I found myself in possession of a small stone which I valued as a memorial of the occasion and as a token that I was now a member of the community of which I had heard so much and had been so eager to join. My fellow-members also, I found, each possessed a similar stone and were all very proud of it. It served as a passport or means of introduction when they travelled for pleasure or business. Some of them wore it openly as a pendant to their watch-chains or had it set in a ring with a square and compasses engraved upon it, or mounted as an ornament for their wives. Personally, I preferred not to advertise the possession of my own stone and kept it in my pocket.

For years I carried it about with me and went my usual way in the world and attended to ordinary business. I continued to attend meetings of the community and to enjoy the company and conviviality I there met. So seductive were these that for long I did not realise that I was learning nothing of any vital use, and that the wisdom I had hoped to learn never reached me. Moreover, I did all that seemed required of me in the way of learning the work of the Society and discharging any task that was given me, yet in no way was I any different or better a man for belonging to it than I might have remained had I never entered it. No knowledge of any value, no secrets or mysteries of any moment, ever reached me, or seemed to be possessed by my fellows. Perhaps after all there were none to impart, or if there were, they did not matter.

The position, after reflection, began to feel a little absurd. I thought of ways of relieving myself of it, by resignation or discontinuing my interest in the Craft, especially as no one I consulted was able to throw me any light upon the reason of its existence. Once, whilst so brooding, I took the little stone from my pocket and slowly turned it over and over, my memory wandering back to the moment when I had received it. I said to myself, "I have been expecting bread, and been given a stone—this stone." Somehow it seemed to have increased somewhat in size, to have become unaccountably heavier. And then, as I scrutinised it, I detected for the first time some minute markings upon it, too small to decipher without the aid of a magnifying glass.

Applying such a glass I found inscribed upon the stone the minute words "Free and Accepted Masonry"; then the Latin words "Descendit e coelo,"—it comes from heaven; and finally, in Greek lettering, the words "Know thyself!" (The quoted words are inscribed on the Foundation stone of Freemasons' Hall, London, laid on May-day, 1775.)

I pondered much upon these words and tried to realise their significance, though to little purpose. I made it in my way to see some of my Brethren and sought permission to examine their stones. To my surprise, in each case I found the same inscription, though they themselves had not discerned it. It was often very faint and in some cases nearly worn away, but there on every stone it was. I pointed it out to some of them. They were momentarily interested, but then fell to talking of other things and thought no more about it. One or two seniors, of high rank and many decorations, grew almost angry at the suggestion that their stone exhibited anything with which they were not already fully conversant; so with them I did not press the matter. No one that I interrogated could give me any helpful explanation.

I was referred to libraries and given the loan of historical and archaeological books. I visited the headquarters of the community and there interviewed antiquaries and other learned and dignified people, but though for some years I strove diligently to trace the meaning, nothing of real value was forthcoming.

Meanwhile, my stone grew gradually larger, heavier; and, as it did so, its inscription became correspondingly more visible and as if demanding more and more insistently to be read and understood. In a twofold sense it weighed upon me; its physical weight was becoming a burden, its unsolved problem an oppression to my mind. How could I get rid of it?

I happen to have a good friend or brother to whom, in emergencies, I have learned to repair for guidance. I don't know who he is, but he is extremely reliable, and though not very communicative and apt to be slow, even sullen, in his replies, and then to answer me in riddles and indirect ways, he has never once misled me. Like my puzzling stone, he too, seems somehow to be identified with myself. A medical man or psychologist would say, of course, that he was my own subliminal or supraliminal consciousness. It matters not which. I only know that he is intimately associated with me, that he has an extraordinary intuitive knowledge of myself and my personal problems, and can settle for me matters which my brain and reason do not and cannot. I have come to call him, as I find Oriental psychologists do, the Teacher or Master in the heart.

To him I referred the matter and sought his guidance. For a long time there was no answer. I tried again and again, and eventually, as my anxiety increased, his aloofness and silence diminished somewhat. But, as usual, his responses were disconnected and enigmatic; mere hints rather than explanations; as though he wished the onus of finding what I sought to know to remain with myself and that I must worry out my own solution with a minimum of help. Piecing together his fragmentary replies, they may be translated and condensed thus:

"You cannot cast away your stone. It is yourself. You cannot evade it and its responsibilities by resigning or remaining absent from the Brotherhood in which you first acquired the stone. Once a Mason, always a Mason: in this world and in worlds to come. You stand solemnly and eternally covenanted, not only to yourself and your Brotherhood, but to the Eternal Sacred Law, to proceed with your Masonic work to the end. That Law does not permit you to stultify an obligation deliberately made upon It, even if made ignorantly. *Ignorantia Legis neminem excusat.* There may be that in you which was not ignorant, and that guided you to undertake that obligation. *Descendit e coelo.* Know thyself!"

Brooding upon this, I realised in my conscience the force and truth of the advice, and that the stone and myself were now more closely identified than ever. It was the inseparable symbol of myself. It was my "stone of destiny," like the Kaabah or sacred Cubical Stone of the Moslems at Mecca; like the Lia Fail in Westminster Abbey upon which Jacob is said to have slept and kings are crowned; both of them stones, moreover, about which the legend runs that they "descended from heaven."

Curious that that legend should now coincide with the inscription on my own stone! Yet what have Jacob and coronations to do with me, or I with them? "Know thyself!" Yes, indeed; for assuredly there may be unplumbed depths and unreached heights of me that my conscious mind does not yet know. But how to reach and investigate them? How is it possible to know more of myself than I do already? —that was my problem.

Thus, baffled, I put the matter by for a while, or rather tried to, but it would not permit itself long to be ignored. The stone continued so to grow in bulk and weight as to become well-nigh as unportable as its meaning grew increasingly intractable.

Ultimately, one day, in despair, I carried it out into a lonely moorland wilderness with the intention of finally grappling with its mystery and unraveling it once and for all, or of leaving it there—if I could. As I went I remembered Bunyan's Pilgrim, carrying on his back the intolerable pack which fell away of itself when he reached the top of a certain hill. I half hoped similar relief might befall myself, but did not expect it. I had again earnestly appealed to my inward monitorial friend for further succour; but this time he had not answered at all.

Weary in body, distraught in mind, I bore my burden, now grown to a weight I could barely carry and finally pitched it down among the ling and bracken of the heath, and in the evening dusk flung myself down to rest, and upon the stone—my stone of destiny—pillowed my head, and from exhaustion fell asleep.

II.

I slept, but my heart waked. Though asleep, I did not wholly lose consciousness, but retained a pleasurable feel of knowing I was asleep, that my fatigued body and brain were at rest, and myself, my released and quickened intellect, was free to act in independence of them. Oh, the rest and blissfulness of that conscious sleep!—paradoxical as it may sound.

Though I knew my tired head and harried brain rested upon the hard stone, that hardness presently seemed to be dissolving and the pillow to become one of the softest down, swathed in fine linen, most white, most cool, lavender-scented. Yes, and more; it became vibrant; intensely, healingly vibrant. Sweet scents exhaled from it; but also sound—oh!—gorgeous strains matching the delicate fragrance, welling sweetly, softly, from afar; the two in perfect concord; unisoned rather; odour melodious, incense musical!

Presently, in this intensifying joy, my eyes opened. It was no longer dusk. Soft golden light was everywhere, through which pulsed now and again, like summer lightning, throbs of rosy and other coloured rays of more than rainbow purity, whilst the ground about me, upon which I lay, was no longer the rough moorland, but fleecy down of most restful violet hue, as though one had passed through the dark-blue vault of the night-sky and lay upon the sunlit upper side of it.

I raised myself and looked round. Standing near me I saw one whom, instantly and instinctively, I recognised as my hitherto unseen friend and brother, the concealed interior monitor, to whom I had previously addressed my appeals for counsel. What a mighty, glorious being he was as he stood there, a dazzle of flame-like hair circling his fine head, his feet also winged with wreathing harmless fire; his person white-robed with a garment that seemed, not put on, but to grow from and be an integral part of him, and about his neck and loins the shimmering blue and gold clothing of—to my amazement—a Grand Lodge Officer. In one hand he bore a tall crystal wand like a deacon's, and his other arm held a golden thyrsos or caduceus.

We both smiled a recognition when our eyes met. I discerned that he was waiting there till I was sufficiently rested.

"Where are we?" I asked.

"In the Aula Latomorum!"

"Freemasons' Hall!"—my thought translated his words, and then as swiftly ran on by habit; "Great Queen Street, London, W.C.2. But surely not there!" And I saw that his mind read mine though I spoke not.

"No, not there. That is far below you now; far removed, yet not so much by distance as by difference of conscious state."

"Then where am I?"

"In the candidate's preparing-room of the Aula Latomorum; the Supreme Universal Lodge of all Builders in the Spirit; what you have heard of as The Grand Lodge Above."

I began to protest that I was unfitted for, and had no title to admission to, such a place, but he checked me, saying: "You have sought, asked, knocked, though you did not know it. That forms your title to admission. Your search for wisdom, your continued askings for light, did not pass unobserved by the Eye that watches here, that never slumbers nor sleeps. Your blind strivings after truth were heard as knocks upon our door, and for you that door will now open. You are being awaited within. Come, we will enter the Lodge!" And he placed a gentle but powerful arm around me.

I still hesitated, but the bracing vitality of his presence and touch counteracted my weakness and gave me tenseness and courage. Nevertheless, as we began to move away, I turned and looked back upon my sleeping body in the gloom at my feet, with its head couched upon the rude dark stone—the poor, poor rags of myself. From it, linking me with it, I saw issuing a slender silvery streak, a phosphorescent filament faintly visible against its violet background.

"That," said my guide, "is your cable-tow, by which you shall be restored later on to the blessing of your material comforts—if, indeed, comforts they be to you," he added with a laugh. "They are a blessing, nevertheless, for without them you could never have reached or entered here. Now come!"

"What is that glorious music?" I asked, as we passed up a great stairway, the steps of which his fire-winged feet scarcely touched. For its tones grew louder, richer, as we ascended, and its waves rolled out upon me like ocean billows.

"Pending your arrival, the Grand Organist is playing selections from the Music of the Spheres for the healing of your bruised spirit. The fragrant music your stone pillow echoed back to you just now was its overtones. This Lodge, the heavens, yes, and the earth beneath, are all built and held together by that music, though few of you in the world below have ears to hear it."

So we passed on.

III.

We reached the first landing of the vast Hall. It was quadrangular, and flanked at each side by a corridor by which one could perambulate the building. My guide conducted me along the four sides. "This," he told me, "is the floor upon which labour all Architects in the Spirit under the guidance of the Universal Great Architect. There are two higher floors; one for the Geometrician who issue the designs for the Architects to fabricate into shape; upon the other labour those still greater souls who are in the secret counsels of the Most High and dwell within His shadow."

We reached the portal of a central hall, the Lodgeroom of the great Apprentice Architects. Without it stood a great being bearing a sword that flashed every way, but observing my clothing and condition, he let it fall and asked in whose name I sought admission. And with a ringing voice, like a silver trumpet, my guide replied for me:

"In the name of the Son of the Carpenter, the Grand Carpenter of the Universe of worlds and men, by whom all things are made!"

And, as the great gates opened, from within, upon rolling waves of sound, welled forth the antiphon:

"Hallowed be that name to everlasting. His kingdom come, without as here within!"

So we entered.

I may not tell all that I saw or that occurred in that wondrous place, that great assembly. But this I will tell, that at one place I found myself before two interlaced triangles of lighted candles, three of which were lesser and three were greater lights, and at their centre, making seven, stood still another light, the greatest of them all and of brilliance so intolerable that I was constrained to fall upon my knees before the candlesticks and shield my eyes from their light with both my hands.

Thus kneeling, self-blinded, words were spoken to me that can never be repeated but that seemed to proceed from the central great candle. And presently I was asked if, voluntarily and of my own free will, I would enter into a great and solemn covenant with the Voice speaking from it, which covenant would not be formulated for me but, as a test of my sincerity and desire, must come as the spontaneous prompting of my own heart. And then, in my ignorance, simplicity, and blindness, but under my compelling joy at the wonders that even so far I had witnessed, I behaved as a child who has been shown some new thing that delights it and forthwith must needs run away to tell the tidings to its friends. And I exclaimed that thenceforward never would I conceal from anyone in the world the fullness of unimaginable splendours that lay so near it yet passed unperceived, but that on the contrary I would reveal them to all men and as far as possible make everyone know about them, and that of the light and bliss in which I stood bathed I would carry back so much into the dark world that no one should fail to see it, and that if needs be I would be content to be ground to dust and cast far and wide in sparklets of powdered light, if by so doing that light might be more widely diffused.

Whilst I still spoke, my hands were drawn from my eyes by another hand, which then took one of mine, and the Voice said, "Rise, brother with the child's heart; of such is this kingdom. Be thou my candlebearer, and let there be light!"

I was raised from my knees, but, rising, my mind seemed to rise in correspondence, to widen out enormously in its perceptions and conceptions as the result of something that thrilled into me from the touch of that hand. All I had before seen and understood seemed but as darkness to what I now saw, and I, who in my impulsive ignorance had said I would become the light of the world, now beheld the great central candle-light of the seven to be no longer a candle, but to be He who Himself bears that name.

"Domine, non sum dignus!" Again I would have fallen to my knees, but the Great Benignity, the Hierophant who walked among the candlesticks, restrained me and, for my support, drew a garment as it were of pure white lamb-skin from the substance of His own person, in which garment and flesh were one, and girded it about my loins as an apron, saying:

> *"This is My Body, given for you, that your body may be given for Me." And again waves of coloured sound poured over me from choired voices singing, "Ecce Agnus Dei, qui tollit peccata mundi!"*

And a great strength passed into me, so that all weakness fled and I stood erect before Him, an accepted Apprentice Mason of the Grand Lodge Above.

Then gathering into His hand the three lesser lights, they blended there into one another and became one light, one candle, which He placed in my hand, bidding me light my way with it until such time as I came to the measure of perfect man and the high stature of a Master Mason, and thereafter to go forth with it to them that sit in darkness and the shadow of death.

When, amid swelling music, my guide led me forth from that great hall, its vast assembly rose to salute their new brother, passing before them, bearing his lighted candle. And thereafter I was free to enter their abodes and workshops where I was shown the work and the methods of those who are indeed the constructive builders and carpenters of everything in the world of manifested form, from the fabrication of a solar system to that of the bodily organisms of all that inhabits it, from the building of a planet to the manufacture of the simplest mechanism of human invention; for what is such an "invention" but a discovery, a finding out, and "coming upon" by the human mind of something of which the pattern already exists upon an, at present, concealed ultra-human level?

Here were visible and exposed the secrets and mysteries in regard to all created forms and physical phenomena. Here the forces constituting natural law were controlled and regulated; here continents, oceans, and waterways were planned, and human racial distribution pre-arranged. In this department worked those who devised the constitution of states, kingdoms, and polities for the lower world; in that, those who compiled tables and codes of law for social use and government, plans of ethical systems, religious, ceremonial, and sacramental forms for human use and educating human understanding in celestial truths. And among these latter were to be seen the originals of the great systems of ritual and symbolism devised to train the human eye and imagination to the perception of spiritual principles to which otherwise they would remain blind—such as those of the Hebrew and the older Christian Churches, the ancient schools of the Mysteries, and also modern Freemasonry, the source of which, so nebulous and uncertain to terrestrial research, here becomes crystal-clear.

For all such institutions exist in the outer world, not from chance compilation or unaided human ingenuity, but because they are "patterns of heavenly things," physicalised reflections of pre-existing fabrications by Architects and Workmen labouring upon a loftier and more enlightened plane of being than that of the flesh, a plane from which they become inspirationally transmitted to the minds of those below or to which some such minds are able consciously to mount and receive direct instruction; as did the Hebrew Initiate, Moses, when enjoined to frame the religio-political system of his people and in doing so to "see that he did all things in accordance with the pattern shown him in the Mount."

For in this celestial "Mount" are made all the patterns or models of whatever is good, useful, and worthy in the terrestrial "valley" below, where nothing is really made, but merely copied and reproduced. From here the prophet, the poet, the artist, the musical genius, the inventor, wittingly or unwittingly draw all the conceptions that become the heritage of man and help on his racial career, but that at the same time convey to him an illusory sense of self-generated progress and a belief in his own cleverness.

Thus was I made free of the great brotherhood of the Supernal Architects, working without haste, without rest, in the world of light. Yet my thought reverted to the builders in the dark world below, where, if they can build nothing other than their own good or evil destiny,

All are architects of Fate,
Working in the walls of Time,—
Broken stairways—where the feet
Stumble, as they seek to climb.

But my flame-shod guide beckoned me, and, remembering that before I could carry light into that tenebrous realm I must go on to the measure of perfect man, I followed him.

IV.

He led me forth and up a great winding stairway to the next landing of the vast Hall, to the Lodge of the Geometricians, and twice was I conducted around its galleries as though the better to adjust myself to that loftier plane of being. Presently, after due preparation and carrying my candle as passport, I was granted admission to its central chamber. And there the Hierophant, whom previously I had met as the Great Architect, now manifested to me in a different and higher guise, as the Grand Geometer.

Now He stood in the midst of a triangle of three great lights, and presently these, too, He gathered into His hand where they blended into one which He placed in my other hand, so that now I stood bearing a pair of candles, one a lesser light that shone but as the moon, and one a greater that blazed as the sun shining in his strength. And I was made to know that I should need both these lights upon the path that still lay before me.

And when the greater light was placed in my hand, my previous illumination seemed but as moonlight in comparison with that which now came to me, and what had up to that moment seemed to me vacuous space I now perceived to be thronged with an innumerable concourse of great beings greeting me into their company, each holding a hand high aloft and chanting over me in chorus:

"Sun, stand thou still in his heights; and moon, stand thou still in his valleys, until all his enemies be overcome in the great day of his perfecting!"

And the Great Initiator placed his hand within his own bosom and drew forth a chalice of red wine and, holding it forth to me, said: "This is My life-blood, given for you that yours may be made Mine. Take, drink!"

And I drank, and gave thanks, and was dismissed to pursue my way.

Hitherto I had perceived as it were with but outward sensible eyes, and had gazed upon but the outward forms and surfaces of what I saw. Now, at this draught of new wine, my inward intellectual eyes became opened too, penetrating beyond all forms, beholding their animating essence; seeing not separate existences and objects, but all life, all objects, in inseparable unity. Here was what Socrates so rapturously tells of in Plato's *Phaedrus*—and I knew that, to tell it, he too must have been called to this same place and been granted this same measure of initiation—that it is a region of which no earthly bard has ever yet sung or ever will sing in worthy strains, one where for the first time one comes to know real existence, colourless, formless, intangible, visible only by the topmost crest of the human mind, the noetic intelligence that sits at the helm of the soul and that alone can share communion with Divine Mind; that cognises the essential substantiality, as distinct from the accidental properties and attributes of things; no longer thinking of what is just, strong, beautiful, righteous, and so on, or of any contrasted relationships, but directly beholding Wisdom, Strength, Beauty, Goodness, in their absoluteness and in their real essential being.

Here, too, I saw the prototypal "ideas" lying behind the patterns and models shown to me in the workshops of the Architects below, and realised the geometrical and mathematical principles upon which those fabrications were based, and how every created thing is made by measure, number, and weight, as the Initiates of the Pythagorean School made known to men in the outer world, so that of a verity I saw that even the hairs of our head are numbered—not in the sense of being counted, but of existing conformably with mathematical necessity—and that not a sparrow falls to the ground apart from that necessity or without recording a fact of, and a change in, the Universal Consciousness.

For on this plane where, as Plato declared, "God geometrises," the Divine Ideas are assimilated by the Geometricians who there labour continually, and thence are transmitted to the Lodge of the Architects below for expression in concrete form. And long would I have lingered here absorbing these inexhaustible wonders, but again I remembered my pledge and my directions, and besought my guide to lead me onwards.

V.

But how shall I relate what next befell me? How voice that which is of the Silence? I had been already led through two new supernal planes of being, one devoted to the building of form, the other to formless self-subsisting principles and abstractions—the ethereal embryos conceived by the Geometers, to which it was the function of the Architects to provide objective embodiment. Now I was to pass to a height surpassing, transcending, both these; one where there existed neither the formal nor the formless, but as it were a primal Chaos from which both had issued and into which both were resolvable; a Matrix beyond thought, beyond imagination, beyond description; and whilst within me was a great urge of my spirit to go further forward and enter it, there yet fell upon me for the first time in that realm of bliss and peace, of colour and sound, of bodily strength and mental clarity, an apprehension that the limits both of my endurance and conscious possibility had been reached, that I could neither know nor bear more than I already knew and bore, and that to attempt to advance farther was presumption and foolishness destined to end in failure and disaster.

"Let strength be perfected out of weakness!" said my guide, reading my thought; "Come, let us go up the Hill of the Lord!" Once more his strong arm was around me, and holding my lesser and greater candles, my moon-light and my sun-light, in either hand, I ascended with him towards the third and topmost storey of the great Aula.

As we mounted, the path became less and less clear; as a highway, leading into open country, terminates in a mere track which finally disappears entirely. And despite the brilliance of the two lights I carried, a twilight seemed to be descending upon us that deepened more and more around us as we rose, until, on reaching a level landing, nothing about me remained visible, or only the most shadowy outlines of what was immediately adjacent.

Although within a building, the building itself no longer appeared as such, but to have become dissolved into something different, indefinable, indescribable—mere "place," to which no epithet or attribute can be attached; no corridors, no departmental chambers, such as I had found on the floors below; no sign of life or activity, but utter desertedness and dereliction, and yet, somehow, a sense that life abounded there upon all sides. Yet thrice was I escorted around what, had it been a visible quadrangle, would have been its four sides, as though to habituate myself to these new conditions.

Deep silence and solitude ruled up here in this dark polar region of the human mind, and here the great music that flooded the lower altitudes failed, it seemed, to reach, as though the air was too rarefied for it longer to be audible or my hearing too gross to respond to it. At times we seemed to be in a dense forest, to be passing beneath the dusky boughs of giant cedars of Lebanon and other mighty growths. At length I enquired of my guide what this place was.

"This," he answered, "is the House of the Sons of the Widow"; and then for the first time a mighty emotion swept through and shook even his strong frame, as he murmured, rather to himself than for my hearing, the words, "Sub umbra alarum Tuarum, Jeheschuah!" as though he too longed to dwell for ever in that place of deep shadow.

And my thought turned to the remembrance of a teaching concerning the bereft Divine Wisdom, the Sophia, the Bride widowed through the ages of Her errant sons until, reverting from the ways of foolishness, they voluntarily return to sonship and She becomes justified of Her children.

We halted, at length, at a place at which, in the gloom, showed the outline of two pillars standing side by side, separated only widely enough for one man to pass between. From here, my guide told me, I must proceed alone, since he could accompany me no farther; but he would prepare me for my entry into that final sanctuary and would wait without until I rejoined him.

Then he began upon me a great and solemn ritual of preparation.

He took from my one hand the great solar light it carried, and placed the candle in a sconce at the head of one of the pillars in front of me;

and then took from my other hand the lesser lunar light and set its candle in a similar sconce at the head of the other pillar; repeating, the while, with intense earnestness the words: "Thou, sun, stand still in his heights; and thou, moon, stand still in his valleys, till his enemies be overcome in the great day of his perfecting!"

He divested me of all my garments, save only the Apron with which the Great Hierophant had invested me in the Lodge below. For my other garments, ethereal though they were, were as the outgrowth of my own nature, the condensed exhalations of my own thought and desire, now become objective and clinging to me as raiment; and of these I must needs stand denuded if spirit is to meet Spirit and, out of my flesh, I am to see God. But my Apron no other hand could take from me than that which gave it, and it remained around my loins to be my strength and support in that day of my perfecting.

Then, from an overhanging tree, he plucked a feathery spray of acacia-leaf and, after weaving it into a fillet, placed it around my head, saying as he did so: "Thou art crowned in the halls of death that hereafter thou may'st wear a Crown of Life that fadeth not away."

Further, he took the golden caduceus or thyrsos he had always carried, and, standing before me, raised it aloft, as a crucifix is held before the eyes of the dying, and exclaimed:

> *"Receive this Golden Bough, thou branchlet of the eternal Life-Tree, and think upon it when thou hangest upon that Tree, that thou may'st become for ever grafted thereinto, and thy leaves and fruit thenceforth be for the healing of the nations!"*

And by a gold cord he placed it upon me, so that it hung suspended against my flesh as a pectoral cross.

Then, with his forefinger, he sealed me at five points with the sign of the cross; upon my brow, upon my throat, upon my heart, upon the palms of both my hands, and upon both feet. And after each sealing with the cross-sign, he sealed me again at the same points with a peace-kiss, as though with his lips to heal wounds which his finger had made; and he said: "Thou art wounded in love in the house of thy friends that by love thou may'st be made whole. These be thy five points of perpetual fellowship with Love Immortal; that in love thou may'st think, may'st speak, may'st feel, may'st act, may'st walk, when thou goest forth among the sons of men."

And having thus done, he turned from me and passed to the twin pillars standing in front of me. There, kneeling between them and with a hand laid upon each, as though to unite them in himself, his voice pealed forth into the distance beyond: "In strength have I striven to establish this son of Thy House, that he may stand firm and steadfast in the great day of his at-one-ment with Thee, Most High!"

Finally, he rose, and taking his rod or wand, passed behind me, so that I saw him no more. But I felt his presence, and that from it was now issuing an energy that was directing, compelling—even propelling me forward; an energy at once of will and of prayer, of will that absorbed and gave direction and intensity to my own will, of prayer that shielded me from all evil as that will urged me on into the valley of the shadow of death; an energy, silent, yet of such gathering intensity that, like a great sea-wave rising to the breaking-point, I knew it must at last break into sound, and that that sound would carry me forward with it.

Presently it broke. It broke upon my hearing, upon my whole being, as one great clear word of power, the vibrancy of which swept me onward. What that word was cannot be related, nor did I then understand it. But as it translated itself at that moment to my understanding, it was the heart-speech of my directing guide saying:

"Father, into Thy hands I commend his spirit, which is also my spirit!"

And, impelled by that word of power, I passed forward along the straight and narrow way between the lighted pillars, into the gloom beyond.

VI.

The ground beneath my feet rose steeply. I felt myself to be ascending a hill in that dusk and stillness, though for some distance a state of twilight remained to me; for memories and remnants of the light that had previously suffused me lingered, and the great twin candles I had borne to this point still cast helpful beams from the pillar-tops for a little way. But the farther I traversed, the higher I mounted, their illumination diminished, until at length twilight melted into utter dark. I remembered and comforted myself with a great word: "The sun shall no more be thy light by day, neither the moon by night; but the Spirit shall be to thee an everlasting light, and thy God thy glory; and the days of thy travail shall be ended." I knew what others have recorded of passing into the Divine Gloom, the agnosia of the human spirit, where vision fails and thought is paralysed, and where that zero-point of consciousness must be touched where nothing is known to be, neither one's self, nor even God; and I knew, and again tried to comfort myself with the reflection, that even this appalling darkness was in fact light, albeit light of intensity so unthinkable as, to eyes not yet opened and inured to it, to appear as darkness. But I had yet to learn that even such comforts as thought and memory provided were staffs that must fail me of support.

In that darkness I now was. In the rarefied atmosphere of the mount I was ascending, my being took on an ever-increasing hyper-sensitiveness, until I felt my flesh, even the tenuous ethereal flesh of my present body, dissolving away, leaving me as but a quivering structure of exposed, unprotected nerves. The feathery fillet of acacia-leaf upon my forehead felt now as a heavy crown of coarse thorns clamped upon my brow, into which the tender, delicate frond-points pressed like steel spikes. The light gold thyrsos suspended from my neck became as a heavy cross, beneath the intolerable weight of which, with bleeding feet and hands, I toiled and staggered upwardly. I paused awhile to rest and with my forefinger swept, from time to time, the increasing blood and sweat from my brow, and in my agony cried aloud:

"Come to my help, ye Sons of the Widow! for I, too, am the Widow's son."

But no answer, no help came; yet the oftener I lingered, the more I faltered, the more conscious I became of the propelling urge of that mighty word of power by which my guide had sped, and still was speeding, me upon my willing quest; and I knew that from a distance—how far, how short, mattered not—he still was watching, directing me; that his rod and staff controlled and safeguarded me.

In the ocean-depths there is a point at which a sinking ship can sink no farther, the pressure upon it from above and the resistance from below so counteracting each other that it remains suspended and undergoes disintegration by the dual forces grinding upon it. In the ocean-depths of Universal Spirit there is a corresponding point of equilibrium, where the human soul, seeking to pass from terrestrial attraction to spiritual freedom, becomes caught and ground between similar upper and nether millstones. That point is the mystical Gethsemane, literally "the place of the wine and oil press," for there the soul reaches the equator-line where the opposing attractive forces of soul and spirit meet, and where the former experiences to its joints and marrow a sundering of its parts. There—as wheat is winnowed from corn-stalk and chaff, as wine and oil are distilled from crushed fruit—the soul's spirit, its sublimated, refined, immortal essence, is dissected from the sheath in which it has matured, is separated and rendered free to commence a new independent life of its own, whilst that sheath itself is left to perish.

That Gethsemane I had now reached. My soul consciously knew the growing division of its kingdoms, "one dead; one powerless to be born," and again and again cried in its anguish for help from the Widow's Sons, yet without avail; and at last resigned itself to the compelling word and will that it felt still to urge it forward, higher.

Beyond Gethsemane rises the Hill Calvary—Kranion or Calvaria, the bald headland, the rocky summit, of no earthly situation, and known to none save the naked human spirit which ascends to it, there to be lifted up high above all terrene ground and magnetic attraction, and pass to birth and apotheosis in the free uncontaminated air of Spirit Absolute.

Reaching that summit, my limbs failing under me, one thing alone saved me from complete collapse, the strength and support that came, that seemed newly and increasingly generated, from the Apron girt about my loins. And then, from that central peak, my feet involuntarily losing touch with the supporting ground beneath, I felt myself lifted up above the earth.

No hand there was that touched or raised me. As one whose limbs become distended, rigid, under the infusion of a strong electric current, so now the charge of the Creator Spiritus passed into me, forcing my frame into vertical erectness and rigidity, extending my arms horizontally, making taut and tense under its strain every fibre of my being. In mid-air, my head held toward heights I could not reach, my feet down-pointing to the earth they no longer touched, my arms wide-flung transversely into void space, I hung suspended upon that invisible impalpable Life-Tree; myself a cross; myself the crucified upon that cross.

For three hours of darkness—hours not of human time, but of that Spirit to which a day is as a thousand years—I hung upon that cross, that Stauros upon which from the foundation of the world Life Creative hangs self-immolated, that worlds may be built upon its pattern and Life Created be fashioned at last into its image.

As there I hung, my thorny crown stabbed its spikes more deeply, more insistently, into my brow, my hands unable longer to move and wipe away the blood and sweat. Yet a joy began subtly to tincture and relieve that pain, as I realised that, under the same strain that my own being knew, the life-sap of the fragile acacia-sprig was also being quickened, was pulsing fast, striving to break to golden bloom; and that, when that bloom broke, light would break for me also and my crown of thorns become a crown of life.

The gold thyrsos upon my breast burned itself into me, until its vertical shaft felt one with my own spinal column, from the base of which the uprising intertwined serpents were as dual streams of a new, larger, richer vitality surging upward through my nerves towards my head, where I knew that—like the dual parts of an electric current that, meeting, flash into light—they would eventually combine and flame to conscious wings, wide-spreading as those of its symbol, far-reaching as my own wide-flung arms.

And my Craftsman's Apron, at once a weight and a support to my straining loins, felt growing into me, to be becoming of my very flesh and substance. I knew now why, traditionally depicted as a loin-cloth, this garment alone was worn upon the Cross by the "King of the Jews," the Supreme Chief of all Initiates, and why all the great painters of the Crucifixion scene had been moved, intentionally or inspirationally, so to depict it and not otherwise—not from any paltry motive of delicacy or prudery, but to point, for those who can understand, the truth that the secret, basic, generative energies procreating the Universe and regenerating human souls must ever remain beyond the ken of all but the Divine Eye.

As with the dying, my consciousness fluctuated from a negative to a preternaturally acute and vivid stage, ranging at times to a wild yet orderly delirium; yet from both these extremes I knew the necessity of holding my will oriented and fixed upon its desired goal. At times it became cosmically comprehensive; at times it would focus upon trivialities and irrelevances. At one moment it would enlarge till, for the little leaf-crown on my head, I wore vast star-belts as a diadem; great constellations filled no more space than the palms of my hands and swam around my person as but dancing fire-flies; my trunk and legs reached down through abysmal leagues of space to the dust-speck of earth below my feet.

At another the heavens would open and expose their joyous contents—a lure and temptation promptly to be rejected as often as it recurred; for, though I thirsted, it was for richer wine than they could give to drink. Now each hair of my head seemed a filament and conduit linking me with angel-hosts and reservoirs of supernatural intellectuality, and now the nerves of my feet ramified into the finest rootlets and tentacles through which I became aware of the activities of nature and of life in the earth below and the minutest details of personal human interest. I heard the crackle of growing grass, the twitter of birds, the cries and laughter of children, equally clearly with the throb of engines, the activities of industry, the clash of armies. No grain of sand, or speck of dust, or cell of tissue, but disclosed its constitution, its potencies, its purpose, its destiny; all straining, striving, building, unbuilding, rebuilding; each sealed with and bearing, wittingly or not, its little cross in one universal effort to become raised to that final cross of transformation upon which I now hung, and thence to pass on to unimagined heights and destinies beyond.

Even my Brother builders in the symbolic Craft—for of them too I became vividly aware in their little dark circumscribed world below—there they were in their Lodges, reeling off memorised rituals, correcting one another at a wrong or misplaced word supposed to affect the efficacy of their work; and some were in banquet halls, and, amid the pop of champagne corks, I heard them toasting one another, extolling the virtues of Masonry, shouting, "Prosper the Art!" and singing of the "mystic tie" that more truly than they know binds all together and advances the building of a Temple conceived of as yet by but few of them.

Darkness, over-intensified, at last of itself becomes as it were a pleasurable light; pain, when ability to feel it is exhausted, a measure of joy; for these opposites are but relative, the poles of a single fact; differing reactions to enforced environment. But neither such light nor such joy was that I longed for. They belonged to feeling, to desire, to thought; not to that deeper factor, the Spirit, which transcends them all, and to which I strove to keep my will one-pointed. But at length feeling died in me; I knew neither pain nor joy. Then desire died; what happened further to me, good or ill, I cared not. Lastly, thought died also; its flickerings and veil-wisps gradually falling away, till stark blankness only remained. Nothing of me still was, save the labouring spirit that strove to be born but could not. It was the zero-point of negative consciousness, the moment of the apparently everlasting NO; where nothing is, and God is not. *Eloi, Eloi! Lama Sabachthani!*

VII.

I revived, yet not I, at length, in light; a new indescribable light, so much more than light because it is also life; life beyond the category of personality; life in the Universal Spirit of light;

> *light rare, untellable, lighting the very light;*
> *Beyond all words, descriptions, languages!*
> *The sprig of acacia had at last burst to golden flower upon my head.*

No tongue may or can speak, nor pen write, of that "sleep in light" as the Egyptian records call it, that conscious rest of the soul in God, that identic union between finite object and infinite Subject, that nirvanic absorption of the spirit's still flame within the Fire of Divine Mind, of the human water-drop in the ocean of that Immaculate Illimitable which is Nothing, but without which nothing is—that impersonal yet self-consciousness which becomes possible only when every activity of sense and emotion has been quelled, every energy of the restless mind stilled, all thought obliterated; and the babe-soul rests upon the naked bosom of that Spirit of which it has been well written:

I am the Silence which is more than Sound.
If therewithin thou lose thee, thou art found!
The Nameless, Shoreless Ocean, which is I,
Thou canst not breathe, but in its bosom drowned!

What previously had seemed utter darkness was now a sea of softest light thronged with life; living light, lighted life. About me thronged the uncountable Sons of the Widow, God's Master Masons, the Lords of Wisdom and sharers of the secret counsels of the Most High, whose inspirations, transmitted to the Geometers and Architects upon the planes below, dictated the plans upon which worlds are built, maintained, dissolved, and yet are but as foam upon the rising and falling waves on the surface of the Universal Life-stream.

And these great Sons, close present to me through my long agony, but invisible till a deeper sight was born in me that could share their intenser light, took me down from my cross; but of the secrets and mysteries that thereupon became known to me I do not here speak, nor of the still higher grades of Initiation that lie beyond that I now testify to. When eventually I left them, I passed through their ranks, as I had passed through them upon my arrival when to my unperfected eyes they had appeared as a vast forest of Libanus cedars under whose swarth boughs I had walked; for were they not as great trees crowning the mountain-top of the world, diffusing over it from their spread branches the dark actinic rays of a Wisdom not yet recognised by men's imperfect vision as light?

I rejoined my former brother and guide at the point where I had left him, between the pillars. Upon seeing me he at once greeted me with a familiar sign in sympathy with my now vanished sufferings, and, kneeling, at the next moment shielded his eyes with his hand as my presence dazzled him with the light it now radiated. Then he rose, and bowing, drew near me and offered me his hand as a Brother of the Third Degree in that Grand Lodge, and as we embraced he exclaimed:

> *"The Master is risen!"*
> *And I to him responded: "He is risen indeed!"*

And we passed back down the grand stairway, up which he had previously brought me, now no longer deserted, but thronged with Geometricians and Architects come forth to hail their new Brother, now journeying back as a light-bearer into the outer dark world. And, upon rolling organ-music once more, came the chanted words: "*To him that hath overcome is given a crown of life!*" and again, "*To him that hath endured to the end is given a white stone!*"

At length we reached the place where, in the gloom, still lay my sleeping body, couched upon a stone. But peering down upon them, the stone was no longer a dark crude mass. It was a crystal cubical stone, upon the top of which rested three cornucopias, bearing corn, and wine, and oil; and against this, my stone of destiny, reposed my head, already faintly aureoled with light. My coronation was complete.

I knew that henceforth both my guide and my stone would be perfectly identified with me and that the contents of the cornucopias were the emblems of my perpetual future nourishment and represented the harvest I had garnered in each of the Three Degrees I had just taken: Bread of Life from the first, Wine of Bliss and Illumination from the second, Oil of Wisdom from the third. Here was the realisation of the familiar words, hitherto but fanciful poetic imagery: "*Thou preparest a table before me in the presence of mine enemies; Thou anointest my head with oil; my cup runneth over!*"Again my good Brother gripped me as a Master Mason. We drew together in an embrace of fellowship so fervent that we seemed to coalesce beyond the possibility of further separateness. "A measure of corn for a penny," he said to me, "and see thou hurt not the oil and the wine." And I understood his hint to be prudent in my use of them.

> *"Ave, Frater, atque Vale!" were his last spoken words to me.*
> *And mine to him were: "Vale, Frater, atque Ave!"*

When I looked about me with the eyes of my flesh I was alone. Sunrise was breaking over the barren heath.

REFLECTION: ILLUMINATION UNBOUND

ASCENDING TO THE GREAT ARCHITECT

The journey into expanded consciousness in *The Masonic Initiation* begins with a profound scriptural reference from Luke 11:34-35, where the single eye emerges as a symbol of undivided vision and inner illumination. In these words—"The light of the body is the eye: therefore, when thine eye is single, thy whole body also is full of light"—the eye signifies more than sight; it becomes a window into the soul's unity, guiding initiates toward a wholeness of heart and mind that illuminates the path to higher wisdom. For Wilmshurst, this single eye reflects the Masonic ideal of inner harmony, suggesting that only through an unwavering, unified vision can one begin to access the deeper truths of existence.

This metaphor of singular vision evokes a state of internal clarity—a focused alignment that draws the seeker into realms of truth beyond intellectual understanding. It is not merely a call to acquire knowledge but an invitation to awaken a light within the Mason's consciousness, which, once kindled, permeates their entire being. In this state of unity, as the "eye" becomes single, the separation between inner and outer worlds dissolves, and the initiate enters what the Craft terms "fullness of light."

To further enrich this foundation, the *Bhagavad Gita* offers a poetic perspective on initiation as "royal lore," a sacred path that purifies and transforms the soul. Here, initiation is depicted as an alchemical process, a gradual cleansing that leads the soul through successive stages of enlightenment, calling the initiate into the "Temple of Wisdom". Wilmshurst's invocation of this sacred lore reflects the Masonic path's essence: a journey of personal transformation that transcends the mere accumulation of knowledge, reaching into the innermost sanctum of the soul.

From an esoteric viewpoint, initiation represents an awakening to new dimensions of consciousness, a shift that extends beyond doctrine or belief into direct experiential understanding. The single eye becomes the lens through which universal truths are perceived, allowing the initiate to see the hidden unity that underlies all things. In this realm of unity, the insights of quantum physics offer intriguing parallels. In *Wholeness and the Implicate Order*, David Bohm describes the universe as a holographic entity where each part reflects and contains the whole. This vision of interconnectedness aligns with the Masonic journey, suggesting that as the initiate's "eye" turns inward, they perceive inner light and the web of unity connecting seen and unseen worlds.

Thus, the Masonic path invites alignment with this cosmic harmony. Through the single eye, the initiate steps toward a mystery as vast as the universe itself, where each revelation is not simply knowledge to gain but wisdom to embody—wisdom that illuminates the path and transforms the seeker.

EXPANDING CONSCIOUSNESS THROUGH INITIATION

For Wilmshurst, initiation is more than ritual; it is a transformative journey touching the soul, guiding the initiate toward an expanded state of awareness. This expansion can be likened to what psychologist Abraham Maslow described as "peak experiences"—moments of profound unity, insight, and connection with something greater than oneself. These moments transcend the limitations of ordinary perception, offering clarity and illumination that alter one's understanding of life and reality at a fundamental level. In the Masonic journey, initiation becomes a gateway to transcendent states, broadening the mind and awakening the heart to a new consciousness.

Maslow's concept of peak experiences resonates with Masonic initiation in that both invite the individual to encounter a reality that feels boundless and interconnected. These experiences echo the transformative states achieved through transcendental meditation and Kriya yoga, where practitioners move beyond the mental to a profound stillness. In these meditative practices, practitioners often report feeling a oneness with all things, a timeless awareness mirroring the Masonic principle of unity. Like Masonic initiation, these practices are not endpoints but doorways into an ever-deepening journey of self-discovery and connection with the divine.

Wilmshurst's vision of life as a "Temple of Wisdom" extends this concept, suggesting that all of existence is an initiation. In this vast sanctuary, every experience becomes an invitation to enlightenment. For the initiate, the world is a sacred space, mirroring the wisdom of Solomon's Temple, where each moment and encounter can reveal divine truths. Just as the stones of Solomon's Temple were selected and placed with purpose, so too are life's experiences arranged, guiding the initiate toward inner refinement and spiritual growth. This perspective challenges the modern Mason: does today's world, with its myriad of diversions, obscure this sacred lens, or can the initiate still find wisdom woven into daily life?

Quantum theory further enriches this understanding, offering insights that parallel the mystical experiences found in initiation. Quantum physics, particularly within consciousness studies, suggests that observation influences the observed—a principle that blurs the lines between perceiver and perceived. Fritjof Capra, in *The Tao of Physics*, draws a connection between these scientific insights and mystical experiences, proposing that the fundamental nature of reality might be accessible through both science and spirituality. This idea of interconnectedness resonates with Masonic teachings, inviting initiates to see their journey not merely as a personal endeavour but as an engagement with the universe—a step toward unity with the whole.

Through initiation, the Mason is encouraged to view each experience openly, look beyond the mundane, and see the eternal truths underlying all things. This is the essence of initiation: a journey that invites the initiate to transcend the self, expand awareness beyond ordinary boundaries, and see the world as a temple of hidden mysteries waiting to be unveiled.

THE FOURFOLD CONSCIOUSNESS IN NATURE'S KINGDOMS

In *The Masonic Initiation*, Wilmshurst presents nature as a hierarchy of consciousness—a ladder of awakening that ascends from the stillness of the mineral kingdom through the growth of plants and the sentience of animals, culminating in human awareness. This "fourfold consciousness" embodies an unfolding journey, where each stage builds upon the previous, mirroring the initiate's ascent toward enlightenment. As Wilmshurst suggests, humanity is not separate from these kingdoms but integrates their essence, embodying a synthesis of all creation's consciousness and carrying the potential for unity within.

Ancient philosophies echo this vision, suggesting that every aspect of creation, from stone to star, contains a divine spark of consciousness. In the *Timaeus*, Plato describes the world as a "living being endowed with a soul," an entity with mind and purpose, underscoring the Masonic reverence for nature as a mirror of universal truths. This idea of progression through nature's kingdoms, with humanity serving as a bridge between earth and the divine, suggests that human consciousness is not merely self-contained but is part of a larger spiritual ascent. In this view, each form of life—from mineral foundation to human potential—contributes to the totality of existence, emphasising humanity's role as an individual and universal link.

Masonic teachings thus invite initiates to consider themselves not just as individuals but as stewards of a shared consciousness, bearers of light that extends throughout creation. Each kingdom contributes essential qualities: the mineral with stability, the plant with growth, the animal with awareness, and humanity with synthesis and insight. This interconnectedness calls the Mason to honour their role within this continuum, understanding their consciousness as part of a broader ascent and embracing a vision of universal brotherhood that links all life.

Modern science offers a complementary perspective, particularly quantum biology and Schrödinger's work. Schrödinger proposed that life exists as a continuum of consciousness across forms, an unbroken field transcending the individual, animating every fragment of existence. This view enriches the Masonic ideal of universal brotherhood, suggesting that humanity's consciousness reflects a larger cosmic awareness, a unified intelligence that permeates all life.

For today's Masons, this understanding renews an awareness of the sacredness of all life. As they journey toward enlightenment, they are reminded that their path is deeply woven with the natural world and all living things. By embracing this unity, Masons transcend individual identity, becoming custodians of life's spiritual ascent and honouring their connection to creation and the divine intelligence animating every stone, leaf, and creature.

UNITY OF LIFE AND SELF-REALISATION

On the Masonic path, life is viewed not as isolated experiences but as a continuum, a flow of consciousness that bridges individual and collective existence. For Wilmshurst, self-realisation arises not in solitude but through understanding life's unity—a fundamental connection that underpins the Masonic journey. Each degree within the Craft offers a profound opportunity for the initiate to glimpse the self as part of a larger whole, presenting a step-by-step progression toward aligning with the cosmic rhythm that flows through all things. In this journey, self-realisation becomes less about discovering oneself as a separate entity and more about uncovering one's place within the greater reality. This interconnectedness deepens the Masonic experience, transforming the rites and teachings into a living journey toward the unity that underlies all creation.

The progression through the Masonic degrees mirrors stages of spiritual evolution, each representing a step upward on the ladder of awareness. As the initiate ascends, they see their journey not as an individual quest but as a path toward unity with all life. This concept resonates deeply with Kabbalistic teachings, particularly the "Ladder of Ascent," where the soul ascends from material entanglements toward spiritual union with the divine. Both traditions go beyond the accumulation of intellectual knowledge, aiming instead for transformation—an awakening to the inherent oneness of life, where the self and the universe merge as a single expression of the divine essence. In both Kabbalah and Masonry, this ladder is more than a metaphor; it is a map of consciousness, a guide for those who seek to transcend ego and enter into the vast unity that connects all beings.

In contemporary society, with its emphasis on separation and individualism, Wilmshurst's vision of unity offers a profound counterpoint. He urges initiates to remember that each life forms part of a larger symphony, a harmonious interplay in which the unity of life transcends the fragmentation often seen in the world today. Through Freemasonry, the initiate learns that true self-realisation is not merely about developing the self but about dissolving personal boundaries, embracing interconnectedness, and awakening to the universal truth that supports all existence. This understanding of unity challenges Masons to go beyond societal expectations and, instead, to cultivate a sense of oneness that respects the divinity within all life. It is a call to view every interaction and every moment as a step toward that unifying principle which echoes throughout the Masonic journey.

David Bohm's insights profoundly deepen the Masonic view of interconnectedness and unity. In *Wholeness and the Implicate Order*, Bohm proposes that reality, at its most fundamental level, exists as an indivisible whole, a seamless unity from which all diversity arises. He argues that the perception of separateness—our tendency to see individuals, objects, and events as isolated entities—is an illusion rooted in a limited, fragmentary view of existence. Bohm's philosophy resonates deeply with Masonic ideals, suggesting that our ordinary experience of division and distinction veils the unity that connects all life. Through Bohm's lens, the initiation process can be understood as a journey of expanding awareness that dissolves the illusion of separation and reveals the interconnected fabric of existence. In this transformative view, initiation becomes more than a rite of passage; it becomes a spiritual alchemy that awakens the initiate to the universal consciousness permeating all things .

For the Mason, Bohm's notion of an "implicate order" presents a new way of understanding the Craft's symbolic journey. Each degree, each teaching, and each ritual within Freemasonry can be seen as a gradual unfolding of this implicate order—a revelation of the hidden unity that underpins all symbols, actions, and intentions. The Mason's journey transcends the limitations of ego-bound perspectives, offering a glimpse into a vast consciousness that interweaves the self with the universe. As the initiate progresses, they are invited to perceive beyond the confines of individual experience, beginning to sense their role as a thread within a cosmic tapestry. This awareness does not negate individuality but situates it within a broader, harmonious reality, where life and self become reflections of a single divine consciousness. In embracing Bohm's vision, the Masonic journey emerges as a path toward enlightenment. This path illuminates the divine harmony within all creation and calls each Mason to recognise their integral part within this unity.

Kabbalistic teachings provide further insight into this profound unity, presenting it not as an abstract or unreachable ideal but as a living, experiential truth. In *Innerspace,* Aryeh Kaplan explores the depths of Kabbalistic understanding, describing the soul's journey as a quest to reunify with the divine essence that sustains all of creation. For the Kabbalist, this unity is not an intellectual concept but a visceral reality that can be directly experienced as the ego dissolves, revealing the self as inseparable from the divine presence. Kabbalah teaches that all life emerges from and is sustained by a single, infinite source, an emanation of divine light that flows through every level of existence. This awareness invites the seeker to see beyond the boundaries of self, recognising that the apparent separation between individuals is merely a veil over an intrinsic unity.

For the Mason, Kaplan's Kabbalistic perspective opens a doorway to profound and humbling self-realisation. The journey to unity within Kabbalah is one of transcending the ego's illusions, releasing the attachments and desires that cloud true vision, and awakening to the interconnected nature of all beings. In this light, the Masonic path parallels the Kabbalistic quest for divine unity, offering each Mason the tools and teachings necessary to undertake a similar ascent toward self-realisation. This journey is not about acquiring knowledge in a conventional sense; rather, it is a gradual peeling away of illusion, a transformation that reveals the self as a microcosm of the greater whole. Through this process, the Mason understands that true wisdom is not something external to be attained but an inner alignment with the cosmic order, a harmonious resonance with the divine essence that animates all life. This unity calls the Mason to a life of humility and service as they realise that their actions and intentions ripple through the fabric of existence, influencing and shaping the spiritual ascent of all.

This journey calls the Mason beyond the self, inviting a vision where life is an intricate tapestry woven with purpose and beauty. Embracing this perspective, the initiate becomes a seeker of knowledge and a living embodiment of unity—a reflection of the Great Architect's design. This is the path of self-realisation as the Craft teaches: a journey leading not only to knowledge but to wisdom and ultimately to recognising that to know oneself is to know the whole.

INITIATION AS A TRANSITION AND DEATH OF THE OLD SELF

On the Masonic path to enlightenment, initiation is a journey of profound inner transformation. Each stage invites the initiate to release parts of their former self, creating space for a new awareness to take root. This journey is more than a progression through symbolic rites; it represents a shift in consciousness, a metamorphosis that gradually dissolves ego, limitations, and attachments to past identities. Here, death becomes a powerful metaphor—a symbolic shedding of the old self that clears the way for an awakening to higher consciousness. Wilmshurst emphasises that this "death" is not an end but a necessary threshold in the soul's evolution, where attachments and beliefs that once defined the initiate are surrendered, creating the possibility for a rebirth into a greater understanding of existence.

This transition finds vivid expression in Masonic ritual, especially in the third degree, where the initiate encounters an allegorical representation of mortality. This symbolic encounter with death is an initiation into the mysteries of self-transcendence, a ritual of dissolution where the ego and its attachments fall away, allowing space for the eternal principles of the Craft to take hold. Through this ritualistic death and rebirth, the Mason emerges renewed, free from the constraints of former perspectives, now guided by a deeper sense of purpose. Passing through this metaphorical death, the Mason symbolically lets go of all that no longer serves them, mirroring universal motifs across mystical traditions. From the alchemical concept of *solve et coagula* (dissolve and coagulate) to the Christian teaching of being "born again," this journey reflects a transformation of the false self to reveal the divine essence within.

This notion of symbolic death as a path to enlightenment remains a vital call for modern Freemasons, reminding them to continually re-evaluate and renew themselves. In today's world, initiation can be seen as a lifelong process of peeling away the ego's layers, each embodying beliefs, identities, or limitations that obscure one's truer self.

This process brings to mind Carl Jung's concept of individuation. This journey requires courage to confront and dissolve the shadow —the hidden or repressed parts of the psyche—toward an integrated whole. For Jung, achieving wholeness involves a profound metamorphosis that resonates with the Masonic call to step into a higher state of being beyond personal limitations.

In this light, Masonic initiation becomes a process that challenges the initiate to look inward, to confront their depths, and to relinquish the layers of self that obscure the soul's light. Each step toward wholeness reveals a new level of understanding, a rebirth into a greater awareness that spirals ever closer to unity and wisdom. This rebirth calls forth the potential within each Mason to rise renewed, each time closer to their essence and the oneness that binds all of life. As each layer of ego dissolves, the initiate draws nearer to inner clarity, a wholeness that is not fixed but unfolds over time in response to the mysteries encountered. This journey is not simply an entry into the mysteries of the Craft; it is a call to embrace transformation as a sacred act, a commitment to letting go of what no longer serves.

As the initiate surrenders the self, what emerges is not emptiness but a life filled with purpose, wisdom, and an abiding connection to the eternal. In this state, the Mason finds that the divine spark within is not a distant ideal but a living presence that calls them to embody love, truth, and light—a deeply personal and universally shared journey.

THE INEFFABLE NATURE OF INITIATIC EXPERIENCE

> *"The Tao that can be told is not the eternal Tao; the name that can be named is not the eternal name."* – Laozi

One of initiation's most profound and mysterious aspects is its ineffability—the quality of being beyond words, defying full expression. Wilmshurst emphasises that the consciousness awakened through initiation is difficult to describe, much like conveying the colours of a sunset to someone who has never seen the light. This transcendent experience, symbolised in Masonic teachings, resists ordinary speech, requiring symbols, allegories, and poetry to approach its essence. As initiates journey deeper into the mysteries, they encounter truths that words can only hint at, and they must surrender to an understanding that transcends intellectual knowing.

Wilmshurst's reliance on symbolic language resonates with mystical literature, where poetry and metaphor gesture toward the ineffable. The *Bhagavad Gita*, for instance, describes a divine vision as an overwhelming clarity that resists full articulation. Similarly, Dante's *Paradiso* portrays divine light as an experience that humbles language, unable to fully capture the splendour of paradise. This humility before the mysteries recalls John Keats's reflections in *Hyperion*, recognising that some truths can only be grasped through experience. These works suggest that there are realms of perception and consciousness that words can never contain, and this same mystical quality lies at the heart of the Masonic path.

For Masons today, poetry and metaphor remain invaluable for exploring consciousness and initiation. These literary forms act as bridges, allowing the initiate to move from intellectual comprehension into inner realisation. Just as poetry speaks to the unspoken depths of the heart, Masonic symbols beckon the initiate toward a truth that must be felt rather than dissected. As physicist Werner Heisenberg noted in *Physics and Philosophy*, even scientific theories often rely on metaphor to convey abstract realities that escape common understanding. Heisenberg's insight reflects a truth mirrored in Freemasonry—that symbols, whether in science or mysticism, are keys that unlock perception, revealing realms that reason alone cannot grasp.

This blending of mysticism, poetry, and science enriches the initiatic path, suggesting that the journey is one of continuous revelation, where each encounter brings the initiate closer to the ineffable. In moments of initiation, the Mason glimpses a truth that defies language; it is a truth that must be lived, a presence felt within the heart and soul. Symbols are not merely representations but living guides, whispers from the depths that urge the seeker deeper into the mystery.

As each new layer of understanding unfolds, the initiate moves closer to a consciousness that transcends the ordinary. In this space beyond intellect, the true language of initiation is silence, and the symbols are shadows of a reality beyond words. This silent, symbolic language continues to speak to those on the Masonic path, reminding them that the journey toward light is one of surrendering the intellect, embracing the heart, and ultimately stepping into the unknown with a spirit open to revelation.

In the quiet moments after initiation, when words fall away, the initiate may feel a sense of unity, a subtle merging with something vast and eternal. In this sacred silence, it is here that the mysteries whisper their deepest truths, truths that can only be known through experience. Each symbol encountered in the Lodge becomes a flicker of this hidden wisdom, a doorway into realms where light and shadow dance harmoniously. In these moments, the initiate feels not just as a seeker but as a part of the divine tapestry itself, woven into the very fabric of the universe.

Thus, initiation is more than a ritual or an ascent; it is an invitation to become attuned to the song of the cosmos, to hear the music beneath the silence. In each heartbeat and breath, the initiate feels the presence of the Great Architect, guiding them toward a life filled with meaning, purpose, and a love that binds all creation. As the Masonic path unfolds, it becomes clear that this journey is not a quest to acquire knowledge but to embody wisdom, to live as a vessel through which the light of understanding can shine. This is the heart of Freemasonry—a journey that leads not to an end but to an eternal beginning, where the light discovered within becomes a beacon for all who seek the path.

CONSCIOUSNESS EXPANSION: SCIENTIFIC AND PHILOSOPHICAL PERSPECTIVES

In exploring the nature of consciousness, Wilmshurst posits that Masonic initiation is not merely an external ritual but a deeply transformative process that expands awareness, enabling glimpses into realities beyond the ordinary. This transformative journey resonates with scientific and philosophical inquiries into altered states of consciousness, where individuals encounter universal truths and a profound sense of unity. For instance, Dr. Richard Maurice Bucke's *Cosmic Consciousness* offers a compelling framework for understanding this expanded awareness. Bucke describes consciousness as evolving through distinct stages, culminating in "cosmic consciousness"—a state of profound unity, enlightenment, and interconnectedness that transcends personal experience. These moments of insight mirror the spiritual awakening fostered through Masonic initiation, marking milestones in humanity's collective journey toward higher awareness.

Similarly, the work of philosopher and psychologist William James underscores the transformative potential of altered consciousness. In his exploration of mystical states, James described experiences of unity and transcendence brought on by aesthetic revelations and altered perceptions, such as those induced by nitrous oxide. He characterised these states as "wholly different from the normal consciousness of men," offering a fleeting but profound glimpse into dimensions of reality that ordinary cognition cannot access. These mystical insights find their parallel in Masonic initiation, where symbolic ritual serves as a catalyst for awakening the initiate to the unity that underlies existence, deepening their connection to the divine.

The ceremonial use of Ayahuasca in Amazonian cultures provides another lens through which to understand these altered states of awareness. Ayahuasca, a sacred brew traditionally made from *Banisteriopsis caapi* and *Psychotria viridis,* combines the MAO-inhibiting properties of the former with the DMT content of the latter, unlocking vivid visionary experiences. Within the ceremonial guidance of shamans, Ayahuasca acts as a bridge between the material and spiritual realms. As noted by Luis Eduardo Luna and Pablo Amaringo in *Ayahuasca Visions,* "Ayahuasca is not merely a tool for altered states but serves as a sacred bridge between the material and spiritual realms." Participants report visions that reveal hidden truths, offer emotional healing, and connect them to a deeper sense of divine unity. This mirrors the Masonic journey, where ritual and symbolism guide initiates toward self-discovery and transcendence, offering insights that integrate the spiritual and material aspects of existence.

For Masons, these intersections of mysticism, science, and ritual point to the initiatic journey as one of expansive awareness. The path is not confined to intellectual understanding or moral growth but encompasses the cultivation of a consciousness that bridges the personal and the universal. This notion finds resonance even in the principles of quantum mechanics, where the observer's role fundamentally affects the observed. Similarly, the Mason's engagement with ritual and symbolism transforms their perception, inviting them to participate in the unfolding of a larger, interconnected reality. Through the degrees of initiation and adhering to the primary duty of prayer and meditation, the Mason, by natural means, moves closer to the universal mind, transcending the boundaries of individual experience to glimpse the unity that underpins existence.

Ultimately, Masonry's exploration of consciousness reflects humanity's ancient quest for understanding—a journey that unites material inquiry with mystical insight. These practices offer a window into a reality where all things are interconnected, and the self is part of a boundless whole. For the initiate, Masonry provides not just a system of moral instruction but an experiential path that leads them closer to the Great Architect's design. Each degree is a step toward expanded awareness, where the mysteries of existence unfold and the initiate aligns with the eternal truths that bind us all.

CHARACTERISTICS OF EXPANDED CONSCIOUSNESS

In Masonic initiation, the transformative experience of expanded consciousness is marked by three essential characteristics: unity of perception, a reevaluation of values, and an integration of sensory awareness. Wilmshurst emphasises that these changes are not theoretical—they reach the heart of the initiate's life, reshaping how they perceive themselves, others, and the world. This shift invites Masons to approach life with a heightened sense of unity, a place where divisions fade and an overarching harmony unfolds in their vision.

The first characteristic, unity of perception, signifies a profound shift in how the initiate views the fabric of existence. It embodies what Wilmshurst calls "seeing with the single eye," a state where the distinctions that typically separate the various aspects of life are replaced by an awareness of their interconnectedness as if woven into a single, expansive tapestry. In this state, Masons begin to see fraternity as not merely an external principle but as an experience of kinship shared with all life, a recognition of a shared purpose and an interconnected destiny. This unity transforms the Mason's relationships, prompting compassion and deeper understanding as they begin to see their journey as part of a collective unfolding. For the Mason, this unity of perception is a revelation that reshapes their way of being in the world, allowing them to see the reflections of their own journey in others' paths.

The second characteristic, a reevaluation of values, calls the initiate to redefine what is meaningful, drawing them away from superficial judgments and external accolades toward a deeper pursuit of inner virtues. This process mirrors the concept of alchemical refinement, where impurities are dissolved to reveal a more luminous, authentic self. In Masonry, this reevaluation encourages initiates to consider what constitutes true "wages" in their journey. Rather than seeking material success, the initiate values wisdom, peace, and spiritual insight as the true fruits of their path. Through this shift, Masons align more closely with the spiritual purpose of the Craft, embracing a life not defined by outward wealth or accolades but by the intrinsic qualities developed within. This inward transformation calls the Mason to cultivate a way of life that reflects their highest ideals and, in doing so, to embody the timeless virtues of the Craft.

The third characteristic of expanded consciousness is the integration of sensory experience, a level of awareness that goes beyond the isolated functions of individual senses and merges them into a harmonious whole. This integration mirrors the mystical experience where the boundaries of sight, sound, and touch blur, creating a synesthetic perception that transcends ordinary sensory divisions. William Blake's famous line, "To see a World in a Grain of Sand," captures this all-encompassing vision, where the initiate can perceive the totality of creation within even the smallest detail. For the Mason, this integration cultivates a profound sense of unity within and without, reflecting the alignment of the inner self with the universe. It is as though each sense expands, allowing the initiate to perceive the world with a holistic vision that reveals the sacredness inherent in all things.

In the context of modern Masonry, this sensory integration endures as a potent symbol of spiritual wholeness, guiding Masons to seek beyond the surface of existence and experience life in its entirety.

This heightened perception, which combines intellect, intuition, and a full sensory connection to life, becomes a guiding light, a call to embrace life with a deeper awareness and harmony. It reminds each Mason that the journey of initiation is ultimately a path to unity, an opportunity to integrate the diverse parts of oneself into a balanced and aligned whole.

Together, these three characteristics of expanded consciousness serve as cornerstones in the Mason's journey, revealing an inner reality that transcends mere intellectual understanding. The unity of perception, the refinement of values, and the integration of sensory experience become pillars of wisdom, leading Masons along a path where each step brings them closer to the divine unity at the heart of the Craft. These traits invite the initiate to look beyond conventional boundaries, experience the interconnected nature of life, and walk forward with a spirit that embraces both the mysteries of existence and the unwavering light that guides the soul toward higher truths.

DESIRE AS THE CATALYST FOR HIGHER AWARENESS

In Wilmshurst's vision of the Masonic journey, desire emerges as the essential catalyst for spiritual growth—a flame igniting the initiate's quest for expanded consciousness. Far from being a mere impulse for external gains, this innermost yearning resonates deeply within the soul, a call to transcend the boundaries of material existence. This profound, soulful desire awakens the initiate to something greater—a longing to touch the divine, to encounter a truth that lies beyond the grasp of intellect alone. Such a desire, rooted in ancient mystical traditions, has long been revered as the driving force for spiritual evolution, an energy that lifts the seeker from the mundane toward realms of higher understanding. For the Mason, this force of inner desire acts as a compass, guiding them toward wisdom and illuminating a path that rises above life's obstacles, pointing to the eternal.

This journey is illustrated in the story of a Hebridean fisherman whose quiet life was marked by an intense yearning for spiritual union. Living in solitude, his entire being was attuned to his quest for divine connection, refining his focus on this sacred aim. Over time, his devotion led him to a moment of mystical revelation, where he glimpsed the divine presence in a way that transformed his understanding of reality. His story exemplifies how purity of focus and a heart stripped of worldly distractions can open hidden pathways to wisdom, granting the seeker access to levels of awareness that lie beyond ordinary perception. In Masonic terms, this concentrated longing—divested of material possessions—becomes a prerequisite for genuine initiation, creating a space for spiritual clarity to arise and deepen.

In today's world, however, sustaining such purity of focus presents unique challenges. With technology's constant demands and the relentless pace of modern life, our attention is often fragmented, making it difficult to cultivate the clarity needed for spiritual growth. The Mason of today faces creating an inner sanctuary amid external noise, fostering solitude, simplicity, and purity of intention. This focus is necessary to nurture the spark of desire into a steady flame that can illuminate the way forward. Philosopher Søren Kierkegaard aptly observed, "Purity of heart is to will one thing," underscoring that an undivided heart and singular intent are essential for accessing the depth of awareness that Masonic initiation invites.

For the Mason, embracing this focused desire taps into an ancient principle: true spiritual advancement requires a heart unbroken in its longing, a passion so intense it becomes both guide and sustainer on the journey. This simplicity of purpose beckons the initiate to release the interruptions clouding their vision, bringing them closer to the divine source. Through this alignment, the Mason's journey becomes a pilgrimage of the heart—an unfolding awakening to the wisdom within and beyond, an integration of their soul with the eternal truths of the Craft.

THE "BAPTISM OF FIRE" AND SPIRITUAL ILLUMINATION

The concept of a "baptism of fire" holds a sacred place in Masonic symbolism, representing a moment of profound inner transformation. At this point, we, as initiates, are called to undergo an intense purification that stirs the very core of our being. This "fire" is not of the physical world but an inner flame, an alchemical blaze that refines and elevates our consciousness, lifting us beyond the boundaries of the material. For those of us who approach this baptism with open hearts, illumination arises as more than an intellectual spark; it is a living, breathing force that transforms our inner lives and outward actions. This transformation is reflected in the universal symbolism of halos and radiant auras around saints and mystics—visible emblems of their communion with divine light. For us Masons, the baptism of fire signals a pivotal shift—a beckoning to shed our earthly concerns and rise toward a consciousness that draws us closer to the eternal.

Throughout history, figures like St. Francis of Assisi and Meister Eckhart have embodied this radiant transformation. With his humility and devotion, St. Francis seemed to emanate a presence that spoke of his inner fire, a light that touched all who encountered him. Meister Eckhart, a mystic of deep insight, often spoke of an inner light that reveals the divine within, calling each seeker to cultivate a consciousness unbound by worldly deceptions. These exemplars, each in their unique way, illuminate truth for us within the Craft: that the fire of spiritual illumination is transformative, not only in our own lives but in the lives we touch. Even in Eastern traditions, sages are described as radiant beings, their luminous presence signifying an alignment with higher wisdom.

Within the Masonic tradition, the baptism of fire is more than an end goal; it is an ever-renewing call that asks us to continually refine ourselves. This baptism is a summons not only to individual enlightenment but to become vessels of that light for the world. It prompts us to examine: do we, as Masons, seek this inner fire as a guiding force? Do we allow it to shape our actions, intentions, and interactions? Through the structured progression of Masonic ritual, we are guided to engage in this transformative work, infusing our very lives with a consciousness that reaches beyond personal ambition, connecting us to a greater unity.

Thus, the baptism of fire becomes more than a symbolic act; it becomes the heart of Masonic practice itself, urging us toward a state where our inner flame radiates outward, lighting a path for others seeking wisdom. By embracing this inner flame, we become recipients of Masonic teachings and expressions of them, embodying the light of spiritual illumination. Each step we take through the Craft draws us closer to this sacred inner fire, where illumination becomes a shared quest, and each Mason steps into the role of a torchbearer, carrying forth a light that invites all who seek to join in the search for wisdom and understanding.

THE POETIC, ARTISTIC, AND MYSTICAL AS NATURAL INITIATES

Wilmshurst speaks to a profound truth when he connects the expanded consciousness of poets, artists, and mystics to the Masonic path. These "natural initiates" possess an inherent sensitivity that allows them to perceive the world with depth and clarity that transcends ordinary perception. Life is a sacred text for these souls, filled with symbols, insights, and revelations waiting to be uncovered. They see beauty, unity, and meaning in grand visions and the quiet corners of existence—the light on a leaf, the whisper of the wind, the silence between words. For us within the Craft, this same sensitivity forms the foundation of our journey, urging us to approach Freemasonry not merely as a set of rituals but as a living experience, a path that calls us deeper into the mysteries of life.

We can see this expanded vision in the works of poets like William Wordsworth, who described a "sense sublime" within the quietude of nature, perceiving in the "light of setting suns" a reflection of life's inherent unity. In Shelley's assertion that poets are "the unacknowledged legislators of the world," we find a recognition of the artist's role as a guide—one who sees, feels, and shapes the spiritual and moral landscape through heightened awareness. Similarly, Tennyson spoke of "seeing into the life of things," touching upon a mystical understanding that resonates with the ideals of brotherhood and universal unity. For these artists and visionaries, their works are more than creative expressions; they are glimpses into a reality that echoes the ideals of our Craft—truth, unity, and the unending pursuit of wisdom.

In Freemasonry, this mystical and artistic sensitivity is expressed in the "mystic tie" of brotherhood. This connection goes beyond individual identities and speaks to a shared inner light that unites us all. This bond is not mere fellowship but a recognition of the unity that threads through all life, a unity we seek to honour and deepen through our Masonic work. For those among us drawn to these ideals, the Craft provides a path that nurtures these intuitions, transforming them into a disciplined journey of spiritual growth. Masonic rituals and symbols serve as touchstones, guiding us to deepen our awareness and align our lives with universal truths, turning the raw materials of our inner sensitivity into polished instruments of enlightenment.

In a world that often emphasises superficial connections, the Craft stands as a sanctuary for those who feel a pull toward deeper truths, a space where the soul's yearning for beauty, wisdom, and interconnectedness is honoured. For many, Freemasonry represents a community and a path that allows the aesthetic, the poetic, and the mystical within us to bloom into true self-knowledge and wisdom. As we walk this path, we find that the Craft becomes not just a personal journey but a way to harness our natural inclinations toward understanding and unity, offering our insights as a light to guide others toward the mysteries.

BAPTISMS OF WATER AND FIRE: SYMBOLIC PATHWAYS

The journey of initiation in Freemasonry is a path marked by rites that symbolise stages of purification and illumination, most notably through the dual baptisms of water and fire. Each of these elements represents an essential phase of spiritual growth, guiding us through layers of transformation that reveal a deeper understanding of ourselves and the divine. The baptism of water signifies the beginning of this journey, a cleansing that invites us to confront and release the aspects of ourselves that obscure our inner light. This purification is more than a symbolic act; it is a call to engage in honest reflection, look deeply into the waters of our consciousness, and wash away the illusions that cloud our perception.

As we move forward, the baptism of fire represents a more profound stage of transformation—a phase where our inner light is ignited, awakening us to the eternal truths that lie at the core of our being. Long revered as a symbol of divine presence, fire is the purifying force that refines our spirit, burning away the remnants of ego and aligning our soul with higher ideals. This baptism is not merely a passage through ritual; it is an initiation into a higher state of awareness, where we are called to let go of the self we once knew and embrace a reality that transcends the intellect, awakening us to a consciousness that resonates with the divine.

These dual baptisms echo across spiritual traditions, reflecting universal stages in the journey of awakening. In Christian mysticism, John the Baptist speaks of a baptism of water. He foretells a baptism of "Holy Spirit and fire", symbolising the soul's journey from cleansing to illumination. Water prepares the vessel, while fire fills it with divine essence, marking the soul's transition from the outer understanding of self to an inner union with the sacred. In Freemasonry, these symbols remind us that true initiation is not a single act but an unfolding process of spiritual evolution.

In Masonic practice, the dual baptisms of water and fire call us to embody these stages continually, allowing each experience of purification and illumination to guide our lives. These elements are not confined to the Lodge—they live within us as guides, shaping how we engage with the world, urging us to purify our intentions, and inspiring us to cultivate a light reflecting the Craft's wisdom. The difference between ceremonial initiation and lived initiation is profound, as each Mason is called to internalise these symbols, transforming ritual into a lifelong journey of growth, where water and fire are companions on the path toward unity with the divine.

Through these elements, our initiation becomes a dynamic, living process—a dance of cleansing and illumination that aligns our lives with the unending light that guides Masonic tradition. As we immerse ourselves in the waters of self-reflection and rekindle our inner fire, we are reminded of the infinite cycle of rebirth and renewal. This cycle invites us to become vessels of strength, wisdom, and compassion. This is the journey of Freemasonry, where every step along the path brings us closer to the divine unity that lies at the heart of existence, calling us to be bearers of light in a world ever in need of illumination.

THE ALLEGORICAL PATH TO DIVINE PERCEPTION

In Freemasonry, allegory is not merely a storytelling device; it is the very language through which the mysteries of existence are revealed. Every stage of Masonic initiation is saturated with symbolic meaning, guiding us toward the light of understanding as we progress along the initiatic path. This journey—from darkness to light—represents our movement from ignorance to knowledge, from the veiled realms of unawareness to the radiant clarity of divine insight. Through allegory, the teachings of the Craft come alive, inviting us to perceive deeper truths about ourselves and the universe. Wilmshurst keenly recognises this, suggesting that the initiatic journey mirrors the soul's own quest for enlightenment, where the symbols and stories within Freemasonry serve as markers on the path of inner transformation.

The use of allegory in Freemasonry resonates with the methods of ancient mystery schools, where initiates were guided toward wisdom through symbolic rites, myths, and metaphorical teachings. These schools understood that certain truths cannot be conveyed through direct instruction; they must be experienced, felt, and discerned through symbols that speak to the soul. In Egypt, Greece, and other ancient cultures, initiates engaged in mystery traditions that used myth and ritual to impart wisdom about life, death, and the divine. Freemasonry continues this lineage, using the same timeless tools of symbolism and allegory to lead us toward self-discovery and spiritual understanding.

The effectiveness of allegory lies in its ability to bypass the logical mind, reaching into our deeper consciousness. When we engage with myth and symbol, we are not simply receiving information; we are entering a dialogue with universal archetypes—images and motifs that have lived in the collective psyche for millennia. Allegories and symbols become the language of the soul, enabling us to see connections between the visible and invisible, the earthly and the divine. As Masons, we are invited to see the Craft's rituals and symbols not as historical relics but as living keys that open the door to greater insight. By internalising these allegories, we develop a symbolic literacy that helps us navigate the tangible world and the unseen forces that influence it.

Consider the classical myth of Orpheus and Eurydice, a tale interpreted as a journey through the underworld of the psyche. Orpheus descends into the dark realm to retrieve his beloved, embodying the soul's descent into the shadow, into the hidden parts of self that must be reconciled before ascending to the light. In Freemasonry, this journey is mirrored in our initiatic rites, where the initiate must metaphorically confront their inner darkness, face the trials of the self, and emerge into a greater state of awareness. Through such allegorical frameworks, we learn that the journey inward is as essential as any outward endeavour. We are reminded that true enlightenment requires exploring both the heights of understanding and the depths of our being.

The importance of allegory in Masonry extends beyond the Lodge; it is a way of perceiving and engaging with life. By applying symbolic understanding to our experiences, we gain new perspectives on challenges, relationships, and personal growth. In our daily lives, we encounter symbols everywhere—in nature, art, and our dreams. When we approach these elements with a Masonic mindset, we see them as reflections of inner processes, guiding us to deeper insights. A storm, for instance, may symbolise turmoil or transformation; a sunrise, the renewal of spirit. By learning to decode these personal and universal symbols, we align ourselves with the ancient wisdom that our journey is both microcosmic and macrocosmic, a dance of the self with the universe.

Allegory also teaches us humility, reminding us that certain truths are beyond the reach of intellectual reasoning. Like the mystery schools' myths, Freemasonry's symbols do not provide easy answers. They are guides, not conclusions. This open-endedness encourages us to cultivate patience, curiosity, and reverence, realising that spiritual understanding unfolds gradually through personal experience and contemplation. When we read allegory with an open heart, we embrace the paradoxes of life, understanding that wisdom is not a static attainment but a living, breathing process of discovery. The circumpunct, with its unbroken circle and central point, symbolises this very journey: the point is our individual self, and the circle is the vastness of all we seek to understand.

Freemasonry's allegorical approach in a world dominated by literalism offers a powerful antidote, inviting us to explore life's mysteries through imagination and intuition. This symbolic way of thinking allows us to engage with life more creatively, helping us to see beyond surface appearances and connect with the invisible patterns that underlie existence. As we deepen our engagement with these symbols, we develop an inner compass that helps us to navigate both the visible world and the hidden realms of spirit. Through allegory, we learn to see the ordinary as extraordinary, to find meaning in the seemingly mundane, and to recognise the divine in the details of daily life.

The study of allegory and symbolism enriches our Masonic path, allowing us to bring the wisdom of the ages into our personal journey. By internalising the symbols of the Craft, we participate in an ancient tradition of seekers who understood that myth and symbol are tools for understanding our place in the cosmos. As we engage with these symbols, we align ourselves with a greater purpose, becoming co-creators in the mystery of life. Freemasonry invites us to understand and live these symbols, embodying the truths they reveal and carrying their light into the world.

In this way, Masonic allegory becomes a map—a guide through the world above and below, helping us to bridge the seen and the unseen, the known and the unknown. We are called not just to study symbols but to allow them to transform us, to let them shape our lives in meaningful ways. In doing so, we become living symbols, reflections of the Great Architect's design, expressing the timeless truths of the Craft in the way we think, act, and engage with the world. Through allegory, we understand that our journey is one of continuous revelation, where each step brings us closer to the divine mysteries, illuminating both our inner and outer worlds with the light of understanding.

EPOPTEIA AND THE INNER VISION OF FULL ILLUMINATION

In the ancient mystery traditions, *epopteia* signified the state of full illumination—a moment of ultimate vision where the initiate transcends all barriers and gains a direct perception of divine truth. Wilmshurst invokes this concept to describe the ultimate goal of Masonic initiation: a journey leading to complete spiritual clarity, which perceives with unified awareness. This eye embodies enlightenment, often spoken of in mystical traditions as a vision that rises above dualities, allowing us to experience the divine as a boundless, encompassing reality. This singular, unified vision lies at the heart of Masonic symbolism, a profound invitation for us to move beyond personal division and embrace a unity that reflects the divine whole.

Across spiritual traditions, we find echoes of this state of illumination in varied forms, each representing the apex of human consciousness—a sun at its meridian, casting away all shadows. Just as *epopteia* encapsulates the journey from initiation to divine vision, these global parallels illustrate that the pursuit of enlightenment is a universal endeavour that mirrors the perfect circumference of the circumpunct. This apex—symbolised in Masonic tradition by the sun's zenith—represents the highest state of awareness, where we perceive the self as part of an unbounded unity, the individual soul in direct communion with the divine.

In Hindu philosophy, *samadhi* and *moksha* describe the culmination of spiritual practice, where the seeker attains a state of pure consciousness and liberation from worldly attachments. In *samadhi*, the individual transcends the ego to experience oneness with Brahman, the ultimate reality. This union parallels the Masonic ideal of illumination, symbolising the initiate's inner ascent. Through *moksha*, the soul achieves a permanent release from the cycle of rebirth, merging with the divine—a state reflecting the *epopteia* of the ancient mysteries. Just as Masonic initiation aims to free us from the shadows of ignorance, *moksha* liberates the seeker from illusions of separation, allowing them to see with the single eye of enlightened perception. In both traditions, the journey inward requires sustained dedication, a commitment to purification, and the courage to see beyond oneself, echoing the ideals embodied in Masonry's degrees.

In Christian mysticism, the Beatific Vision represents the soul's union with God—a direct, unmediated experience of divine presence that fulfils the soul's deepest longing. In this vision, we "see God face to face" and understand the Creator's boundless wisdom and love. The Beatific Vision mirrors *epopteia,* lifting the soul beyond human perception into the eternal light of divine truth. For us, this is a reminder that initiation is not merely an intellectual pursuit but a deeply experiential one. The single eye of unity calls us to strive for inner clarity where divine wisdom flows freely, aligning the self with the light of truth.

Sufi mysticism describes *fana* and *baqa* as stages in the journey to divine unity. *Fana,* the annihilation of the self, dissolves the ego and allows the soul to experience unity with Allah. This dissolution is followed by *baqa,* where the self is re-established within divine consciousness. Together, these states reflect the journey of the ancient Epopts, where the initiate moves from self-dissolution to spiritual reintegration, guided by a connection to the divine. In Masonry, we shed attachments to become vessels for divine unity, paralleling the Sufi's journey from self-annihilation to spiritual reintegration.

Within Kabbalah, *Tiferet* and *yechidah* represent stages of alignment with the divine. *Tiferet,* the heart of the Tree of Life, symbolises harmony and balance. At the pinnacle, *yechidah* signifies ultimate oneness with God. In this state, divisions vanish, and the soul merges with the divine essence. These stages mirror the Masonic progression from balance to illumination, where our single eye sees the origin of all things in divine unity. As *yechidah* unites the soul with God, Masonic initiation invites us to align our consciousness with universal light, embodying the wisdom of the Great Architect.

THE CIRCUMPUNCT'S GUIDING LIGHT

In Freemasonry, allegory and symbolism offer us more than mere ritual; they serve as guides, illuminating the path to spiritual transformation and deeper understanding. Central to this symbolic landscape is the circumpunct—the point within the circle—which embodies one of the Craft's most profound teachings. This symbol carries a wealth of meaning, with the point representing the individual soul and the encompassing circle symbolising the infinite, unbroken unity of the divine. This simple, powerful image reminds us that while we are individual points, we are never separate from the greater whole. As Wilmshurst notes, "It is by recognising the point within us, and by circumscribing our desires within bounds, that we begin to understand our place within the divine scheme".

The circumpunct has held spiritual significance throughout history, appearing in Egyptian, Greek, and Christian iconography. In Egypt, it was linked with the sun god Ra, symbolising life's central force radiating through creation. In Greek philosophy, particularly within the teachings of Pythagoras, the circumpunct represented the Monad, or the source from which all existence flows. Early Christian mystics saw it as a depiction of God as the centre of all existence, whose presence is everywhere yet whose nature remains boundless. Each tradition embraced the circumpunct as a reflection of cosmic unity, guiding us to perceive ourselves as individual and universal beings.

For Masons, the circumpunct reminds us of our dual nature: as individuals, we are distinct, yet we are inseparably connected to the unity of all life. This symbol urges us to balance the inner and outer, self-knowledge and universal understanding. In the same way that the point within the circle is centred, we are called to centre ourselves, developing an inner stillness that allows us to act as conscious participants within the Great Architect's design. The circumpunct is not only a symbol to ponder but a guide for living, challenging us to achieve harmony within and reflect it outward. Wilmshurst captures this sentiment by stating, "To comprehend the Great Architect, we must first establish an inner temple, marked by self-control and unity".

In the context of personal transformation, the circumpunct aligns with alchemical symbolism, representing the merging of spirit and matter. Alchemists saw this symbol as a representation of the Philosopher's Stone—the perfected state of being where all opposing forces are harmonised. This process of inner refinement is mirrored in our Masonic journey through the degrees which encourage us to purify our character, align with truth, and embody the ideals of wisdom, strength, and beauty. The circumpunct, as a symbol of wholeness, reflects the alchemical adage *solve et coagula*, dissolve and reform, guiding the initiate toward a synthesis of the physical and spiritual realms.

Finally, the circumpunct speaks to the essence of Masonic brotherhood. Encircled by the teachings of the Craft, we understand that individual enlightenment is not an isolated endeavour but a contribution to the collective light. Meditating upon this symbol reminds us that our personal growth enriches the fraternity as a whole. Through the circumpunct, we are called to become beacons of light, serving as guides for others on the path and strengthening the bonds that unite us within the unbroken circle of the Great Architect's creation. As Jung remarked, "He who looks outside, dreams; he who looks inside, awakens," highlighting the journey toward inner clarity that not only benefits the individual but shines forth to uplift others.

Through the circumpunct, we connect to a lineage of seekers across time and culture, each striving for unity with the divine. It reminds us that our journey is not separate but part of the boundless pursuit of wisdom—a quest that transcends the self and brings us ever closer to the heart of the Masonic path. The circumpunct, standing at the intersection of the individual and universal, teaches us to live in harmony with both worlds, illuminating a path to wisdom that is both personal and eternal.

THE MASTER'S JOURNEY TO WISDOM AND UNITY

In the final stages of the Masonic path, the Master Mason reaches a profound culmination, standing as one who has integrated wisdom and unity within themselves. Our ascent is not an ordinary one; it signifies the culmination of a journey woven with resilience, self-refinement, and divine insight. Wilmshurst portrays this ultimate stage not as an endpoint but as an invitation into a more profound relationship with the divine. Here, the Master Mason becomes a living symbol of the Craft's ideals, embodying wisdom that transforms each thought, intention, and action.

This ultimate journey is symbolised in Masonry through the five-pointed star and the acacia—two powerful images that offer layered meanings to the initiate. The five-pointed star, or pentagram, represents the inner spark of divinity, a light that transcends personal limitations to reflect body, mind, and spirit harmony. Across cultures, the pentagram has symbolised the perfected human form, a balance between earthly and spiritual realms. In Masonic teaching, each point represents the refinement of the five senses, guiding the initiate to sharpen these faculties as instruments of deeper perception, ultimately transforming each sense into a tool for spiritual understanding. This ideal resonates with Pythagorean thought, where the pentagram embodies the "golden ratio"—a universal harmony that reflects the divine order within all creation.

Further, this star symbol plays a significant role in the Order of the Eastern Star, where each point represents virtues like loyalty, fidelity, and purity, drawn from biblical figures. This connection serves as a reminder that the journey to enlightenment is not isolated; it connects each Mason to a vast community, each striving toward their own inner refinement. Thus, The pentagram becomes a mirror of our higher potential, a symbol that reflects the balanced, integrated self central to the Masonic pursuit.

Accompanying the star is the acacia, an evergreen symbol of the soul's resilience and immortality. In ancient Egypt and the Mediterranean, the acacia was revered as a plant of regeneration and eternal life—a symbol of continuity that speaks to the soul's unending journey. For the Master Mason, the acacia represents faith in the soul's endurance, its power to transcend the confines of physical existence and merge with the eternal. It is not merely a promise of life after death but a symbol of the spiritual legacy left by those who have travelled this path. Through the acacia, the initiate understands that each life, each step along the journey, contributes to a larger unity, an eternal bond with the divine that transcends the self.

As Wilmshurst articulates, reaching this union of wisdom and self signifies a "new beginning," where the Master Mason comes into a boundless relationship with the divine. This resonates with mystical insights from figures like Meister Eckhart, who spoke of the "birth of the Word in the soul"—an awakening to the divine presence within paralleling the Kabbalistic concept of *yechidah*, the soul's ultimate union with the divine essence. Here, the self is no longer separate but dissolves into an all-encompassing unity, a timeless continuum in which the initiate understands their place in the cosmic order. In Masonic terms, achieving this unity is akin to becoming one with the circumpunct—the central point within the unbroken circle—symbolising a soul harmonising with the divine pattern that sustains the universe.

For the modern Mason, this journey is an invitation to embody unity and stability in a fragmented world. Carl Jung's concept of individuation mirrors the Masonic ideal of wholeness, describing a process in which all aspects of the self are integrated into a coherent, balanced whole. In individuation, as in the Masonic journey, the initiate transcends inner conflict to achieve a unity that aligns with the wisdom of the Great Architect. Jung suggests that this inner unity is the foundation of wisdom, creating a self that perceives reality deeply and acts from an authentic, integrated centre.

The Masonic journey toward wisdom and unity is not confined to one tradition; its echoes resound across world philosophies. In Hindu mysticism, *samadhi* represents a state of profound inner light, where the soul perceives itself as unified with Brahman, the universal essence. In Christian mysticism, the *Beatific Vision* offers the soul a direct experience of divine love and wisdom, aligning with Masonic ideals of spiritual clarity. In Sufism, *fana* (self-annihilation) and *baqa* (rebirth within the divine) symbolise the dissolution of the ego, transforming personal consciousness into divine presence. Similarly, in Kabbalah, the stages of *Tiferet* (beauty and harmony) and *yeshivah* (oneness) embody the soul's journey toward divine union. These states mirror the Masonic vision of the soul's ascent, each expressing humanity's potential to transcend individual limitations and align with the infinite.

These apex states, where the soul reaches its "sun at meridian," reinforce the idea that the pursuit of enlightenment is universal. The circumpunct—a central point encircled by unity—symbolises this shared aspiration, reflecting a spiritual truth that transcends time and culture. For the Master Mason, this realisation is deeply humbling, for it connects their path to a lineage of seekers spanning generations and geographies. This is the shared legacy of Freemasonry: a path that leads each initiate beyond themselves, affirming that our journey contributes to a wisdom that unites all humanity.

As Wilmshurst eloquently describes, the final stage of the Master's journey is not a closure but an opening into the greater mystery, a call to live as a "living stone" within the eternal temple of humanity. The Master Mason, embodying this inner unity, serves as a living testament to the ideals of the Craft, radiating wisdom, peace, and resilience into the world. This ultimate stage, where wisdom and unity converge, invites each initiate to become a reflection of the Great Architect—a guiding light that illuminates the way for others. In this apex state, the initiate has transcended mere knowledge, embodying wisdom that aligns with the eternal and fulfilling the highest aim of Freemasonry: to bring each soul into harmony, wisdom, and peace within the vast, unbroken circle of existence.

CHAPTER FOUR - THE MASONIC INITIATION

THE PAST AND FUTURE OF THE MASONIC ORDER

"First, that which is natural; after, that which is spiritual."

THE PAST

Beginnings, whether of nations, religions, institutions, or even of the world and life itself, are notoriously obscure and difficult of precise fixation. The reason is that nothing actually "begins" to be; rather, there merely takes place a transformation into new conditions of something that pre-existed in other conditions. Call the point or moment at which the change occurs a "beginning" if you wish; it will be found that such beginning is but an effect generated by, and issuing from, anterior causes. Life itself does not, at physical birth, begin to be; it merely then enters physical conditions and assumes physical guise. A corresponding change occurs at the birth or beginning of human institutions—they are developments and formalisations of something which previously existed in a fluid incohesive condition. This is the case with Masonry, and accounts for the tradition that it is as old as man himself, whatever forms it has assumed, and that it is of Divine origin.

Modern Speculative Freemasonry had a beginning in the early years of the 18th century, but only in the sense that in 1717 originated that which afterwards developed into, and now subsists as, the English Masonic Constitution. Masonry itself existed long before that time, and in two forms: (1) exoterically, in the Operative Building Guilds, and (2) esoterically, in a variety of secret communities of mystics and occultists, having no relation to the practical building trade but often using builders' terminology for symbolical purposes of their own.

Modern Masonry is a blend of both of these; its constitutions, charges, rituals, and instruction lectures incorporate elements drawn from each of them. The Ancient Charge, for instance, which is delivered to every Masonic candidate on admission to the Order today, is an example of what has come over from the Operative Masons. It is patently an instruction of the kind one would expect to find given to a youth on becoming entered as an apprentice to a handicraft and embarking upon adult and civic responsibilities; it is a mere admonition to him to be a moral man, a worthy citizen, a creditable workman and member of his trade-guild, to fear God, honour the King, love his country, and generally educate and improve himself. It does not contain the least reference to any knowledge or wisdom of an extraordinary kind, or suggest any vestige of acquaintance with subjects of a mystical or occult character.

But on turning to the ceremonial rituals, especially that of the Third Degree, and to the "Traditional History" and instruction lectures, we find, mixed up with references to the Operative Builders' trade, matters of a highly esoteric and mystical nature, having no possible operative or materialistic connection and not to be thought of as associated with the technical equipment of a workman in material stone and brick.

This esoteric element descended, of course, not from the Operative Guilds, but from less public organisations of symbolic or mystical

Masons, and it is the latter alone whose necessarily obscure history and purpose repay investigation at this time of day.

These organisations were the representatives of a stream of Hermetic tradition and practice, the upper reaches of which go back into pre-Christian times, into Egypt, and to the Rabbinical mystics and Kabbalists, among whom existed a secret, guarded lore of the Cosmos and of human life; a lore which found only partial, though cryptic, expression in the Hebrew Scriptures in terms of building. With them, the building and the subsequent vicissitudes of Solomon's Temple (whether this was ever an historical material erection or not) provided a great glyph or mythos of the up-building of the human soul, whether considered individually or collectively; and as the course of Hebrew history advanced and the stream of circumstances and mystical tradition widened into its Christian development, the same symbolic terminology continued to be used. Accordingly, the Gospels, the Epistles, and the Apocalypse are found to teem with Masonic imagery and allusions to spiritual building. It is in these that the human soul becomes expressly declared to be the real Temple prefigured by the previous historic or quasi-historic one. A spiritual Chief Corner-stone, rejected by certain builders, is mentioned; one in which the entire social fabric is to grow together into a single universal Temple.

St. John himself, as the "beloved disciple" or most advanced Initiate of the Christian Master, becomes, according to the esoteric tradition, his Chief Warden and entrusted—as every Senior Warden in our symbolic lodges is—with the task of keeping order in the West and, after the days of his flesh, of occultly controlling from the heavens the development of the law of Christ in the Occidental world. Hence he became, and still is acknowledged as, the Masonic Patron-saint, and is found spoken of in the Rosicrucian reference in Dante's *Paradiso* as:

> *He that lay upon the breast*
> *Of Him who is our mystic pelican,*

And from the Cross was named for office blest;

whilst one of his known pupils, St. Ignatius—who is reputed to have been the little child whom the Lord once took and set in the midst as a type of fitness for realising the kingdom of heaven—is found expounding religion in these purely Masonic terms: "Forasmuch as ye are stones of a Temple which were prepared beforehand for a building of God, the Father, being hoisted up to the heights by the working-tool of Jesus Christ, which is the Cross, and using for a rope the Holy Spirit; your faith being a windlass, and love the way leading up to God. So then ye are all Companions in the way, spiritual temples, carrying your Divine principle within you, your shrine, your Christ and your holy things, being arrayed from head to foot with the commandments of Christ." (*Epistle to Ephesians*)

The pronounced Masonic imagery used by Ignatius (who was martyred at Rome in A.D. 107) tends to corroborate the tradition that the Square, Level, and Plumb-rule, now allocated to the Master and two Wardens of a Lodge, were originally associated with the Bishop, Priest, and Deacon, when serving at the secret altars of the persecuted Christians. Put together, the three tools form a Cross, which, on the worshippers being disturbed by the secular authorities, could quickly be knocked apart and appear but as builders' implements.

The most popular religious book of the earliest Christian centuries was *The Shepherd of Hermas*, a collection of teachings, visions, and similitudes, couched in terms of Masonic allegory and veiling (as the title implied) the hermetic or esoteric instruction of some "Shepherd," as the Hierophants and Adept-teachers of the Mysteries were, and in the canonical Scriptures are, uniformly designated.

To define the position which, after the event known as the Christian Incarnation, seems to have been assumed by all the mystical Builders, the spiritual Alchemists, the Rosicrucians, and the diverse other schools of the secret Gnosis who accepted that fact as the central pivotal one of human spiritual evolution and the culmination of earlier Mystery-systems, it may be said that they regarded themselves as one great Fraternity in the Divine Mysteries under the unseen but actual guidance of Jesus Christ, "the Carpenter" (Tekton), as Supreme Grand Master, with the greater Initiate, St. John the Divine, and the lesser Initiate, St. John Baptist, as Senior and Junior Grand Wardens; the winter and summer solstices (the times of the sun's lowest annual declension and meridian height) being allocated to the two latter as festival days or time-points peculiarly favourable for spiritual contact between the Grand Lodge Above and the lesser Lodges below.

All down the stream of history will be found the similitude of the human soul to a stone and directions for working it from a crude to a perfect state. The career of the patriarch Jacob begins with a stone. The Dervishes of the Arabian Desert are given a cubed stone smeared with blood on their initiation. The sacred object and palladium of the Moslem faith is the Raab eh or Cubical Stone. The stone is found described as *Lapis exilis* and *Lapis ex Coelis*; it is always said to have come from heaven, whence it is now in exile in this outer world. As a protest against materialising the idea of it, one finds exclamations such as Cornelius Agrippa's famous *Transmutemini! Transmutemini in viventes lapides!*—become ye transformed into living stones!

Those more advanced mystics, the spiritual Alchemists, have provided us with a wealth of obscure lore concerning the "Stone of the Philosophers"; and all through the Christian centuries, behind the activities of public elementary religion and the official work of the Church, can be traced evidences of this higher, esoteric, more abstruse and difficult work of mystical Masonry and stone-working being wrought by abbots, monks, and laymen, either in solitude or in communities of lesser or greater size, yet in severest concealment.

The history of this movement in England cannot be written in detail here, but a few points of it may be cited as evidence of the fact that, beyond all operative-trade connections, the primary work of Masonry was one of mystical religion and had to do with the arcana of the human soul; that it was an intellectual and a spiritual science promoting the development of the individual initiate and, through him, the advancement of the general weal.

The English Masonic Constitutions of 1784, for example, reproduce a memorandum "concemynge the Mystery of Maconrye," said to have been written early in the 15th century by King Henry VI with his own hand—probably for private rather than for state purposes, since he himself is alleged to have been made a Mason. Transposing his words from archaic into modern English, the King's memorandum indicates as follows: that Masonry is a spiritual science; that it originated in the East (in both a mystical and a geographical sense) and reached the junior human races in the West through travelling Phoenicians (misdescribed as "Venetian"); that its development had been greatly advanced by Pythagoras (curiously mis-called by the English names "Peter Gower"), who, after receiving his own initiations, founded the great Crotona school and instructed others in the science; that the science itself involves knowledge of and power over hidden forces of Nature, so that the expert Mason can perform acts which to the uninitiated would appear miraculous; that progress in the science comes by instruction, practice, and silence; that the science is to be imparted only to worthy and suitable men, since abuse of it and of the powers arising with it would result in both personal and general evil; that Masons understand and can effect the art of alchemic transmutation and possess a universal symbolic language of their own by which they can intercommunicate, whatever their race or country; that they have the "skill of becoming good and perfect," apart from all motives of fear and hope such as influence lesser minds and are held out by popular religion; that not all Masons realise their attainments or become perfect, for many fail in capacity, and more still in the arduous personal effort essential to the acquisition of this wisdom.

The genuineness of the King's memorandum has been questioned, though prima facie it is well attested. But whether a genuine script of his or not, its contents, within their limits, accurately represent the nature of Masonry itself.

No one can read English or European history from the period of that memorandum onward without realising that to that history there has been an inner side not cognised or treated of by academic historians, or without feeling behind the march of external events—and as it were connected with or even directing them—the concealed presence of minds more than normally capable: initiates, possessing and wielding the very powers testified to in Henry VI's memorandum. The lives and literary remains of such men as—to name no others—Paracelsus, Abbot Tritheim, Basil Valentine, Jacob Boehme, George Johan Gichtel, Thomas Vaughan, and Elias Ashmole provide above-surface indications of a strong current of sub-surface activity, a current of which no record exists or is ever likely now to be made. But to that current one must look for the perpetuation of the secret Masonic science, and to its projection, in a highly diluted and elementary form, into publicity in modern speculative Masonry.

The religious Reformation of the 15th century was the first great episode in a far-reaching revolutionary movement in the intellectual, social, and political life of the West, a movement the end of which is not yet. Amid the intensifying unspirituality and materialism of the times and the impending disintegration of public instituted religion, a decision seems to have been come to by some far-seeing enlightened minds to put forward the old mystical Gnosis and tradition in a simple form and to attempt to interest a small section of the public in it. This suggestion is incapable of rigorous proof and will perhaps commend itself only to those who are in any measure conscious of the inner mechanism controlling the visible clock-face of historic events. But be this as it may, we find, about the year 1600 and onwards, the first small signs of a movement that has eventuated in the vast modern Masonic Craft, with its as yet further indeterminate possibilities.

The first recorded reception of a non-operative Mason to an operative Lodge occurred at Edinburgh in 1600. The Operative Lodges were then becoming obsolete and defunct, and by 1620 Operative Masonry had become entirely superseded in London by Speculative, the members of the former working no longer in guilds but striving still to keep alive their old form of fellowship. The first traceable initiation, on English soil, of a non-operative Mason occurred at Newcastle in 1641, and the second—that of Elias Ashmole, already a student of arcane science—at Warrington in 1646.

Accretions to the ranks of the Craft proceeded to be made, but were at first few and gradual, owing to disturbed political conditions. The Charter of the Royal Society, dated 1663, as drawn up by Dr. (afterwards Sir) Christopher Wren, seems to have been prepared with a view to giving official sanction not to science as at present secularly understood and pursued, but to science of a more occult character such as Masonry as before defined deals with, for the preamble of that document refers to private meetings of certain men devoted to the investigation of the "hidden causes of things" in the public interest.

In 1717 four old London Lodges combined to constitute a new nucleus. From them the first Grand Lodge was formed and thus Modern Masonry was born, at an inn, the Apple Tree Tavern, in Lincoln's Inn Fields.

In 1721 Dr. Anderson was entrusted with the drawing up of the Constitutions of the new community. The conditions of the Craft in that year may be deduced from a statement of the eminent antiquary Dr. Stukeley, who writes: "I was the first person made a Freemason for many years. We had great difficulty to find members enough to perform the ceremony. Immediately after that it took a run, and ran itself out of breath through the folly of its members."

Abuses supervened from the admission of all and sundry without due qualifications. In 1724, a Brother protested in a public journal that "the late prostitution of our Order is in some measure the betraying of it. The weak heads of vintners, drawers, wigmakers, weavers, etc., admitted into our Freemasonry, have not only brought contempt upon the Institution, but do very much endanger it."

In the same year, the first benevolent fund was established "for poor brethren," which has since developed into the great Charity organisations now connected with the Craft. In the course of the next fifty years, the numbers of the Craft so increased that central headquarters were found advisable, and on May-day of 1775, the foundation-stone of the present Freemasons' Hall in London was laid with great ceremony.

Despite the fact that men were being admitted to the Order who were little qualified to appreciate the science of Masonry, and that consequently the understanding of that science was becoming increasingly debased, elements of the original intention still remained, and echoes of it can be caught in some of the recorded incidents of the occasion. In the Foundation-stone itself was inserted a plate perpetuating the event and the names of the then Grand Master, his deputy, and the Grand Wardens; and stating that Masonry was of heavenly origin, "descendit e ccelo"; and concluding with the maxim of Solon in Greek characters, "Know thyself." At the religious service performed upon the occasion was sung an anthem of praise to the Great Architect:

"Who deign'd the human soul to raise
By mystic secrets sprung from heaven"

whilst a specially composed ode affirmed of the new *Aula Latomorum* that:

"Religion, untainted, here dwells;
Here the morals of Athens are taught;

Great Hiram's tradition here tells
How the world out of chaos was brought."

From these extracts, it is clear that, at least to its leading minds, Masonry was a secret science of soul-building, and that the great central legend and mythos expressed in the Traditional History in the Craft's Third Degree referred to no events in earthly time or history, but to Cosmic events of a metaphysical and mystical character.

Further, from the preface to the Constitutions of 1784, it is made clear that the practical builder's art is to be considered only as the substratum of Speculative Masonry; that the history of the Operative side is negligible, for when Speculative Masons became a separate body of men, the science had no further concern with practical building; and that the Speculative work is a personal mystical one, rising like a pyramid "tending regularly up to a summit of attainments, ever concealed by intervening clouds from the promiscuous multitudes of common observers below."

Freemasons' Hall being completed, it was, on 23rd May 1776, triply dedicated, again with great ceremony; firstly to Masonry; a second time to Virtue; and a third time to Universal Charity and Benevolence. The last-named of the three purposes came in course of time to dominate completely at least the first of them. The Craft became a great money-raising institution for relieving its own needy members and their relatives, and as a charitable society does excellent work which commands the devoted interest of many good Brethren who know nothing, and seek to know nothing, of Masonry itself in its only proper and primary aspect of spiritual science, and who regard it merely as a luxurious item of social life and maintain their connection with it solely from philanthropic motives.

From the facts thus roughly outlined, it is clear that the pre-1717 Brethren were men of a very different calibre, and held a vastly higher conception of Masonry, from those who subsequently came to constitute the Craft and have expanded it to its present great dimensions. Of the latter class, whatever their merits, virtues, and good works in other respects, they cannot be said to have been either theoretic or practical mystics, nor to have cultivated the knowledge of Masonry as that science must be primarily understood. They cannot say of themselves as their predecessors truly could and did:

We have the Mason Word and second sight,

for growth in the life of the spirit and the enhanced faculty and inward vision that come therewith have not been within the ambit of their desire. As one of the most deeply learned and understanding writers upon the subject affirms, (the authoress of *A Suggestive Inquiry into the Hermetic Mystery*), "The outward form (or present practice) of Masonry is too absurd to be perpetuated were it not for a certain secret response of common sense to the original mystery. The Initiated moved one another on by words of power. The Masons ape this but have lost the magic key to open the door into the Hermetic garden. They want the words, which are only to be found by seeking them in the subjective fundamental life, from which they are as far out as the tools they use. The true tools also may be found on the way in; they will be given one after another as they are wanted."

Another learned author, who had every motive to speak well of the Craft—the late Brother John Varker—was constrained to write in 1872, in his able and most instructive *Notes on the Scientific and Religious Mysteries*, that: "As the Masonic fraternity is now governed, the Craft is fast becoming the paradise of the bon vivant, of the charitable hypocrite who forgets the version of St. Paul and adorns his breast with the 'charity jewel'; (having by this judicious expenditure obtained the purple, he metes out judgment to other brethren of greater ability and morality but less means); the manufacturer of paltry Masonic tinsel, etc. No other institution is so intrinsically valuable as Craft Masonry, or capable of such superhuman things. As now governed, few societies perform less. None profess such great objects; few accomplish so very little real and substantial good. May reformation be speedy and effective!"

Such facts are not pleasant to contemplate, nor would they be proclaimed here without good purpose and a constructive motive. But it is well to face them before proceeding further, since what remains to be said will not only deal with a happier aspect of the subject, but is based upon the premise that the otherwise deplorable perversion and materialisation of the true Masonic intention has been both an inevitable and a necessary prelude to a spiritual efflorescence which in due course will manifest itself and of which the beginnings are already perceptible.

In no censorious or reproachful spirit, therefore, are such observations as the foregoing recorded. They might indeed be extensively amplified if to do so would serve any useful purpose, but no one with intimate experience of the Craft will fail to recognise either their truth or the cogency of their reproach. It is undeniable that, through ignorance of the true principles of Masonry, the Craft has suffered itself to become debased and overrun with members lacking alike the intellectuality, the temperament, and the desire to appreciate those principles. To-day's newspaper, for example, contains the advertisement of a turf bookmaker who proclaims himself to be "on the square," and on the strength of that qualification seeks to engage the services of a betting-tout. It is well known that commercial houses to-day find it advantageous, for business purposes, to insist upon their more important employees being members of the Order.

In the Order itself, advancement is notoriously connected with social position and the extent of a member's contributions to the Charities. Honours, and even medals, are bestowed for money payments to this or that subscription list. Any man with a title, from a mayor to a prince, needs only to be a Mason a matter of months to find himself elevated to some figurehead position in the Craft, without the least merit of a purely Masonic kind or any understanding of the science itself. The central ideas and teachings of the Craft are left unexplained; ceremonies are discharged quite perfunctorily, and with the majority are of entirely subservient importance to the indissociable feasting and wearisome rounds of speechmaking that follow; and the general ignorance of Masonic truth provides ample scope for the self-assertion of men whose ideas of moral grandeur and Masonic virtue are evidenced by an ambition to attain office in the Craft and to adorn their persons with as much purple and jewellery as they can acquire.

It is all woefully wrong and misconceived. Of course, worthier traits exist. The heart of English Masonry is sound, if its head be obtuse and muddled and the work of its hands not of the character it might and ought to be.

When the worst has been said that can be charged against the methods of modern Masonry, it amounts merely to an exhibition of venial human weakness, vanity, and sycophancy, the growth of which, whilst obscuring and falsifying Masonic principles, has been due to failure to grasp what those principles imply and entail. Many tares have sprung up among the corn; but good corn has not failed to grow, and that the two can grow together in the same field is a tribute to the richness of the soil from which both spring and the nourishing power of the Masonic intention, which, like sunlight, shines impartially upon both and quickens whatever seed is sown within its field, whether tares or wheat.

There are few received into the Craft to whom Masonry does not bring, if but dimly and momentarily, some measure of new vision, some impulse towards its ideals; few who do not feel it to contain something far greater than they know or than appears upon its surface-presentation. Moreover, in the deep heart of every man exists a responsiveness to ultimate truth, and a fondness, amounting sometimes to a passion, for it when expressed in ceremonial grandeur and impressiveness—a sub-conscious reminiscence, as Plato would explain, of truth and glories it has once known and must one day know again, and which Masonic ritual does something to revive, as was of course the intention of all the Initiation systems of the past and is still the intention of our present Order.

And how often one finds minds which are denied, or which would repudiate, the use of symbolic ritual in their Church, leap to it with admiration and affection in their Lodge, as though the Protestant rejection, in the religious sphere, of the rich symbolism and sacramentalism wisely once devised for instructing eye, ear, and mind, and exalting the imagination towards spiritual verities, had starved them of their rightful nourishment. It is not surprising that to many such minds Masonry becomes, as they themselves say, a religion, or at all events a precious fact to which their souls respond however inarticulately, and that for them the door of the Lodge is, as was once said of the Altar-rails, "the thin barrier dividing the world of sense from the world of spirit."

THE FUTURE

In the fact that, amidst so much imperfect apprehension of its meaning and intention, Masonry should not only have survived, but should continue to make an ever-widening appeal to the imagination, exists the proof that, inherent in it, however deeply veiled, is a vibrant, indestructible vital principle which awakens a never-failing response, whether loud or feeble, in its devotees. The light is in the darkness, though as yet that darkness comprehendeth it not. The modern Craftsman may not as yet "have the Mason Word" in his own possession, like his earlier Brethren; but, nevertheless, that Word itself abides within the Masonic system, and he faintly hears and responds to its overtones; it is, for most, a Lost Word, but it patiently awaits recovery; and many to-day are impatiently seeking to find it.

That vital principle became implanted in the Order system by those wise, far-seeing, now untraceable minds which, as we have said, some three centuries ago conceived and inspired, if they did not directly devise, the formation of the Order as a means of perpetuating in an elementary way the ancient Secret Doctrine through a period of darkness and disruption, and until such time as that Doctrine, and the Mysteries that once taught it, can again be revived in a larger way.

The evidences of the presence in the Masonic system and texts of the ancient arcane teaching are threefold. Firstly, the grading of the system itself into the three traditional stages of spiritual perfecting, involving in turn the discipline and purification of the body and sense-nature; the control, self-knowledge, and illumination of the mind; and, finally, that entire abnegation of the will and death of the sense of personality which lead to union with the Divine Will, beyond personality and separateness. Secondly, the incorporation of the myths of the building of Solomon's Temple and the death of Hiram, both of which are allegories and portray not historic, but metaphysical, truth of profound importance. Thirdly, the insertion into the texts of the Ceremonies and side-lectures of a number of pieces of esoteric teaching common to all the Initiation-doctrine of East and West, but not known to be such by the average Brother who is unfamiliar with that doctrine, and so cryptically expressed and so interwoven with more elementary moral teaching as only to be recognisable to the more fully instructed observer. Examples of this esoteric teaching and of its implications are given in the second section of this volume, dealing with "Light on the Way."

The compilation of the text of the present Rituals and Instruction Lectures is supposed to have been, and no doubt was, undertaken in or soon after 1717, by Dr. Anderson and others whose personality is now of no moment. (Royal Arch Masonry was introduced into England in 1778 by a Jewish Brother, Moses Michael Hayes.) Nor is it material to inquire how far those compilers were deliberately obscuring and crypticising occult knowledge they personally possessed or, if personally lacking it, were unconsciously led into perpetuating greater wisdom than they knew. The subject has been ably and exhaustively discussed in a work of very high value to the Masonic student, *Studies in Mysticism*, by Brother A. E. Waite, who takes the view that the compilers did not for the most part know what they were doing, yet that they wrote as if guided by a blind though unerring instinct "which made even the foolish old scholars of the past see through their inverted and scoriated glasses something of what Masonry actually is, and therefore, in the midst of much idle talk, they provided, unconsciously to themselves, a master-key of the Sanctuary."

This is probably a true verdict, for from various evidences Anderson and his colleagues show little signs of having been esotericists of any depth or ability. But, be it accurate or not, the fact remains that our system was so designed and devised as to be a true compendium of universal Initiation; one that reproduces the salient features of every system that has existed, or that elsewhere still exists, for advancing human perfecting.

In that fact lies the strength, the vitality, the attractive power, of the Masonic system; the subtle charm that it casts over minds sensitive to its implications, but as yet unable to interpret them or to understand their own responsiveness to them. And in the demonstration and elucidation of the doctrine concealed in the system lies the hope of the Craft gradually educating itself and fulfilling its original design in the years now before it.

The point up to which these observations are meant to lead can now be stated. It is that before the true spirit and inward content of Masonry could be appreciated upon a scale sufficiently wide to constitute the Order a real spiritual force in the social body (as one hopes and sees indications that it will become), it has been necessary in the first instance to build up a great, vigorous, and elaborate physical organisation as a vehicle in which that spirit may eventually and efficaciously manifest. In view of the importance of the ultimate objective aimed at, it matters nothing that from two to three centuries have been needed to develop that organisation, to build up that requisite physical framework, or that the material of which it has been constructed has not been so far of ideal quality.

With the larger prospect in view, we can afford to look both charitably and philosophically upon momentary matters that may be regarded as regrettable and as falling far below the standard of even the surface and letter of Masonic principle; we can be content that the Order has been composed so largely of men little understanding or capable of assimilating its profounder purpose; that its energies have run off from their true channel to the subsidiary ones of social amenities and charitable relief; that its higher ranks have been filled, not with adepts and experts in spiritual science, capable of ministering wisdom and instruction to the humbler ranks below (as the symbolism of our great hierarchical system surely implies their doing), but with "great kings, dukes and lords" and other social dignitaries, displaying no signs of possessing arcane wisdom and placed in their complimentary or administrative positions (which they nevertheless admirably and efficiently fulfil) merely to give the Order social sanction and—as the nauseous doggerel runs—"our mysteries to put a good grace on."

The growth of a great institution—a nation, a Church, a system of the Mysteries—is a slow growth, proceeding from material apparently unpromising, and involving continual selection, rejection, and refining, before something becomes finally sublimated from it and forged into an efficient instrument. To take the most appropriate analogy, the erection of Solomon's Temple was a work of years, of diversely collected material and engaging numerous interests; but not until it was completed, dedicated, and consecrated as a tabernacle worthy of the Shekinah, did that Presence descend upon it, illumining and flooding the whole House and enabling the earthy vehicle to fulfil a spiritual purpose.

So now, too, with the Masonic Order. As a physical vehicle, a material organisation, it is as complete, as elaborated, and as efficiently controlled as perhaps it can ever be expected to be. It now stands awaiting illumination. That illumination must come from within itself, as the Divine Presence manifested within the symbolic Temple. The Order awaits the liberation and realisation of its own inner consciousness, hitherto dormant and repressed by surface elements now proving to be of no, or of illusory, value. No sooner is the deeper and true nature of the Masonic design revealed to Brethren than upon all hands they leap to recognition of it and desire to realise it; and, for such, there can be no going back to old ways and old outlooks. The people that have sat in darkness have seen glimpses of a great light; they will now cultivate that light themselves, and be the means that others behold it also. In this way, the Craft throughout the world will become gradually regenerated in its understanding and so fulfil the destiny planned for it by those who inspired its formation three centuries ago. And it will become in due course the portal to still higher and more important spiritual eventuations.

The coming change must be, and will be, worked out not from anything emanating from the higher ranks of the Craft—the Grand Lodge and Provincial Grand Lodges—but from the floor of the individual private Lodge. For the private Lodge is the Masonic unit. The higher ranks are but recruited there from at present for complimentary or administrative purposes, although when the time comes for those hierarchies to realise their own symbolic value, it will be their members who will descend upon the Lodges of common Craftsmen, no longer as makers of merely complimentary speeches, but as real authorities upon Masonic wisdom and instructive missionaries and purveyors of Masonic truth. The private Lodge is the point from which the transformation must be achieved.

One such Lodge in a town or district, that applies itself to Masonic work upon the lines indicated in these pages, will be as a powerful leavening influence and set up wholesome reactions in neighbouring Lodges. Some resistance, and even derision, may be anticipated at first from those content with old standards and not yet ripe to appreciate a higher one, for the "nations" of less refined understanding may always be expected to "rage furiously together" at any suggestion involving departure from habitual methods or implying a possible reflection upon their wisdom. This, however, can be met with patience and charitable thought, and will soon disappear before a quiet, resolute adherence to principle. Moreover, the problem of the admission of unsuitable applicants for membership of a Lodge will soon settle itself when the standard of Masonic interpretation has been thus raised.

Let it here be emphasised that nothing in this volume is intended to advocate the least departure from or alteration of current Masonic working, or any deflection from loyalty to established usage or the governing authority. Those forms are so efficiently contrived, so perfectly adapted to the work of the Order, that, save perhaps in a matter of detail here and there, they can be altered only to their disadvantage and at the peril of disturbing ancient landmarks fixed where they are with greater wisdom than is perhaps at present recognised. Even as things are, in the haste to get through ceremonial work as quickly as may be, there is an unfortunate tendency already in official quarters to clip and curtail certain ceremonies, thereby depriving the Brethren of some valuable and significant pieces of ritual which, if continued to remain unworked, will soon become obsolete and forgotten.

Nevertheless, a little flexibility in matters of Lodge procedure would be permissible and is even desirable when Degrees are conferred. Merely to reel off a memorised ritual in a formal, mechanical way too often results in but mechanical effects, and the subject of the Ceremony goes away perhaps unimpressed or bewildered. There is nothing to prevent the delivery of the official rite being supplemented by unofficial words of explanation and encouragement such as would lend that rite additional impressiveness, a more intimate and personal bearing, and awaken in him who undergoes it a more deep and real sense of becoming vitally incorporated into living truth and into a Brotherhood to whom that truth is no mere sentiment but a profound reality.

Moreover, with a view to inducing favourable atmosphere and conditions for the conferment of a Ceremony, before the candidate enters, the assembled Brethren should always be notified from the Chair that they are about to engage in a deeply solemn act which claims the concentrated thought and aspiration of each of them, to the intent that what is done and signified ceremonially may be realised spiritually in both themselves and him to whom they desire to minister. Further, the ceremonial preparation of the candidate before being brought into the Lodge should be treated, not with levity or as a mere incidental formality, but as a profoundly sacramental act, in the significance of which both the officiating deacons and the candidate himself should be instructed. Let all Brethren be assured that there is no detail of Masonic ceremonial but is charged with very deep purpose and significance; this will appear to them more and more fully and luminously in proportion to their faithful endeavour to realise the intention of even simple and apparently unimportant points of ritual.

Sundry other matters may here be mentioned as deserving the consideration of the Craft. The first is the co-ordination of the Rituals with a view to securing uniformity of working and instruction throughout the Craft, coupled with a certain but slight amount of desirable revision. An official standardised Ritual would be beneficial and would no doubt be widely adopted even if its adoption were left optional to Lodges preferring to continue their present form of working. Upon all new Lodges, constituted after the date of standardisation, the official working should be imposed, so that, in course of time, virtual uniformity of procedure would be achieved.

The present divergences in the working of Lodges are not great and are easily capable of adjustment so as to secure a common footing of work throughout the Craft. Some Lodges use points of working not used in others and which they are rightly jealous in desiring to conserve; for example, many Lodges neither work nor know of the traditional five signs connected with the Third Degree, and merely communicate three of them, omitting two which are of great significance. On the other hand, some Lodges retain details brought over from the Operative bodies, details now obsolete and without moment to Speculative Masonry and which nowadays might well be dropped.

The "Ancient Charge" delivered to Entered Apprentices on their reception is an instance of an Operative tradition, for which, if it be not abandoned altogether, an alternative Charge, more suited to present conditions and more in consonance with Speculative Masonry, might well be substituted. For a Charge that was intended for, and that was delivered to, youths upon entering an Operative Building Guild is unsuited to men already immersed in civic, family, and business responsibilities, and seeking now to acquire knowledge of a purely mystical character; it is absurd and grotesque to counsel a middle-aged experienced man to perform elementary duties of citizenship, or to express to—perhaps an ecclesiastical dignitary who joins the Order—the hope that he "will become respectable in life"!

Revision of the Rituals would, of course, be a delicate task; one not to be undertaken at haphazard or to meet the chance whims and uninstructed notions of this or that Brother, but one calling for the enlightened guidance of minds conversant with Initiation-science; otherwise the Craft may lose more than it may gain, and good plants may be pulled up and thrown away in mistake for weeds.

As an example of a point needing revision and excision, let me instance those passages in which a candidate is enjoined to extend charity and relief to those needing it "if he can do so without detriment to himself or connections." These qualifying words surely vitiate the whole spirit of "Charity." If Charity means anything—and mere financial help is not charity, but only one form of its practical manifestation—it involves a wise but unstinted selflessness, a self-sacrifice at whatever personal cost. To hedge round that supreme virtue with a cautious verbal reservation in one's own favour is a limitation entirely unworthy of Masonic magnanimity, and the words come as a shock to one's moral sensitiveness.

To come to the next point: the Festive Board. In previous pages, it has been indicated that the customary practice of refreshment and social conviviality is not only practically useful, but has a deep sacramental value. It is, of course, technically extra-Masonic and non-official, or perhaps quasi-official; but it provides real and useful opportunities for fraternising and intellectual opportunities for enlarging upon Masonic matters not dealt with in the Lodge sanctuary itself; whilst, in its symbolic and higher aspect, it illustrates that relaxation from labor, and that refreshment derived from the inter-communion of those united in a common work, which in the providential order are arranged for us both in this life and hereafter.

The value, or otherwise, of the Festive Board depends, therefore, upon its good use or its abuse. If it be regarded and used as the natural extension of the more formal work of the Lodge, it can exercise a ministry of great service; if, on the other hand, it be but an occasion for junketing and social frivolity under the cover of Masonry, but with little or no Masonic relevance, it is apt to become a thing of reproach; the sublimities of the Lodge-work are falsified by it, and any good issuing from that work is forthwith neutralised. The test of true Masonic devotion and sincerity would be the honest answer each Brother can give to the question: "How far would my interest in Masonry extend and continue if the practice of the Festive Board did not exist and Masonic proceedings were confined to the formal work of the Lodge?" With this reflection, the matter may be left to the good judgment of the Craft.

There must also be mentioned a question which has already rankled as a thorn in the side of Grand Lodge and will doubtless become still more troublesome: the "Women's question"; and if I approach it, it is not with the idea of presuming to offer suggestions to the governing authority of the Craft, but of defining the position for the guidance of the average Brother.

As things stand, Grand Lodge is the trustee of a system which it has inherited, which it is pledged to continue upon established lines, and which it has no power to alter if it wished, save at the request and by the common consent of those whose interests it exists to conserve. It has no power to sanction the admission of women into the order, nor is there any desire in its ranks that it should; indeed, the fact that women can today take elsewhere precisely the same degrees as the Craft confers is a fact unknown to the majority of Brethren.

Whether Grand Lodge should extend official recognition to societies professing to be Masonic and admitting members of both sexes is another matter, and depends upon the view to be taken of the regularity or irregularity of the societies in question. Can such societies produce satisfactory evidence of their regularity and right to recognition, or have they sprung into existence through the treachery or disloyalty of members of the Craft? That is not a question falling to the present writer to determine, nor has he sufficient material before him to do so. The only conclusion he can come to for himself, and the only advice he can offer to others, is to abide loyally by the existing ordinances of the duly constituted authority. The Craft so far has been the "Men's House," and must so remain until such time as circumstances—which do not now exist and for a long time to come are unlikely to exist—clearly warrant a departure from the present position.

It may be that the "Men" do not make the best use of their "House"; it may be that the now banned societies have sprung into existence because of that fact; it may be—and there are grounds for supposing it—that in those societies Masonry is worked with greater decorum, a far fuller understanding, a deeper reverence and appreciation of what it implies, than in the orthodox Craft. But the fact remains that we are committed and pledged to our own Constitution for the present and we shall do neither it nor our individual selves a service by departing from strict loyalty to it.

Upon the general question of the fitness of women to receive the Masonic or any alternative form of Initiation, I must record an affirmative conviction of the same strength as the negative one I make to the suggestion that women should be admitted to the Craft or that visiting relations between the latter and the unauthorised societies should be sanctioned; for, in existing conditions, such relationship is undesirable and might prove disastrous to both.

Although the sexes meet upon a common footing in the field of both religious and secular affairs, and although the whole modern tendency is towards equality of rights, function and responsibility, Masonry at present stands outside both the religious and the secular categories, and by the majority of its members is viewed merely as a social luxury and a casual appendage to other activities of life. Until it is accorded a far higher appreciation than this, until it can be viewed from a standpoint not merely of ordinary morality but from one involving a high standard of personal sanctity; until the mental conception of it is sufficiently lofty and compelling to neutralise emotional frailty and the chances of moral lapse, Masonry is far better reserved as the "Men's House," even though that House be, in the prophet's words, one "of untempered mortar" and lacking the advantage of feminine association.

The human soul is essentially sexless, yet to the feminine side of humanity is notoriously credited exceptional intuitive power and capacity for the finer apprehension of truth, and upon this account, in the days of the Eleusinia, women were never excluded from initiation into the Mysteries, but were allotted special rites of their own, and, in the processions of the Thesmophorim, passed along the public street bearing upon their heads the volumes of the Sacred Law—an eloquent symbolic tribute and testimony to the superior power of the feminine understanding to intuitise the finer sense and implications of that Law.

It was to a woman—the mysterious Diotima of Megara—that the amazed Socrates owed his supreme initiation into that last Mystery of Love about which he speaks in the Symposium with such awe and moving eloquence; yet a woman with whom stands exhibited, in purposed contrast, that opposite pole of womanhood, the futile, mindless Xantippe whom he had wedded.

There have been Egerias, Aspasias and Hypatias, besides those known to history; and Dante's hierophantess, Beatrice—but types that "eternal womanly" which, Goethe truly divined, always exists with us to lead the male intellect ever upward and on. It is almost needless to point to the mass of work done by women still living in the exposition of mystical philosophy and religion, or to say that such great mines of instruction in matters of Masonic moment as *Isis Unveiled, The Secret Doctrine,* and *A Suggestive Inquiry into the Hermetic Mystery,* have come from the pens of women learned and enlightened in things pertaining to the Craft to a degree seldom evidenced by its own members.

In every interest, then, it is desirable that the "women's question" should rest where it is. Nothing can prevent those, of whichever sex, who are really builders in the spirit, from privately fraternising in that spirit. To such, formal collaboration, however agreeable it might be were it permissible, can be dispensed with, for their work is not dependent upon facilities of a formal character, and they will be the first to recognise the wisdom of Order accepting and the expedience of conforming to current technical necessity. When the time and conditions arrive for present barriers to be removed, it will be because the Craft itself will have removed them by entering into a fuller realisation of its purpose than now obtains, and because Grand Lodge will have been influenced to alter its laws by an authority higher even than itself—the Grand Lodge Above.

To pass now from these considerations of things of the moment to the larger vista towards which those things are leading, what is the prospect before the Order?

That prospect is perhaps sufficiently indicated by the familiar words written at the head of this paper: "First, that which is natural; after, that which is spiritual." For nearly three centuries the Craft has been developing from a small germ to a great robust body characterised by tendencies of a purely natural kind, manifesting natural human weaknesses, and displaying the inexperience, the irresponsibility, and the limitations of outlook common to all youth. It has meant well, even when it has misconceived its purpose. If it has provided a field in which numbers of men, blind to the Order's real significance, have sought merely social amusement and personal distinction, it has also proved a source of light and guidance to many obscure souls not subject to those vanities and who have realised and profited by its implications, and some of who from the portal of the Craft, have passed on in silence to more advanced methods or colleges of spiritual instruction. A sacramental system is not invalidated by the default of those accepting its jurisdiction; and as saints often flourished in the Church amid most unsaintly conditions, so not a few Masons have won to the light despite the surrounding darkness of their Brethren.

But now is coming a change, and it is significant that it comes not from the higher ranks of the Craft where, with all desire for the Craft's best interests, every tendency is towards conservatism and the sufficiency of old standards, but from the rank and file, from the younger, newer blood now flowing into the veins of the Order. It is, of course, not a movement even remotely resembling disaffection, but now, as never before, Brethren in numbers are asking from Masonry bread of life; they are caring less and less for ceremonies and ancient usages unless these can be shown to have supporting justification; they look to the leaders and teachers of the Craft for, not a perpetual reiteration of complimentary but unsatisfying speeches, but for instruction in real Masonic light and wisdom.

The future of the Order cannot be appraised without reference to the general social life surrounding it; for it is not something apart and detached from that life but an integral element of it, and between the two there is perpetual interaction and reaction. The gradual disintegration of the Churches affects the Craft, tending both to increase it numerically and to advance the exploration of its concealed spiritual resources. Religion will not die—the religious instinct can never die—nor will "the Church" in some form cease to exist and to fulfil a certain ministry. But today a supplementary form of ministry is required and Masonry can provide it. A regrouping and redistribution of energy is taking place, in the course of which we may come to find that that powerful psychological phenomenon, a new group-consciousness—the Masonic consciousness—has been in process of formation; a consciousness which may become in time as potent a factor as was the Church-consciousness of mediaeval days, or as was the moral power of the Delphian Mysteries during the seventeen centuries of their great influence.

When the time ripens, the Mysteries—as a science of life and an art of so living as to qualify for attaining ultra-natural life—will come to be restored. For long past, both within and without the Church, the tide of human persuasion and events has been deadest against the tradition of regeneration into that ultra-natural life, as originally taught and practiced. But that which has been is that which, in the course of cyclic recurrence, shall be again, and upon a higher level of development than before.

It is not that the Christian Church is not a steward of the Mysteries —or at least that portion of it which does not reject the authentic sacramental signs and channels through which those Mysteries may be realised, but, from reasons too complex and lengthy here to detail, there has been failure on the human side to realise them, as they are now presented, with the result that the Christian Ecclesia has degenerated into a state analogous to that into which the pre-Christian Mystery-systems had fallen when the new era began. To the clear-seeing eye the narrative in the Gospels, apart from all questions of historicity, is a drama of Initiation written for that time, for every eye to see, and for every mind to profit by; for what previously had been but adumbrated and approached by a few individuals in the concealment of the Mystery-schools, became, at the Incarnation, objectified, universalised and made generally accessible; in other words the Gospels became a manual of Initiation-instruction to the whole world according to the measure of individual capacity to receive it, notwithstanding that large tracts of knowledge remained unproclaimed in those Gospels but were reserved for more private communication.

The recurrent cycle of the Church's year, with its feasts and fasts, its symbolic seasons pointing to inhibitions and expansions of the soul's consciousness, is a true chart of the path to be followed by those who themselves seek initiation under the mastership of the Great Hierophant and Exemplar of regenerative science; while in the Sacrament of the Altar is portrayed, albeit under different symbolism, the actual process of Initiation and the same transmutative changes in the body and mind of the recipient as are emblematised to the Masonic candidate in the Craft Degrees.

Truth remains static, although temporal expressions and ministries of it follow the temporal order, and are born and die. When this form of the Mysteries becomes neglected or abused, or that steward of them decrepit or ineffective, another—in the Divine providence and patience—stands ready to carry forward their torch; truth becomes "fulfilled in many ways lest one good custom should corrupt the world." The Masonic system was devised three centuries ago, at a time of general unrest and change, as a preparatory infant-school in which once again the alphabet of a world-old Gnosis might be learned and an elementary acquaintance made with the science of human regeneration.

However misunderstood and misapplied, however materialistically conceived, have been its rites, the soul and consciousness of every voluntary participant in them stands imperishably impressed with the memory of them. The maxim "Once a Mason, always a Mason" expresses an occult truth not realised by those who are unaware of the subjective value and persistence of one's deliberated objective actions; though the Church implies the same truth when it deems the act of sacramental baptism to bring a given soul within the fold of Christ forever. In each case, and especially so when the deliberate will of the neophyte assents to the act, a new addition is made to the group-soul of the community into which the individual becomes incorporated; and, in the case of the Masonic initiate, the aggregate and volume of what we have termed the Masonic Consciousness is enlarged.

Reactions and consequences follow of a nature perhaps too abstruse to dilate upon here, but to which the Roman Initiated poet referred in the well-known words:

Magnus ab integro saeclorum nascitur ordo.
Iam redit et Virgo; redeunt Saturnia regna;
Iam nova progenies coelo demittitur alto.

Meanwhile, tinctured and affected by this metaphysical influence from the subjective world, the work of the Craft proceeds within this bourne of time and place; beginning, as we have shown, crudely and following the grosser tendencies of the natural order, until a moment is reached when a new birth becomes possible. Then the natural gives way to the spiritual, and the great material organisation, a "body prepared," becomes the requisite physical vehicle for a correspondingly great office as a minister of real Wisdom.

Operative Masonry preceded and became spiritualised into Speculative, and the gross beginnings of the latter are now becoming sublimated into a more subtle conception and tending to a scientific mysticism at once theoretic and practical. We may look forward to the gradual increasing spiritualisation of the Craft and to its becoming—in a future the nearness or distance of which no one can presume to indicate—the portal to a still more advanced expression of the Sacred Mysteries.

For, foretold the Great Master, the time will surely come when in the present ways of neither this "mountain"—neither this Church nor that Craft—nor any Jerusalem that now serves as a place of peace, will men worship the Universal Father, but after another manner and mystically, that is, after the manner of the eternal Mysteries. "For salvation is of the Jews," He added, and it has previously been explained that by "Jews" is implied the Initiates of those Mysteries, acting under the Grand Mastership of Him who was named "the King of the Jews."

The Churches, therefore, may be left to continue to discharge their proper ministry, whilst those who feel the need of a larger science, an alternative and perhaps richer fare than the Churches provide, may find it in the ancient Gnosis to which Freemasonry serves as a portal of entrance. By following the path to which that portal leads, they may be brought to a deeper knowledge of themselves and of the mysteries of their own being; to which end, and which end alone, the Masonic Craft was designed.

That Craft will only become what its individual members make it. If they see in it only a ceremonial procedure, as such it will remain, and their initiation will be but one in name and not in fact. But if they strive to realise and make their own the living spirit and intention behind the outward rites and formal usages, the dramatised quest of light and of the Lost Word may result for them in a blessed finding of that which they profess to seek, and what they find themselves they will become able to communicate to other seekers, until the Craft is justified of all its children, and itself becomes—as it was intended to become—a great light in a dark world.

REFLECTION: FOUNDATION OF STONE, TRANSMUTATION OF SPIRIT:

OPERATIVE TRADITION TO ARCANE SIGHT

ECHOES OF THE QUARRY

As we approach the threshold of Masonic initiation, we are not merely stepping into a new fraternity or tradition but into a timeless and sacred landscape. This moment is an awakening, an invitation to journey inward and rediscover the unchanging wisdom that resides within the self. To begin is not to merely start but to open ourselves to the mysteries—ancient truths that call out to the eternal essence of our being, shaping and being shaped by the legacy of countless seekers who have walked this path.

The ritual of the Entered Apprentice stands as both a gateway and a mirror, reflecting the initiate's potential while gently urging the soul toward its highest purpose. Symbols that seem at first glance static and ornamental reveal themselves, in time, as living keys, each unlocking hidden truths within the Craft and, more profoundly, within the initiate. As we encounter Jacob's Ladder, its rungs ascending through the virtues of faith, hope, and charity, we find a reflection of our spiritual ascent. These are not merely virtues to admire but steps that guide us to harmonise our aspirations with divine principles. At its pinnacle, charity is revealed—not as the simple act of giving but as the all-encompassing love that binds the universe together, urging us toward unity with the Great Architect.

This symbolic ladder connects our earthly experience to a greater reality, echoing the ancient rites of the Eleusinian Mysteries, where initiates passed through layers of understanding to glimpse the eternal. Like those ancient ceremonies, Masonic initiation is not simply a ritual to observe but a transformative process that unfolds through experience, introspection, and the quiet illumination of the soul. Each rung climbed is a step away from ignorance and toward the light, a journey through our passions, past our limitations, and into the clarity of higher awareness.

Yet, this journey is not solitary. The initiate enters a lineage of seekers, united across time by their shared pursuit of light and truth. Each symbol of Freemasonry serves as a bridge connecting the individual to this timeless current, as living expressions of wisdom. The compass, the square, and the ladder are not merely tools but echoes of universal truths that speak directly to the heart, urging the soul toward wholeness.

As we reflect on this transformative beginning, we are reminded of Wilmshurst's insight: that initiation is not merely an external act but an internal awakening. It is a call to step beyond the surface of life, to transcend the transient and align with the eternal. A century later, his warning remains as vital as ever—Freemasonry must remain a living flame, kindled in the hearts of its members, lest it fade into mere form and tradition. To allow this fire to burn brightly, we must approach each ritual and symbol with reverence and openness, allowing them to awaken within us the same timeless truths that have guided Masons for generations.

Joseph Fort Newton once remarked, "Rituals, when rightly understood, become a language that speaks directly to the soul." This understanding is at the heart of the Masonic path. Our journey as Masons is not toward an external destination but inward, where the soul discovers its unity with the divine. Engaging deeply with this journey, each Mason becomes a "living stone," part of a vast and eternal Temple built not of hands but of spirit, where the pursuit of wisdom and light continues unbroken.

ORIGINS OF MODERN SPECULATIVE FREEMASONRY

The formation of the Grand Lodge of England in 1717 stands as one of the most transformative moments in the history of Freemasonry. It marked the beginning of organised speculative Freemasonry, a profound evolution that took the Craft beyond its operative roots. This shift was not merely administrative or structural; it was a symbolic reimagining of the tools and practices of medieval stone-masons into metaphors for the inner work of the soul.

In its operative form, masonry was bound to the physical world and focused on constructing grand cathedrals and enduring monuments. The compass, square, and level were practical instruments, tools wielded by skilled craftsmen to ensure balance, precision, and stability in their work. But with the advent of speculative Freemasonry, these tools were imbued with a deeper significance. The square became a guide for moral rectitude, the compass a reminder to circumscribe our passions within due bounds, and the level a symbol of equality. Together, they formed a language of the soul, aligning the Mason's character with universal principles.

This evolution was not an isolated phenomenon but part of a larger cultural movement. The early 18th century was a time of intellectual and spiritual awakening, where thinkers sought to reconcile reason with faith and science with mysticism. Freemasonry, emerging in this fertile ground, drew deeply from both exoteric practices and esoteric traditions. Its rituals, symbols, and teachings became a bridge between these two realms.

The exoteric dimension of Freemasonry retained its connection to craftsmanship, emphasising practical morality and the application of

Masonic principles in daily life. But beneath this visible layer lay the esoteric core—a reservoir of wisdom drawn from Hermeticism, Kabbalah, Rosicrucianism, and other mystical traditions. These influences imbued the Craft with a profound depth, offering initiates a path of self-discovery and spiritual enlightenment.

Manly P. Hall, in his seminal work *The Lost Keys of Freemasonry*, described the Craft as "a university, teaching the liberal arts and sciences of the soul to all who attend to its words." For Hall, Freemasonry was not merely a social institution but a spiritual discipline designed to awaken the latent divinity within each initiate and a call to Masons to see the connection between their inner and outer worlds, between the temple they built within themselves and the greater universe.

However, this balance between the exoteric and esoteric has not been without its challenges. In *The Meaning of Masonry*, Wilmshurst cautioned against the risk of Freemasonry becoming "an exoteric system concerned with social entertainments and charitable activities," warning that the Craft might lose its spiritual sanctity if it failed to engage with its inner mysteries. This tension remains relevant today as modern Freemasonry navigates its dual identity. On the one hand, it is a fraternity committed to fellowship and public service; on the other, it is a repository of ancient wisdom, a guide for the soul's journey toward light.

The esoteric influences that originally shaped speculative Freemasonry still linger within its rituals and symbols, but their depth is often obscured by a focus on outward forms. The mystical teachings of Hermeticism, emphasising the unity of all things, and Kabbalah, with its intricate map of spiritual ascent, provide profound insights into the Masonic journey. Yet, these teachings are not always explicitly explored within contemporary Lodges. The Rosicrucian ideal of hidden knowledge, accessible only to those who seek it sincerely, mirrors the Masonic principle that true understanding comes through personal effort and introspection.

In reflecting on these origins, we are reminded that the tools of the operative Mason were never abandoned; they were transformed. They became symbols of inner craftsmanship and instruments for building a Temple not of stone but of spirit. The compass that once traced the curves of an arch now traces the boundaries of the Mason's conduct. The square that once tested the angles of a cornerstone now tests the integrity of the Mason's actions. Each tool remains a reminder that the inner work of the heart must match the outer work of the hands.

As we consider the divine symmetry between Freemasonry's exoteric and esoteric dimensions, we are called to ask: does modern Freemasonry honour this dual legacy? Do its practices and teachings inspire Masons to look beyond the surface and seek hidden wisdom within? The answer lies not in the Craft as an institution but in each Mason's journey. The rituals and symbols are there, waiting to reveal their secrets to those who approach them with reverence and curiosity.

In this light, the origins of modern speculative Freemasonry are not merely historical facts but a living foundation. They remind us that the true work of the Mason is not to preserve the past but to embody its principles in the present. By engaging deeply with the esoteric traditions that shaped the Craft, we ensure that Freemasonry remains a path of enlightenment, a bridge between the material and the mystical, a journey from darkness to light.

THE ANCIENT CHARGE AND OPERATIVE FOUNDATIONS

In its earliest days, the Ancient Charge was more than a guide to ethical behaviour; it was a solemn commitment, elevating labor to an act of reverence and devotion. The operative masons, who shaped stone into cathedrals and structures of enduring beauty, understood that their work extended beyond the physical realm. Each tool in their hands was not merely a means to an end but a symbol of precision, discipline, and purpose, reflecting a harmony that resonated with the divine order of creation. This ethos, captured within the *Regius Manuscript* and the *Halliwell Manuscript* pages, illustrates the profound interconnectedness between physical craftsmanship and moral character.

The *Regius Manuscript* calls upon masons to live with integrity, declaring,

> *"Be steadfast and true, and well keep counsel;*
> *For the same shall help you well."*

Such directives were not limited to the practicalities of the Craft but echoed a universal call to align one's labour with ethical and spiritual values. Similarly, the *Halliwell Manuscript* reminds us of the collective responsibility inherent in Masonry, stating,

> *"every man shall his fellow help,*
> *For to his craft is all his help."*

These ancient words reflect an understanding of fellowship and shared purpose, where the labour of one contributed to the collective good—a principle that transcends time and remains central to Freemasonry.

As Freemasonry evolved from an operative to a speculative tradition, the Ancient Charge underwent a transformation, which mirrored the philosophical expansion of the Craft itself. This evolution was not a departure but an alchemical refinement, preserving the foundational principles of the operative masons while inviting deeper contemplation of the soul's journey. The tools of the trade—the square, level, plumb, and chisel—were reimagined as metaphors for ethical alignment and spiritual growth. The square came to symbolise moral rectitude, guiding actions to remain just and balanced. The level reminded Masons of equality and the interconnectedness of all beings, while the plumb urged them to walk uprightly by the highest principles of truth and virtue.

Wilmshurst captures this transition with profound clarity, asserting that "the true secrets of Masonry are concerned with the development of the divine possibilities latent in the soul of man". In speculative Freemasonry, the operative mason's labour of shaping stone became a metaphor for the speculative Mason's labour of refining the self. The act of constructing physical edifices transformed into the sacred task of constructing an inner temple—a place of harmony, wisdom, and alignment with the Great Architect's design.

This transformation is beautifully articulated by René Guénon, who described Freemasonry as the inheritor of ancient wisdom, preserving sacred traditions in the heart of its rituals. Through this lens, Freemasonry emerges as both a custodian and a vessel of timeless truths, bridging the practical and the mystical. The Ancient Charge, reinterpreted through the speculative lens, calls each Mason to participate in a journey of self-discovery, transforming the rough ashlar of unrefined character into the perfect ashlar of moral and spiritual integrity.

Yet the Ancient Charge is not confined to the lodge's rituals. It is a living directive that challenges modern Masons to apply its principles in a world that prioritises superficial achievement over genuine growth. It reminds us to approach our work within and beyond the lodge with our operative ancestors' discipline, focus, and reverence. Are we, like them, crafting lives as skilfully as they crafted cathedrals? Are we ensuring our moral and spiritual foundations are as solid and enduring as the structures they built?

With its rapid pace and shifting values, the modern world presents unique challenges to the continuity of the Ancient Charge. Wilmshurst warned against reducing Freemasonry to "an exoteric system concerned with social entertainments and charitable activities," cautioning that such a focus risks losing the inner sanctity of the Craft. Masons must balance outward action and inner growth to honour the Ancient Charge fully. Charity and fraternity, while noble, gain greater resonance when grounded in the transformative principles that lie at the heart of the Craft.

Today, the Ancient Charge serves as a call to continuous self-refinement. Each decision and action becomes a brick in the edifice of one's character. Through acts of patience, humility, and perseverance, the Mason builds a life of virtue and a legacy that contributes to the collective good. Wilmshurst reminds us that the goal of Masonry is to "arouse the hidden powers latent in man," urging each Mason to embrace the Ancient Charge as a framework for personal and societal transformation.

The Ancient Charge also challenges Masons to consider their responsibilities within a broader context. In an era of ethical dilemmas and societal divisions, the principles embedded within the charge offer a guide to navigating complexity with integrity and compassion. By embodying the values of justice, equity, and service, Masons can exemplify the harmony and unity that the Craft envisions.

Ultimately, the Ancient Charge remains as relevant today as it was in the time of operative masonry. It calls us to be both builders of character and architects of a better world. In preserving this sacred directive, Freemasonry offers a sanctuary where timeless values and inner transformation converge. Each Mason, by embracing the lessons of the charge, contributes to the grand edifice of truth, light, and virtue—a legacy that honours the past while illuminating the path forward.

MYSTICAL AND ESOTERIC ASPECTS OF THE CRAFT

At its heart, Freemasonry is a spiritual journey, a quest that leads the initiate from the temporal toward the eternal. Nowhere is this more evident than in the Third Degree, where the initiate undergoes a symbolic death and resurrection, echoing the ancient mysteries that have guided seekers for millennia. This profound ritual invites the Mason to step beyond the realm of the familiar and into the depths of self-discovery, where the symbols and teachings of the Craft unfold as gateways to eternal truths.

The transformative power of the Third Degree lies in its ability to connect the Mason with timeless wisdom encoded in Hermetic, Kabbalistic, and alchemical traditions. Hermeticism, rooted in the teachings of Hermes Trismegistus, offers a cosmological vision of unity, where the macrocosm and microcosm mirror one another. This principle, encapsulated in the Hermetic axiom "As above, so below," serves as a cornerstone for the esoteric dimensions of Freemasonry. Each ritual and symbol reflect universal principles, guiding the Mason to align their inner life with the divine order.

Similarly, the Kabbalistic Tree of Life provides a map of spiritual ascent, with its ten Sephiroth representing stages of consciousness and divine attributes. The journey up the Tree parallels the Masonic path, inviting the initiate to ascend from material limitations to spiritual illumination. This symbolism is most evident in the Third Degree, where the initiate's figurative death represents the surrender of ego and attachment, while their resurrection signifies the soul's rebirth into higher awareness.

The alchemical tradition, focusing on transformation and refinement, also resonates deeply within the Craft. The Mason's labour of perfecting the ashlar mirrors the alchemist's quest to transmute base metals into gold. This process, known as the Great Work, symbolises the inner alchemy of self-transformation, where the Mason refines their character and reveals the divine essence within.

As Manly P. Hall eloquently stated, "Freemasonry is a spiritual movement designed to unite the initiate with the spiritual source of his life". The rituals and symbols of Freemasonry are not static relics but living tools, inviting each initiate to engage actively with the mysteries of existence. The Third Degree, in particular, offers an unparalleled opportunity for self-reflection and spiritual growth, guiding the Mason through the ultimate mystery of life, death, and rebirth.

However, in the modern era, the mystical essence of Freemasonry often lies dormant, overshadowed by an emphasis on fraternity, social engagements, and public service. While these aspects of the Craft are valuable, they risk obscuring the deeper purpose of Freemasonry: to awaken the soul to a realisation of the divine mysteries. Wilmshurst's words challenge Masons today to reconnect with the spiritual roots of the Craft and to prioritise the mystical elements that give Freemasonry its transformative power.

To reinvigorate the teachings of the Third Degree in modern practice, Lodges must embrace their role as sanctuaries of spiritual exploration. This begins with an intentional focus on the symbolism embedded within the rituals. For instance, the allegory of Hiram Abiff, central to the Third Degree, offers profound lessons on the soul's journey and the triumph of integrity over adversity. By delving into the esoteric meanings of this allegory, Masons can uncover layers of wisdom that transcend the ritual's outward form.

Moreover, Lodges can incorporate teachings from the Hermetic, Kabbalistic, and alchemical traditions to deepen members' understanding of the Craft. Workshops, discussions, and guided meditations on these traditions could provide Masons with practical tools for integrating their spiritual insights into daily life. Such practices would honour the Craft's heritage while ensuring its relevance in an era that prioritises the material over the spiritual.

The mystical path within Freemasonry is as relevant today as it was in the past, but cultivating its transformative potential requires a conscious commitment. Each symbol, each gesture within the ritual, may awaken the initiate to the mysteries of life and the cosmos. Yet this potential can only be realised when Masons approach their work with sincerity, reverence, and an open heart.

Freemasonry offers more than moral instruction or fellowship; it provides a framework for personal and spiritual evolution. The journey through the degrees is not merely a progression through ceremonial waypoints but a call to engage with the hidden dimensions of existence. As the initiate moves through the degrees, they are invited to leave behind the concerns of the profane world and step into a sacred space where transformation can occur.

In today's society, where outer achievements often overshadow inner growth, the teachings of the Third Degree offer a counterbalance—a reminder that true success lies not in what we accumulate but in who we become.

Ultimately, Freemasonry's mystical and esoteric aspects are not optional embellishments but the very essence of the Craft. They call us to transcend the mundane and to align ourselves with the eternal principles that underpin all creation. By prioritising these teachings, contemporary Lodges can ensure that Freemasonry remains a vibrant and transformative force in the lives of its members and the world.

GUARDIANS OF BALANCE: THE DUAL PATH OF THE SAINTS JOHN

Freemasonry's profound symbolism finds a central focus in the figures of St. John the Baptist and St. John the Evangelist.Beyond their historical or religious identities, these two Saints represent the dual aspects of the Masonic journey: action and reflection. Together, they guide Masons toward a harmonious balance between outward engagement with the world and inward contemplation of the self. Their presence in the Craft embodies wisdom, zeal, introspection, and dedication to higher ideals, serving as archetypes of a life shaped by Masonic values.

St. John the Baptist, associated with initiation and preparation, calls Masons to embrace the zeal and discipline necessary to embark on the Masonic path. His austere life in the wilderness and his call to repentance mirror the early stages of the Masonic journey, where the initiate is urged to confront their inner imperfections and prepare themselves for enlightenment. He symbolises action, urging Masons to take decisive steps toward the light.

In contrast, St. John the Evangelist represents wisdom, reflection, and the soul's journey inward. Known for his deeply spiritual Gospel and visionary revelations, he guides the inner mysteries, calling Masons to contemplate the higher truths of existence. He reminds us that the ultimate goal of Masonic labour is not merely outward accomplishment but the cultivation of inner peace and understanding.

This duality of the Saints John reflects the Masonic principle of equilibrium, where the active and contemplative life must coexist harmoniously. Their symbolism is beautifully captured in the emblem of the circumpunct—a point within a circle flanked by two parallel lines. The circle represents the infinite, unbroken unity of the divine, while the central point symbolises the individual soul. The parallel lines, representing the Saints John, serve as pillars of equallibrium, guiding the Mason between the realms of action and introspection. They illustrate the Masonic journey of aligning the self with universal harmony.

The cosmological significance of the circumpunct extends beyond Masonry, finding parallels in ancient spiritual traditions. In Egyptian cosmology, the circle represented Ra, the sun god, radiating life and order. In Hermeticism, the circumpunct symbolised the Monad, the source of all existence. These connections reinforce the Masonic teaching that the soul, while distinct, is inseparably connected to the greater whole. By meditating on this symbol, Masons are reminded of their dual responsibility to refine themselves and contribute to the broader harmony of existence.

ESOTERIC CONNECTIONS: THE SAINTS JOHN AND MYSTICAL TRADITIONS

The dual roles of the Saints John resonate deeply with esoteric traditions such as Rosicrucianism, where they are seen as guardians of spiritual wisdom and transformation. St. John the Baptist embodies the fiery zeal of the alchemical process, the burning away of impurities that prepares the soul for transformation. St. John the Evangelist, with his contemplative vision, aligns with the alchemical stage of illumination, where the purified soul reflects the divine light.

In Freemasonry, these esoteric connections are not merely academic; they are living teachings that guide the Mason toward inner and outer alignment. The Saints John represent the pillars of the inner temple, reminding Masons that true wisdom arises when action is tempered by reflection, and reflection is given purpose through action. Their symbolism invites Masons to embrace the dual aspects of their nature, striving for a balance that honours both the physical and the spiritual.

THE ROLE OF THE ESSENES AND THE PATH OF PURIFICATION

St. John the Baptist's life and teachings are remarkably similar to the Essenes' practices, an ancient Jewish sect devoted to ritual purity, communal living, and spiritual preparation. Like the Essenes, who sought enlightenment through strict discipline and separation from worldly distractions, John exemplifies the Masonic ideal of purification as a prerequisite for illumination. His call to "make straight the way of the Lord" mirrors the Masonic charge to prepare oneself for the journey toward light, emphasising the need for moral and spiritual readiness.

The Essenes' communal focus and dedication to higher principles also resonate in Masonic Lodges, where fellowship and shared commitment to virtue are central. Their belief in an impending divine revelation parallels the Masonic teaching that enlightenment is a gradual unveiling accessible to those who diligently seek it. By understanding these connections, Masons can see St. John the Baptist as a historical figure and a timeless archetype of preparation and transformation.In Freemasonry, Saints John—the Baptist and the Evangelist—serve as profound symbols of balance, guiding Masons along the dual paths of action and introspection. Their feast days, June 24 and December 27, align with the summer and winter solstices, marking pivotal points in the natural cycle of light and darkness. These celestial events provide Masons with opportunities to reflect on the deeper symbolism of the Saints John, offering a framework for personal growth and Masonic education.

The celebration of St. John the Baptist occurs at the summer solstice, the longest day of the year and a time of abundant light. It symbolises outward action, zeal, and the courage to confront life's challenges with purpose and resolve. St. John the Baptist's call to repentance and his austere life in the wilderness mirror the beginning of the Masonic journey, where the initiate is called to confront inner imperfections and prepare for spiritual growth. His feast day is ideal for Masons to gather and reflect on the importance of outward action, courage, and discipline in their practice. This time could also inspire discussions or workshops on how to apply Masonic principles to daily life, emphasising service, purpose, and living with intention.

In contrast, St. John the Evangelist's feast day at the winter solstice, the longest night of the year, symbolises inward reflection, wisdom, and the search for inner light. Known for his spiritual Gospel and visionary revelations, the Evangelist reminds Masons that the ultimate goal of their labours is not external accomplishment but the cultivation of deeper understanding and harmony with the divine. His feast day offers a natural pause for introspection and renewal, encouraging members to meditate on their spiritual progress, consider goals for the coming year, and seek inner illumination. It is a moment to emphasise the importance of wisdom, humility, and the quiet pursuit of self-knowledge as a complement to outward action.

Together, these solstitial celebrations embody the cyclical nature of the Masonic journey. They remind Masons that periods of outward labour must be balanced by times of inward contemplation. This equilibrium ensures that Masonic work is infused with wisdom and guided by higher principles, reflecting the universal harmony symbolised by the circumpunct—a point within a circle flanked by two parallel lines representing the Saints John. This emblem unites the infinite nature of the divine (the circle) with the individual's journey toward balance and enlightenment (the central point), supported by the dual archetypes of action and reflection.

Despite their profound symbolism, the Saints John are often under-appreciated in modern Freemasonry, where their deeper esoteric significance risks being overshadowed. To reinvigorate their presence within the Craft, Lodges could embrace their roles as archetypes of a balanced life and stewards of Masonic values. Their duality represents the Masonic principle of equilibrium, harmonising the active and contemplative aspects of existence.

Lodges can deepen their connection to the universal rhythms symbolised by the Saints John by creating opportunities for celebration and education around the solstitial cycles they represent. For St. John the Baptist's feast, gatherings might focus on action, zeal, and outward purpose, reflecting on how Masonic teachings inspire members to engage with the world meaningfully. For St. John the Evangelist's feast, moments of quiet reflection, meditative lectures, and discussions on the pursuit of wisdom and inner harmony could provide a counterbalance, fostering introspection and personal growth.

As Wilmshurst reminds us, "The true Mason, and the true meaning of Masonry, can only be found by those who will 'search for it as for hidden treasure.'" The Saints John, as guardians of this treasure, call Masons to harmonise action with reflection, outward labour with inward understanding. Their duality reflects Freemasonry's core principle of equilibrium—a balance essential for personal and collective growth.

By embracing the teachings of the Saints John and aligning Masonic practices with the solstitial cycles they represent, Lodges can cultivate a deeper, more vibrant engagement with the Craft. These celebrations serve as reminders that the Masonic journey is not a linear path but a cyclical dance between light and darkness, action and introspection, outward service and inner peace. In this way, the Saints John continue to illuminate the way for all who seek the eternal truths of Freemasonry.

THE MYSTICAL STONE AND INNER TRANSFORMATION; THE PHILOSOPHER'S STONE AND HISTORICAL ESOTERICISM

The symbolism of the stone within Freemasonry speaks to the deepest truths of the human experience. At its most profound, the journey from the Rough to the Perfect Ashlar represents the lifelong process of inner refinement, where raw potential is shaped into purposeful wisdom and beauty. Each Mason begins as a Rough Ashlar, marked by imperfections yet imbued with the divine spark necessary for transformation. This path is not merely a metaphor but a living practice requiring dedication, introspection, and resilience.

In modern society, the journey toward the Perfect Ashlar faces challenges unlike any other time in history. Social media, materialism, and pursuing superficial validation present obstacles to genuine self-reflection. These pursuits encourage the construction of a polished outer facade while neglecting the inner labour required for true self-mastery. Likes, shares, and curated digital personas mask the unrefined edges of the soul, offering a fleeting illusion of perfection but leaving the inner stone untouched and unpolished.

Freemasonry calls upon its members to resist these illusions and engage in the authentic work of inner transformation. To embrace the journey from Rough to Perfect Ashlar is to reject external validation in favour of deeper, quieter growth. This is the work of smoothing the character's rough edges—arrogance, impatience, and selfishness—until the inner stone aligns with the divine principles of wisdom, strength, and beauty.

Practical steps for this transformation begin with self-awareness. Masons are encouraged to reflect regularly on their actions, aligning their daily lives with Masonic virtues. Meditation, study, and honest dialogue with trusted Brethren can provide the tools for chipping away at imperfections. Charity, patience, and humility become the working tools that shape the inner temple, creating a foundation of integrity and purpose.

Once achieved, the Perfect Ashlar is not an endpoint but a state of being. It represents the Mason who has become a vessel of light, contributing to the world with clarity and wisdom. Each moment of self-refinement strengthens the individual and the Craft itself, ensuring that the collective temple remains.

As Wilmshurst writes, "The true work of Masonry lies not in the perfection of the ritual but in the perfection of the individual". This principle reminds us that every Lodge meeting, every symbolic gesture, is an opportunity for transformation—a chance to shape the stone within and reflect the divine architecture in our lives.

THE PHILOSOPHER'S STONE AND HISTORICAL ESOTERICISM

The Philosopher's Stone, long celebrated in alchemical traditions, represents the pinnacle of spiritual and material transformation. In Freemasonry, this mystical symbol parallels the Perfect Ashlar, serving as an allegory for elevating the soul from its base state to one of enlightenment and harmony. While the Rough Ashlar embodies potential, the Philosopher's Stone captures the fulfilment of that potential—the culmination of the Masonic journey toward unity with the Great Architect.

Throughout history, figures like Paracelsus and Elias Ashmole have bridged the worlds of alchemy and Freemasonry, leaving an indelible mark on the Craft's esoteric teachings. Paracelsus, a Swiss physician and alchemist, revolutionised the understanding of transformation by emphasising the spiritual dimension of healing. His belief that the divine essence could be found in all creation resonates with Masonic teachings, where every symbol and tool holds a deeper, universal meaning.

Elias Ashmole, one of the earliest recorded speculative Masons, exemplified the integration of alchemical and Masonic philosophies. His writings reflect a commitment to inner refinement and the pursuit of universal truths, aligning with the alchemical stages of transformation: calcination, dissolution, purification, and coagulation. These stages mirror the Masonic degrees, offering a personal and spiritual evolution roadmap.

- **Calcination**: This initial stage represents the burning away of impurities. The Entered Apprentice degree symbolises the confrontational act of acknowledging one's flaws and false perceptions. Through humility and self-examination, the Mason begins the process of inner purification.
- **Dissolution**: In this phase, the ego dissolves, allowing the individual to let go of attachments and illusions. For the Fellow Craft, it signifies the move from physical labour to intellectual and spiritual exploration, breaking down barriers to self-understanding.
- **Purification**: The Master Mason degree reflects this stage, where the self undergoes a symbolic death and rebirth. Here, the Mason's virtues are refined, and the soul aligns more closely with universal principles, represented by the polished Perfect Ashlar.

- **Coagulation**: This final phase marks the integration of the purified self with the greater whole. The Mason, now a living embodiment of Masonic values, contributes to humanity's spiritual edifice, becoming a beacon of light and transformation.

The Philosopher's Stone invites Masons to see their journey not as a solitary endeavour but as a contribution to a collective legacy. By transforming themselves, they add strength and beauty to the spiritual temple of the Craft. This work is subtle and internal, demanding integrity, patience, and a willingness to surrender superficial pursuits for enduring truths.

Modern Masonry, rich in fraternity and tradition, must not lose sight of these esoteric foundations. As Wilmshurst cautions, "The outer form of Masonry is but a veil, concealing the inner light which it is the Mason's duty to reveal". To honour this duty, Lodges can incorporate workshops, study groups, and meditative practices that explore the alchemical dimensions of the Craft, ensuring that its mystical heritage remains vibrant and accessible.

The Philosopher's Stone, like the Perfect Ashlar, challenges us to look beyond appearances and seek the essence of transformation. In a world that prizes speed and surface, it calls us to slow down, reflect, and engage in the labour that shapes the self into a vessel of truth and light. Through this alchemical process, Masons fulfil their highest calling, aligning their lives with the eternal principles of the Craft and contributing to the grand design of the Great Architect.

KING HENRY VI'S VISION OF SPIRITUAL MASONRY

In a memorandum attributed to King Henry VI, Masonry is described as a "science of the spirit," a profound discipline intended to unlock deeper truths and uncover the mysteries of existence. His words suggest an understanding of Masonry as a path transcending mere Craft or fraternity, portraying it as a sacred pursuit of wisdom and insight. To King Henry, Masonry connected the physical with the metaphysical, guiding its practitioners toward harmony with the natural world and its unseen, divine forces. This vision of Masonry elevates it beyond any social function, framing it as a pathway to enlightenment, a science that unveils the hidden order of the cosmos.

King Henry's perspective suggests a view of the Craft that aligns with ancient mystical traditions, where initiates were taught to perceive reality through the five senses and the inner eye of spiritual understanding. His characterisation of Masonry as a "noble science" implies that its teachings hold the potential to bridge the material and the spiritual, revealing how natural laws resonate with spiritual truths. In this light, Masonry emerges as an organisation and an esoteric school of thought dedicated to transforming the initiate by expanding their perception and aligning them with universal principles.

A PATH FORWARD

To revitalise Freemasonry as a custodian of mystical knowledge, individual Lodges and Grand Lodges must embrace the spirit of exploration these organisations exemplify. The Craft should encourage Masons to delve into its rich symbolic language, fostering a culture of study, reflection, and personal transformation. Masonic institutions can transcend the limitations of social perception and reconnect with the spiritual essence that has defined Freemasonry for centuries.

Ultimately, pursuing mystical knowledge is not about retreating into secrecy but engaging more deeply with the Craft's timeless truths. Freemasonry fulfils its role as a bridge between the material and spiritual worlds through this commitment to inner transformation and sharing wisdom. As Wilmshurst eloquently states, "The real secrets of Masonry are concerned with the nature of man and his relations with God and the universe". In preserving this sacred science, the Craft ensures that its light continues to shine for generations to come.

REVITALISING MASONRY THROUGH THE PRIVATE LODGE

The private lodge is the beating heart of Freemasonry—a sanctuary of learning, reflection, and transformation. Here, within the sacred confines of the lodge, the Craft's wisdom is preserved, and its light kindled anew with each gathering of Brethren. Yet, the lodge is not merely a place; it is a living tradition, a microcosm of the Great Work where individual effort and collective purpose unite in the pursuit of enlightenment.

For Wilmshurst, the private lodge represented far more than a local chapter of the fraternity; it was the crucible in which the true spirit of Masonry was forged. He saw the lodge as a space where the deeper mysteries of the Craft could be explored, where Masons could engage in the transformative work of refining their characters and deepening their understanding of the world and themselves. It was a place of reverence and study, a haven where the ancient wisdom of the Craft came alive in the hearts and minds of its members.

We can reclaim its role as an intellectual and spiritual engagement centre to revitalise Masonry through the private lodge. This begins with mentorship, where experienced Brethren guide new initiates not only through the rituals but also through the symbolic and philosophical dimensions of the Craft. In this vision, a Worshipful Master is more than a ceremonial leader; he is a teacher and guide, fostering a culture of inquiry and growth within the lodge.

Structured educational programs can play a vital role in this revitalisation. Lodges can offer workshops on the symbolism of Masonic tools, lectures on the history of speculative Freemasonry, and study groups focused on the esoteric traditions that underpin the Craft. These initiatives transform the lodge from a meeting place into a true school of wisdom, where Masons come to perform rituals, delve into their meanings, and apply their teachings to daily life.

The private lodge also serves as a bridge between the past and the future. Its rituals and traditions preserve the wisdom of those who came before, offering modern Masons a connection to the ancient currents of Hermeticism, Kabbalah, and alchemy that flow through the Craft. Yet, the lodge is also a space of innovation, where Masons can adapt these timeless teachings to address the challenges and opportunities of contemporary life.

Imagine a lodge where each meeting is a journey of discovery, where Brethren gather to explore the depths of Masonic philosophy, share their insights, and support each other in their pursuit of light. In such a lodge, the rough ashlar of each member's character is shaped and smoothed through study, dialogue, and mutual encouragement. These Brethren build a stronger fraternity and a brighter and more enlightened world.

This vision of the private lodge as a sanctuary of wisdom and transformation is not merely an ideal but a necessity. In a world that often prioritises superficiality over substance, Freemasonry offers an alternative path that values introspection, integrity, and the quiet work of self-improvement. By embracing this vision, private lodges can become beacons of light and learning, inspiring Masons to carry the teachings of the Craft into their lives and communities.

A CALL TO THE CRAFT'S ETERNAL LIGHT

As we approach the culmination of this journey, we are called to reflect on the timeless question that lies at the heart of Freemasonry: What does it mean to seek the light? This question is not merely a rhetorical flourish but an invitation to embark on a path of self-discovery, transformation, and service. The light we seek is not a distant star or an external ideal—it is the spark within us, waiting to be kindled into a flame.

Freemasonry is more than a collection of rituals and symbols; it is a way of life, a philosophy that challenges us to rise above the mundane and engage with the eternal. Its teachings remind us that true strength lies not in outward appearances but in the inner work of refining our character and aligning ourselves with the principles of wisdom, strength, and beauty. In this way, the Craft calls us to become architects of our souls, building inner temples that reflect the harmony of the cosmos.

The conclusion of this work is not an ending but a beginning—a call to action for every Mason who reads these words. Freemasonry's survival and vitality depend on its members' dedication to preserving its teachings, engaging with its mysteries, and embodying its ideals. Each Mason is a steward of the Craft, entrusted with its legacy and responsible for its future.

To answer this call, we must first look inward. The journey of the Mason begins within the self, where the rough ashlar of our character awaits the careful shaping of discipline, reflection, and moral courage. In the quiet moments of self-examination, we uncover the light of truth and wisdom, illuminating the path before us.

But the work of the Mason does not end at the lodge's threshold. It extends into the world, where we are called to live the values we profess—to act with integrity, seek justice, and bring compassion and understanding to our relationships and communities. In this way, the light we cultivate within ourselves shines for others, guiding them toward their journey of self-discovery and transformation.

The modern Mason faces unique challenges and opportunities. In a world of instant communication and global connectivity, we have the tools to share the wisdom of the Craft more widely than ever. To navigate this landscape, we must hold fast to the principles of Freemasonry, using them as a compass to guide us toward authenticity and purpose.

Wilmshurst reminds us, "The true Mason is not he who merely wears the badge, but he who understands the meaning of the symbols and applies them to the building of his own soul." This is Freemasonry's challenge and promise: to live so that our actions reflect the light we seek, embody the virtues we profess, and leave the world a better place than we found it.

Freemasonry's greatest strength lies in its ability to inspire and transform. Its rituals and symbols are living guides to a better future. As we conclude this centennial celebration of Brother Wilmshurst's masterpiece, let us remember that the light of the Craft shines not in its buildings or ceremonies but in the hearts and minds of its members. Each Mason is a torchbearer, carrying the flame of wisdom, integrity, and unity.

Let this be our call to action: to rise as Masons, embrace the inner work of transformation, and carry the light of Freemasonry into the world. May we honour our inherited legacy and pass it on with reverence and care. May we, through our lives and actions, illuminate the path for those who follow, ensuring that Freemasonry remains a beacon of light for generations to come.

> *"He who has gazed into the depths of truth knows that this world is but a shadow of the eternal. What once was sought as ultimate knowledge becomes a journey, as endless as the stars, ever pushing the soul toward new horizons of understanding."*
> *—Johann Wolfgang von Goethe, Faust*

POSTSCRIPT

W.L. WILMSHURST

And now let me close this book, as every Lodge is closed, in peace and concord with all my Brethren, and with the ancient prayer that the Order may be preserved of God, and its members be cemented with every virtue. If, in what has here been written, Masonry has been given a conception spiritualised beyond the measure of its common understanding, I have but followed the example of our Ancient Brethren, who, lifting up their eyes to hills whence cometh strength, wrought their Masonic work upon the highest eminences of the mind and discerned the Mysteries of the Craft, not with eyes of the flesh, but with the vision and understanding of the spirit. And they it was who perpetuated for us of later time an Order and a Doctrine by the right interpretation and use of which we, too, might ascend where they had risen, and from the same Mount of Vision behold the same things that they had seen.

Few, perhaps, ascend to those high hills today, in this more than usually troubled and dark age. But some are ready and eager to do so, and for them especially it is that this book is written. All must ascend thither at last. But, at the moment, the World-spirit is dominant in all our institutions. Wisdom is little apparent; for want of vision the people perish; and the quest of light has to be pursued under conditions of peculiar adversity. But there is a mystery of Darkness no less than one of light, and, in the sculpting hands of the Great Architect of the House of Life, the darkness and the light are both alike and serve as twin pillars that, finally, will establish that House in strength.

Those, then, who cannot, or are not yet prepared to, mount the higher path of understanding the things of the Craft, must nevertheless be thought of in charity, and spoken of in faith and in hope. For, placed as we all are in different and unequal degrees of perception upon the chequer-work floor of Life, around all alike—black and white, wise and foolish, learned and uninformed—runs the unifying, surrounding skirtwork and border of a common Providence; about us all are flung the Everlasting Arms; whilst, from the mutual interplay of the light and darkness in us all, becomes gradually generated the realisation of that Wisdom in which, even now, we are all one, though of that unity few as yet are conscious. And since Wisdom will at last be justified of all her children, we need not complain of her processes, which, as they work out through the ages to a beneficent conclusion, temporarily involve the sharp and painful contrasts that we find.

Twenty-four centuries ago, at a time of similar darkness and degeneracy to the present, an aged seer and golden-tongued poet, who through a long life had contemplated the Ancient Mysteries of light and Wisdom, spoke of the difficulty of conveying them to a world not yet able to appreciate them; and yet recognised the truth that, in the opposition of the World-spirit to them, the Divine purpose was nevertheless being effected. In sending forth this book, then, and exhibiting the Mysteries of Masonry in a light towards which, doubtless, some who read it will not at once be responsive, let me appropriate that poet's words, and welcome any in appreciation of what I have written with the same serenity as his; the same confidence of forward-looking faith in its ultimate acceptance:

Knowledge, we are not foes!
I seek thee diligently;
But the World with a great wind blows,
Shining—but not from thee!
Yet blowing to beautiful things,
On, amid dark and light;
Till Life, through the trammellings
Of laws that are not the Right,
Breaks, clean and pure, and sings
Glorying to God in the height.
—Euripides, Bacchae *(trans. Murray)*

AFTERWORD

As we conclude this exploration of the profound teachings and timeless insights of Freemasonry, it is fitting to express deep gratitude for the wisdom of Brother Walter Leslie Wilmshurst. His works remain a beacon for those seeking to understand the deeper meanings of the Craft, inviting us to look beyond the surface of rituals and symbols to uncover their transformative power. His vision of Freemasonry as a living tradition—a spiritual journey that harmonises action with contemplation—resonates as strongly today as it did in his time.

Brother Wilmshurst urged Masons to strive not only for personal enlightenment but also for the perpetuation of the Craft as a guiding force for humanity. His writings challenge us to keep the flame of Freemasonry alive, kindled in our hearts and illuminated through our actions. As he so eloquently wrote, "The true Mason, and the true meaning of Masonry, can only be found by those who will 'search for it as for hidden treasure.'" This call to seek light with sincerity and dedication is as vital now as ever.

In a world that often seems dominated by division and distraction, the principles of Freemasonry offer a counterbalance—a path toward unity, wisdom, and moral refinement. The lessons of the Craft remind us that true progress begins within ourselves, through the steady work of self-improvement, introspection, and service to others. By embodying the teachings of Freemasonry, we can contribute to a broader transformation, illuminating the way for those around us and for future generations.

The future of our Craft is bright. Freemasonry endures not because it is rigid and unchanging, but because it is rooted in principles that transcend time and adapt to the needs of every era. Today, as we stand at the crossroads of tradition and modernity, we are called to uphold these principles with renewed vigour. Through our commitment to learning, mentorship, and the cultivation of virtue, we ensure that the ideals of Freemasonry remain a vital force in an ever-changing world.

Let us, as Masons, honour the legacy of those who have come before us—not only by preserving their teachings but by living them. Let us be steadfast in our pursuit of wisdom and light, mindful that each step we take enriches not only our individual lives but the collective strength and spirit of the Craft.

May this journey continue to inspire us to embody the Masonic virtues of truth, charity, and brotherly love, and may we carry forward the light of Freemasonry with hope, integrity, and purpose. As we do so, we honour the wisdom of the past, embrace the challenges of the present, and shape a future worthy of the principles we hold dear.

So Mote It Be.

ABOUT THE AUTHORS

WALTER LESLIE WILMSHURST

Wilmshurst (1867–1939) was a British Freemason, mystic, and philosopher whose contributions to Masonic literature remain influential within esoteric and initiatic circles. Known for his profound understanding of Freemasonry's inner teachings, Wilmshurst sought to illuminate the spiritual and mystical dimensions of the Craft. His writings go beyond the ceremonial aspects of Masonry to explore its potential as a path to inner transformation and spiritual enlightenment.

Wilmshurst's most renowned work, The Meaning of Masonry, delves into the symbolism and deeper esoteric meanings behind Masonic rituals, aiming to reconnect Masons with the spiritual ideals that underpin their practices. He argued that Freemasonry, at its core, was intended to be a progressive journey toward self-knowledge and alignment with universal truths. His commitment to this vision led him to examine Freemasonry as part of a larger mystical tradition, often referencing ancient wisdom traditions, Hermeticism, and Christian mysticism to emphasise the Craft's potential for guiding individuals to higher understanding.

A man of quiet introspection, Wilmshurst led by example, living in a way that reflected his values of humility and spiritual integrity. His dedication to bridging Eastern and Western mysticism within the Masonic framework made him a respected figure, both in his era and and in the decades that followed. Through his work, Wilmshurst continues to inspire generations of Freemasons, inviting them to rediscover the Craft as a path of inner illumination and transformative power.

MICHAEL DUNLAP

A Cyber Threat Intelligence Analyst by day and aspiring Author, Michael has dedicated his life to unraveling both the digital and esoteric mysteries that connect the modern world with ancient wisdom. His professional background aligns seamlessly with his passion for Masonic studies, as both fields feed his insatiable curiosity and drive to uncover hidden truths. For him, the pursuit of knowledge—whether through data or spiritual teachings—serves as a continuous journey to "hunt deeper," finding insights that lie beneath the surface.

Michael's first publication, *Sacred Wisdom of Hermes Trismegistus: An Experiential Guide,* reflects his dedication to exploring the Hermetic traditions that underpin much of Freemasonry's symbolic language. Building upon this foundation, this Centennial Edition of *The Masonic Initiation* marks the culmination of several years spent with Walter Leslie Wilmshurst's seminal work as his guide. With this new edition, Michael seeks to honour Wilmshurst's legacy, communicating the Craft's teachings in ways that resonate with today's Brethren.

As the Director of Music at his mother lodge, Lodge Kiama No. 35, Michael actively contributes to the vibrancy of the Masonic experience. He is also a member of the Australia and New Zealand Masonic Research Council (ANZMRC), the Masonic Library and Museum Association, and the Quatuor Coronati Correspondence Circle. Inspired by Masonic scholars like Wilmshurst, Mackey, Newton, Earnshaw, and Ward, he champions Masonic education as a continuous journey, empowering each Brother to discover personal truths within the symbols and teachings of the Craft.

Michael's esoteric influences are drawn from a rich array of mystical and philosophical sources, including A.E. Waite, Joseph Campbell, Baal HaSulam, Swami Vivekananda, and Sadhguru. Through his speaking engagements and written work, he encourages fellow Masons to embark upon their own path of self-illumination, discovering the timeless wisdom that unites seekers across traditions.

Outside his professional and Masonic pursuits, Michael enjoys exploring nature's beauty through ocean photography, playing golf, and immersing himself in the natural world along the Australian coast. He resides with his family in Wollongong, Australia, yet remains closely connected to his roots in the United States, traveling whenever possible to visit family and friends.

ABOUT HIS LODGE

LODGE OF THE LIVING STONES NO 4957

In a letter, dated July 1923, W.L. Wilmshurst had written:

> 'I cannot...point to any lodge under our constitution where the esoteric side of Masonry receives prominence. The conditions under which Masonry is at present conducted and the virtually indiscriminate admission of new members make it almost impossible for a lodge to be carried on upon ideal lines.'

He resolved to do something about this and laid the groundwork in his presidential address to the Huddersfield and District Installed Masters Association in November 1924 when he suggested that brethren who shared his ideal might meet: 'with the intention of conforming to it, and here and there even a small new lodge might be formed for that special purpose.

Three years later, on 16th December 1927, The Lodge of Living Stones was consecrated in Leeds. Wilmshurst was installed as the first Master and outlined the purpose and aims of the lodge:

'This lodge has been formed to meet a demand that nowadays is increasingly heard in the Craft for a fuller understanding and realisation of the latent teachings of our Order than usually obtains. It is our design to try to meet the need of a growing minority of brethren who are not content with the routine formalities and social amenities of their lodges, but feel that the Craft was intended to mean more than this and who are eager to learn what that "more" is.'

The Lodge has initiated very few Candidates in its ninety years but still meets regularly and frequently to promote the deeper interpretation of the Craft ceremonies.

http://www.lodge-of-living-stones.org.uk/

BIBLIOGRAPHY

Anderson, James. *The Constitutions of the Free-Masons*. 1723.

Ashlag, Yehuda Leib (Baal HaSulam). *The Zohar with the Sulam Commentary*. Bnei Baruch Kabbalah Education & Research Institute, 2003.

Ashmole, Elias. *Theatrum Chemicum Britannicum*. Thomas Harper, 1652.

Assmann, Jan. *The Mind of Egypt: History and Meaning in the Time of the Pharaohs*. Harvard University Press, 2003.

Augustine. *Confessions*. Translated by F. J. Sheed, Sheed and Ward, 1943. Original work published c. 397–400 AD.

Black Elk, and John G. Neihardt. *Black Elk Speaks: Being the Life Story of a Holy Man of the Oglala Sioux*. University of Nebraska Press, 2004.

Bronfman, Edgar M., and Beth Zasloff. *Hope, Not Fear: A Path to Jewish Renaissance*. St. Martin's Press, 2008.

Burckhardt, Titus. *Alchemy: Science of the Cosmos, Science of the Soul*. Fons Vitae, 1987.

Burkert, Walter. *Ancient Mystery Cults*. Harvard University Press, 1987.

Campbell, Joseph. *The Hero with a Thousand Faces*. Princeton University Press, 1949.

---. *The Power of Myth*. Doubleday, 1988.

Cassian, John. *The Conferences*. Translated by Edgar C. S. Gibson, SPCK, 1894. Original work published c. 420 AD.

Climacus, St. John. *The Ladder of Divine Ascent*. Translated by Archimandrite Lazarus Moore, Holy Transfiguration Monastery, 1959.

Copenhaver, Brian P., translator. *Hermetica: The Greek Corpus Hermeticum and the Latin Asclepius in a New English Translation, with Notes and Introduction*. Cambridge University Press, 1992.

Desaguliers, John Theophilus. *A Course of Experimental Philosophy*. Vol. 1, 2nd ed., W. Innys, 1745.

Eliade, Mircea. *The Sacred and the Profane: The Nature of Religion*. Harcourt, 1959.

Faivre, Antoine. *Access to Western Esotericism*. State University of New York Press, 1994.

Granach, S. M. "Ceremonial Rites of Passage for Adolescent Boys: Essential Components for Contemporary Initiations." 2001. *ProQuest*, https://search.proquest.-com/openview/37182e86ad939d86690d2b9c50d695e3.

Guénon, René. *Symbols of Sacred Science*. Sophia Perennis, 2004.

Gurian, Michael. *The Wonder of Boys: What Parents, Mentors, and Educators Can Do to Shape Boys into Exceptional Men*. TarcherPerigee, 2006.

Hall, Manly P. *The Lost Keys of Freemasonry*. Macoy Publishing, 1923.

---. *The Secret Teachings of All Ages*. Philosophical Research Society, 1928.

Hamill, John. *The Craft: A History of English Freemasonry*. Crucible, 1986.

Holy Bible. *The New Oxford Annotated Bible, New Revised Standard Version*. Oxford University Press, 1991.

Immordino-Yang, Mary Helen, et al. "The Brain Basis of Emotion and Feeling: A Neurally Informed Guide for Educators." *Mind, Brain, and Education*, vol. 12, no. 2, 2018, pp. 109-119.

Jacob, Margaret C. *Living the Enlightenment: Freemasonry and Politics in Eighteenth-Century Europe*. Oxford University Press, 1991.

Jung, Carl G. *Memories, Dreams, Reflections*. Edited by Aniela Jaffé, Vintage Books, 1989.

---. *Psychology and Alchemy*. Princeton University Press, 1968.

---. *The Philosophical Tree*. Vol. 13, *Collected Works of C.G. Jung*. Translated by R.F.C. Hull, Princeton University Press, 1968.

Kaplan, Aryeh. *Meditation and Kabbalah*. Samuel Weiser, 1982.

Kerning, J. B. *Letters on the Royal Art*. Goodreads, 2024.

Kingsley, Peter. *In the Dark Places of Wisdom*. The Golden Sufi Center, 1999.

Lodge of Living Stones. *History*. Lodge of Living Stones, http://www.lodge-of-living-stones.org.uk/history.htm. Accessed 18 Nov. 2024.

Mackey, Albert G. *The Symbolism of Freemasonry*. Masonic History Co., 1882.

Makdisi, George. *The Rise of Colleges: Institutions of Learning in Islam and the West*. Edinburgh University Press, 1981.

Neihardt, John G. *Black Elk Speaks: The Complete Edition*. University of Nebraska Press, 2014.

Newton, Joseph Fort. *The Builders: A Story and Study of Masonry*. Macoy Publishing, 1914.

Origen. *On First Principles*. Translated by G. W. Butterworth, Harper & Row, 1966. Original work published c. 220–230 AD.

Plato. *Phaedrus and the Seventh and Eighth Letters*. Translated by Walter Hamilton, Penguin Classics, 1977.

---. *Timaeus and Critias*. Translated by Desmond Lee, Penguin Books, 1971. Original work published c. 360 BC.

Preston, William. *Illustrations of Masonry*. 1772.

Raphael, Marc Lee. *Judaism in America*. Columbia University Press, 2003.

Robinson, Sam. *The Rosicrucian Path of Inner Light*. Rosicrucian Order, 2019.

Rosenblum, Bruce, and Fred Kuttner. *Quantum Enigma: Physics Encounters Consciousness*. Oxford University Press, 2011.

Scholem, Gershom. *Major Trends in Jewish Mysticism*. Schocken Books, 1946.

---. *On the Kabbalah and Its Symbolism*. Schocken Books, 1965.

Seneca. *Letters to Lucilius*. Translated by Richard M. Gummere, Harvard University Press, 1917.

Sharma, Arvind. *The World's Religions: A Contemporary Reader*. Fortress Press, 2008.

Stevenson, David. *The Origins of Freemasonry: Scotland's Century, 1590–1710*. Cambridge University Press, 1990.

The Book of the Dead: The Hieroglyphic Transcript and Translation into English of the Papyrus of Ani. Translated by E. A. Wallis Budge, Dover Publications, 1967.

The Corpus Hermeticum. Translated by G. R. S. Mead, Watkins Publishing, 1906.

Tononi, Giulio. "Integrated Information Theory of Consciousness." *Nature Reviews Neuroscience*, vol. 17, 2016, pp. 450–461.

Waite, A. E., translator. *The Hermetic and Alchemical Writings of Paracelsus*. Watkins, 1894.

Wilmshurst, Walter Leslie. *The Meaning of Masonry*. Bell Publishing, 1922.

---. *The Masonic Initiation*. William Rider & Son, 1924.

Yates, Frances A. *The Rosicrucian Enlightenment*. Routledge, 1972.

Zohar, Danah, and Ian Marshall. *The Quantum Self: Human Nature and Consciousness Defined by the New Physics*. Morrow, 1990.

PUBLISHERS NOTE

This expanded centennial edition of *The Masonic Initiation* includes the original text by Walter Leslie Wilmshurst, which is in the public domain. The content of Wilmshurst's work has been carefully preserved, with only minor structural adjustments for improved readability, where necessary. No words from the original text have been altered or removed, ensuring Wilmshurst's ideas and expressions remain true to his vision.

All images used in this publication are licensed from Adobe Stock.

This edition, featuring commentary, reflections, and supplementary material, has been prepared to honour Wilmshurst's legacy and illuminate the enduring value of his teachings for modern readers.

Milton Keynes UK
Ingram Content Group UK Ltd.
UKHW051320031224
3298UKWH00055BA/522

9 781763 7977